To be unique you have to learn from your life and customize the knowledge you learn from others.

Just as the earth is transformed into a flower by the plant, let your knowledge be transformed into wisdom by your effort.

BEING THE BEST

Practical Advice for Peace and Happiness

Jayaram V

Published by
Pure Life Vision LLC
New Albany, Ohio

Being the Best: Practical advice for peace and happiness
Copyright © 2014 by Jayaram V. All rights reserved.
Published and Distributed Worldwide by Pure Life Vision LLC., USA.
First edition 2014

Thank you for purchasing an original copy of the book. This book is copyrighted under Berne convention. Printed in the USA. All rights reserved. No part of this publication may be reproduced stored in a retrieval system, or transmitted in any form or by any means, electronic, mechanical, photocopying, recording, scanning or otherwise, without the prior written permission of the publisher or the author. Requests to the publisher for permission or for bulk purchase of the book should be addressed to Pure Life Vision LLC, P.O. Box 707, New Albany, OH 43054.

Limit of Liability/Disclaimer of Warranty: While the publisher and the author have used their best efforts in preparing this book, they make no representation or warranties with respect to the accuracy or completeness of the contents of this book and specifically disclaim any implied warranties of merchantability or fitness for particular purpose. No warranty may be created or extended by sales representatives or written sales materials. The advice and strategies contained herein may not be suitable for your situation. You should consult with a professional where appropriate. Neither the publisher nor author shall be liable for any loss of profit or any other commercial damages, including but not limited to special, incidental, consequential or other damages.

Publisher Cataloging-in-Publication Data

V, Jayaram
Being The Best: Practical advice for peace and happiness
    p. cm
    Includes bibliographical references
    ISBN- 13: 978-1-935760-23-8
    1. Success-Psychological Aspects. 2. Self help techniques. 3. Quality of Life   I. Title

    BF637.V2 2010
    158— dc22   2014917644

Printed in the United States of America
Designed by Jayaram V
10 9 8 7 6 5 4 3 2 1
First Edition

About the Author

Jayaram V is a well-known author of 12 books. He combines the mystic knowledge of the spirit with his experiential and practical knowledge of the world. His knowledge is derived from a variety of sources, including science, business management and information technology. For over 45 years Jayaram explored various branches of knowledge, including philosophy, mysticism, spirituality, history, and behavioral sciences, to understand the big picture, our purpose and place in creation. His writings reflect his composite personality and diverse knowledge. Before his writing career, he worked in various administrative and managerial positions in three continents which had given him the rare opportunity to meet people from different backgrounds and understand human nature from different perspectives. Through his writings and speeches, he provides his insights into the nature of reality, yoga, spiritual transformation, and mystic symbolism. He also writes about human personality, consciousness, and behavior, combining the transformational wisdom hidden in the ancient scriptures of India with the recent researches in human psychology and mental health. Jayaram has written hundreds of articles on various subjects and authored several books, which include Think Success, Brahman, An Introduction to Hinduism, Selected Upanishads, the Bhagavadgita Complete Translations and the Awakened Life. Since 2000, he has been actively engaged in writing about spiritual, religious, and material aspects of human life. Jayaram V can be contacted at the following address: http://www.jayaramv.com.

Also By Jayaram V

1. Think Success, 2nd. (Revised) Edition.
2. The Awakened Life.
3. Brahman.
4. The Bhagavadgita Complete Translation.
5. The Bhagavadgita Simple Translation.
6. Essays on the Bhagavadgita.
7. Introduction to Hinduism.
8. Selected Upanishads.
9. Brihadaranyaka Upanishad.
10. Chandogya Upanishad.
11. Thoughts and Quotations.

Being The Best

Practical Advice For Peace and Happiness

Jayaram V

There is no better example of perseverance that what Nature does to improve and perfect life upon earth.

Contents

Preface 13
Five Great Thoughts That Can Change Your Life 17
The Psychology of Happiness 21
Proven Techniques to Make Money and Grow Rich 35
Why People Avoid Having Goals 40
How To Become An Expert In Any Field 43
Enjoying The Simple Pleasures Of Life 48
How to Develop Curiosity and Sustain it 52
Dealing with People and Relationships 56
When You Lose Your Job 62
When Your are Criticized 65
What Do you Think Success Means? 69
On Writing Skills and Becoming a Writer 72
What Makes you Happy 77
The Powers That Shape Your Life and Destiny 81
Three Rules for Peace and Stability 85
How to Cope With Suicidal Thoughts 90
Understanding the Meaning and Mechanics of Success 95
Coping With Stress in Daily Life 99
How to Avoid Stereotyping 101
Seven Simple Techniques to Peace and Happiness 107
How to Deal With Unpleasant Situations 109
The Roots of Unhappiness 113
What Success Truly Means 119
A Brief Guide to Relationships 121
How to Survive in a Recession Economy 125
Problems and Problem Solving 129
Two Success Factors Used by Successful People 134
Intention, Attention and Manifestation 138
The Basis of Happiness 141
The Art and Science of Persuasion 151
Cultivating the Virtue of Patience 154
Fear, What Can you Do about it? 158
Don't Look for Happiness at the End of the Journey 161
How to Motivate Yourself and Keep Your Morale High. 164
Are you Bored With Your Life 168
The Success Mindset 171
A Brief Study of Intuition 175
Improving Intuition 179
How to Create Happiness in Your Life 182
Cultivating Wisdom and Intelligence 185
Focus on the Positive Aspects of Life 190
Understanding and Accepting Your Emotions 193
Listen to the Messages Life Delivers 198
How to Use Defensive Pessimism 202

Dealing with Emotions 206
Core Values For a Principle Centered Life 211
Knowing and Being Who You are 215
How to Reduce Anxiety By Changing Your Thoughts 218
The Power of Positive Thinking in Daily Life 223
Taking Responsibility for Your Life 226
The Self-confidence Gospel 231
How to Deal with the Monotony of Life 236
Finding Happiness in the Simple Pleasures of Life 239
How to be Assertive and Tolerant 243
Thinking Outside The Box 245
How Should We Deal With Our Bad Memories? 250
Being Alone and Feeling Lonely 254
How to Manage Worldly Success? 257
Recommended Reading 261

For Padma, Harshita and Oscar

Those who quarrel about frivolous matters should lift their heads and look at the stars.

Preface

This book is not about religion. It is not about the scriptures. It is about self-effort, keeping yourself motivated, taking responsibility for your life, and living with curiosity, an open mind, and appreciation to fulfill the simple purpose of your life, which is happiness here.

This is my second book on self-help, after my first one, Think Success, which was published a few years ago. This volume contains 58 essays on improving your physical and mental wellbeing by reaching your goals, overcoming your shortcomings, improving your relationships, solving your problems and finding peace and happiness in you and around you. These articles have no correlation with one another, even though sometimes they may deal with identical themes.

While writing them I did not think about putting them together into a book. I wrote them for the visitors to my websites. However, I did it with a clear purpose and tried to provide them with useful information and solutions, according to my knowledge, research, and understanding, to the commonest problems we face in today's world. Since people found them useful and inspiring, and according to the comments I received from them, I decided to put them together into a book and reach out to more people.

The purpose of this book is to awaken you to your potentials and possibilities with right information so that you can cultivate and sustain a proper frame of mind, when you need it most. It is not that you do not know the information or you have never read it before. However, you may not find all the information in one place when you need it. In this book I have presented a diverse range of ideas, in one place and the good thing is you do not have to read them all at once. You can read them according to your convenience.

Human life is such that the same problem can be resolved in various ways, according to the individuals and the circumstances involved. No one can say which one of them is the best. Sometimes the best solutions can fail, if those who use them do not understand the principles involved or do not have faith in them. You must believe in the solutions for the solutions to work. Further, any solution to any problem you want to resolve must suit the specific circumstances in which you live.

It means that you should either find your own solutions or customize the general solutions that you may find in the self-help books according to your specific needs. The essays presented in this collection provide you with several practical solutions to improve your thinking and problem solving ability. Hence, I am confident that you will find them useful.

Jayaram V

You can find answers to any problem, provided you are willing to learn and think.

The greatest gift that you can give to your children is to teach them to think objectively and rationally, and express their uniqueness.

Five Great Thoughts That Can Change Your Life

Your life is shaped by what you think and believe. Every day, numerous thoughts arise and subside in your mind as you engage in different activities. You may not pay attention to them or remember them clearly. However, if you observe them closely, you will realize that your thoughts are shaped and driven mostly by a few dominant desires, expectations, ideas, beliefs and thoughts. They guide your thinking and actions, irrespective of your professional background and personal beliefs, and influence the quality, nature, and course of your life.

You can use this knowledge to your advantage by consciously choosing and remembering a few affirmations or ideas that can potentially transform your thinking, behavior and attitude for good. The following five affirmations are chosen for such a purpose. You can use them directly or customize them according to your needs to change your thinking and attitude about your life, the world, and the nature of your existence. You should frequently affirm them until they are integrated into your consciousness and become a part of your personal philosophy and awareness.

1. You do not live forever: You have to remember this universal truth as frequently as possible because people do not think about it at all, and live and act as if it does not apply to them. You can see how such escapism manifests in their lives and makes them ignore the value of life, or the importance of time and relationships. As people overlook their mortality, they become careless in their thinking and actions, indulge in frivolous activities, and waste many opportunities that would help them enrich their lives or live according to their best ideals, dreams and desires.

Ask yourself whether you incorporate the inevitability of death in your planning and outlook, and whether you take your time and actions seriously. Do you value your life, your goals, and the relationships you build? Do you take time to relax and look at the world around you? Are you lost in your job, the pressures of life, or some social, political, or ideological cause that prevents you from being yourself or spending time with your near and dear? Have you ever felt the need to recognize and appreciate your existence and the rarest opportunity you have as an intelligent and self-aware person to consciously experience life? According to you, what is the most precious thing in your life? If your answer is life, you are thinking in the right direction.

There are many ways in which people fill their days with meaningless activities and let their lives slip by. Take a deep breath and think. What is the most important thing in your life? It is not your religion, your race, your nationality or your company. It is your life, which becomes diminished with the passing of each moment. Your life is like a bank balance, which keeps dwindling, whether you spend it or not, and cannot be increased except fractionally. Do you realize how precious it is?

You have a unique opportunity to be alive and conscious in a vast universe, surrounded by the richness and diversity of life that manifests in innumerable forms. It lasts but for a short time, and will never repeat again. Even if you think you are going to have another birth, it will not be the same. Therefore, live your life fully, and use every opportunity to be alive and happy. Find your purpose, set up a few important goals, choose your priorities, and live with the gratitude of being born as a human, and being active, alive and conscious.

2. Things change: Your life not only diminishes with each moment but also keeps constantly changing. The world in which we live is impermanent. Neither you nor your behavior nor your possessions last forever. Death and destruction are encoded in the structure of the universe, while we live in a sea of impermanence, surrounded by innumerable objects that are in a constant flux. The impermanence is a great source of misery as we are caught in the duality of likes and dislikes.

While our existence is finite and transient and physically and emotionally creates enough problems for us, on the positive side you may consider it a blessing because it gives you a precious opportunity to improve your life and situations according to your needs and expectations. Imagine how the world would be if everything is frozen in time, with no scope to change or improve anything. Would you like to live in such a world? People are bored even when there is so much impermanence around them. Imagine how boring it would be, if nothing changes, and if you are condemned forever to the circumstances in which you were originally born!

Fortunately, the world gives you many opportunities to experience life differently and become a different person if you desire so. Many people are afraid to change, because they cannot trust themselves and do not like to stay out of their comfort zones. They resist change because they do not want to take the risks and face the problems it may create. Hence, they try to secure their lives against impermanence by building walls of defense.

While it may give them the illusion of security, it also makes them prisoners of their fears. The best way to deal with impermanence is to face it and accept it boldly as an integral part of your life and plan your life accordingly, without being reckless or negligent. Use the opportunities that change offers, with courage, detachment, equanimity and sameness to improve your life and destiny.

3. Manifest your uniqueness: We marvel at the uniqueness of a product or a gadget, but we do not realize or appreciate how unique we are. We are the unique creations of Nature, born with a huge potential to make a difference in the world in our own unique ways. Each of us sets in motion a chain of events that will have far reaching consequences for our civilization. Each of us will be the starting point for several generations of new people who will descend from us or who will be benefited by our actions. The markets may tell you that if you have a unique product or service, it will sell, but is there anything that is as unique as you?

Your uniqueness is your wealth. There is none like you and none can think, act, or live like you. Even if you are largely conditioned by society, you are still unique. You can use your uniqueness to your advantage and creatively manifest it in your thinking, problem solving, and actions to stand apart in a sea of humanity and prove your worth. Therefore, before sheepishly believing in anything or following anyone, remember that you have a mind and a will of your own and you are not under any compulsion to meekly accept anything or blindly follow anyone.

You can manifest your uniqueness and freedom by knowing yourself, finding your unique strengths and talents, expressing your individuality, speaking for yourself, and cultivating an inner sense of detachment, courage and confidence. Knowing that you are unique and frequently remembering it, you can learn to be yourself and stand for yourself.

4. Excel in whatever you do: You do not have to be perfect all the time, but you should try to achieve perfection and excellence in whatever you do. It can by any task, but you must do it as sincerely and perfectly as you can so that when you complete it and see the results, you will not only feel good about yourself and your skills, but also increase your chances of success and prosperity. Discipline, knowledge, skills, respect for rules, commitment quality, and genuine love contribute to excellence in any field.

The road to excellence is never ending. It is a continuous journey in which you move from one level of perfection to another. Hence, focus upon your goals and tasks and give your best, without worrying about results. At some stage, your effort will bear fruit. To excel in any field, you must set standards of performance, learn from your peers, question your assumptions, challenge your ideas and solutions, and do not settle for less. Put your one hundred percent in whatever you do, with detachment and a sense of duty, but without being vain, anxious, or proud.

5. Relax in the silence of your inner space: There is too much noise in our lives. As our civilization progresses, we create more noise and distractions. The mobile phones and the Internet make sure that you cannot have quiet time for yourself. All this puts a lot of strain upon us. We may not be aware, but the noise puts a dent upon our ability to think clearly, stay in control, and remain healthy and happy, making the need for peace even more important and urgent. At the end of the day, despite your problems and pressures, you must be able to sleep well. If you can sleep well, it is a sign that you are in control.

There are many techniques which you can use to calm your mind and experience peace even in busy surroundings. One of the ways to do it is to consciously prolong the silence between your two thoughts, so that you can stop your mental chatter, and experience temporary relief. You can practice it every day as a part of your meditation, or anywhere and at any time. The human mind can only think one thought at a time. Therefore, before your mind jumps from one thought to another, take a deep breath and prolong the silence between any two thoughts. As you close your eyes and still your mind, hold on to the silence as long as you can, without letting any new thought enter. As the gap between two consecutive thoughts increases in you, you gain control over your mind. With your mind increasingly resting in silence, your awareness also deepens.

The Psychology of Happiness

What is happiness?

Happiness is a state of mind. You are familiar with it. You know what it means. You also know from experience how to make you or others happy in your own unique ways. Life teaches us many lessons and from them we learn the many possibilities by which we can minimize our sorrows and maximize our happiness and fulfillment. We may not always succeed in our aims. Yet we live with the conviction that happiness is possible, attainable and repeatable by making adjustments to our thinking and attitude. Our choices and conclusions about happiness may not always be rational or healthy. Yet we know by instinct that the situations and the people who may increase our happiness.

Happiness is both long term and short term. We may experience it momentarily from the simple joys and pleasures of life, and in retrospect from the sum of our achievements when we reflect upon them and see how far we fared. Whether it is long term or short term we know from experience that like everything else in this world happiness is neither permanent nor continuous.

Life is mostly about escaping from harm, danger and suffering rather than living in perpetual happiness. Whether you are rich or poor, young or old, and whether you live in the most affluent part of the world or not, it is not possible to always remain happy. One moment you are happy and the other moment pensive. Even a baby knows that if she has to be happy, she has to make sure that she gets enough positive attention from her parents. That is how life is, a great ride that lasts for a lifetime in the rollercoaster of emotions.

Happiness is a positive emotion we experience as joy, fulfillment, inspiration, satisfaction, pleasure, contentment, encouragement, exhilaration, enthusiasm, pleasantness, delight, enjoyment and so on. When you are happy, you feel good, blessed and on the top of the world. You feel you are charged with energy and enthusiasm, and live with greater confidence and optimism.

Yet, your capacity for happiness depends upon your overall feelings about yourself and your current life situation. Your happiness will not last for long unless you feel good about yourself and your life in a general sort of way. While happiness is a universal emotion, it has so many layers to it that it is not easy to define. Although we live on the same planet, we live in different worlds. What happiness is to one may not be happiness to another. When life becomes so hard and challenging, for many people thinking about happiness is a luxury if not selfishness. For them life is about making sacrifices, compromises and adjustments, not happiness. Nowadays we are so preoccupied with daily problems and pressing deadlines that for most of us happiness means just not having any serious problems in life. Ordinary problems you are going to have anyway. Therefore, not having serious problems is a cause of happiness.

While such thinking about happiness is justified from certain perspectives, thinking about happiness from the perspective of problems may not be the right approach. Our lives are such that we are never really free from problems, except when we are dead or when we enter a deep sleep. Besides, even if we try to focus our minds elsewhere, the media, our friends and the internet make sure that we know what has been going on in the real world in real time.

It appears that happiness, which is what most of us want to experience in our lives, does not get as much attention as it deserves. Most people go through a struggle if you ask them to recall a few occasions in which they experienced real happiness. They would eventually recall a few experiences, but it is rarely without making an effort. It is not that they have not experienced happiness or do not care for it. They might have experienced happiness on many occasions, but they do not remember them because their minds are elsewhere. What happened then is not a priority now. Those events have happened and gone.

You may think about them occasionally and like to repeat them if possible, but on a moment's notice you may not recollect them because your mind remains preoccupied with many current issues and problems that consume your attention. It is also probably true that the moments spent in the expectation of experiencing great events in life are more exciting than the events themselves. Most people do strive for happiness with their limited means and want to be happy; yet when they are happy, they mostly treat it just like any other experience and file it away in the cupboards of their minds.

Happiness is...

Before we examine the philosophy and psychology of happiness, let us examine briefly how people perceive happiness in their lives and what beliefs and opinions they usually associate with it. People view and experience happiness in various ways, which are listed below.

1. Happiness is a pleasant feeling.
2. Happiness is a subjective feeling expressed in various ways.

3. Happiness depends upon the satisfaction of needs.
4. Happiness is linked to the values one follows.
5. Happiness does not mean one is completely free from worries.
6. The way people experience and express happiness is universal.
7. As we grow older, we tend to become less happier.
8. Our happiness arises from both intrinsic and extrinsic factors.
9. The body language associated with happiness is common across all cultures and peoples.
10. We may not define happiness clearly, but we know what it means.
11. People differ in their empathy and sensitivity towards the happiness of others.
12. Happiness may arise from our perceptions, memory or even imagination.
13. Expectations reduce happiness.
14. Even animals seem to experience happiness in their own unique ways.
15. When you are happy, you experience the world and relationships differently.

The psychology of happiness

Due to individual difference in their temperament, disposition and attitudes, people vary in their ability to experience different emotions. Certain factors predispose them to be happy and certain factors predispose them to be depressed and unhappy. Such factors may also keep changing frequently in the life of an individual, making happiness an unpredictable and varying emotion.

For example, extroverts and introverts may differ in their ability to respond to different situations and experience different emotions. Similarly, healthy people are more predisposed to be happier than people with constant health problems. Exercising is proven to be effective in uplifting people from temporary depression. Release of certain chemicals into the bloodstream is also found to induce positive emotions in people. Studies in neuroscience suggest that different areas of the brain are responsible for different emotions such as happiness or depression.

Such findings indicate that genetic, chemical and biological factors may be responsible for much of our emotional behavior. Positive thinking, resilience, religious beliefs, knowledge and education, aesthetic sensibility, extroversion and introversion, self-esteem, and aversion to risk are a few personality traits that are linked to our happiness. In the following discussion, we examine the psychology of happiness from different perspectives so that we not only gain a deeper understanding of the subject but also know how to sustain and prolong our happiness.

The philosophy of happiness

Even the most hardened criminal occasionally suffers from guilt and remorse. Newspapers sometimes report that a certain person did not show any remorse in the court for his or her alleged misdeeds, thereby implying that he or she deserves a worse punishment. While people may vary in their ability to display their emotions publicly, it is true that due to our conditioning virtue and happiness are closely inter linked.

If your actions are in harmony with the established code of conduct and moral norms, you have greater chances of experiencing peace, happiness and higher self-esteem. Philosophers like Aristotle, Plato and Thomas Jefferson in the past argued that virtue was imperative for human happiness. The practice of virtue makes you feel good about yourself, and experience a subtle sense of pride for sticking to the mortal path, which is a challenge for many as they trade their virtue for success and a temporary sense of achievement.

Immanuel Kant believed that more than virtue, the exercise of will power to achieve good was important and in that pursuit one might have to sacrifice even the desire for happiness. Human beings are not interested in the mere act of living, but living appropriately according to their sense of judgment. Their sense of propriety and morality may vary, but no one really feels happy to be on the wrong side of life or committing morally depraved actions that degrade human life or dignity.

Genuine happiness arises from doing good and being good. There is a definite correlation between altruism and happiness. By nature, we are conflicted beings, driven by self-interest on the one hand and the need for belongingness and appreciation on the other. There is a higher nature in each of us that prompts us to perform good actions, which not only define our character and elevate our self-esteem but also lead to our individual and common good.

We learn from history, from our religions and from our own observation that happiness arising from evil and negative actions is temporary, and in the long run will lead to sorrow and suffering. From this perspective, we reach the universal moral norm that it is better to be poor and righteous rather than rich and evil. This is the moral aspect of happiness.

Social dimension of happiness

There is a social dimension to happiness. We learn early in our lives from our parents and peers that our happiness should not lead to the misery of others or increase their misery. A robber may feel happy by stealing from another. A hunter may feel happy after hunting a few wild animals and making trophies out of their heads. Spiritually, it is best described in many religions as dark and evil happiness, or sadistic happiness, that will be short lived with worst karmic results.

True joy arises from helping others, and being helpful. We also feel happy and at peace when we care for others. This social dimension of happiness should never be ignored. The US constitution guarantees its citizens life, liberty and the pursuit of happiness. The three are interconnected. There is nothing depressing for a human being than having no freedom, living in fear and submission, and feeling oppressed by the weight of authority. You are happier when you have the freedom to exercise your will and make choices for your wellbeing. This, in brief, is the social aspect of happiness.

Wealth and happiness

There is a material side to happiness. Wealth may not make you a happy person, but if you are predisposed to happiness, wealth may increase your chances of happiness. Wealth does not mean material wealth. If you have the wealth of a talent or a skill and if you make use of it abundantly in your life, you will experience greater satisfaction than when you do not find opportunities to use it.

Happiness stems from the abundance of having things, reaching goals, making use of your talents, achieving success, having good health, doing a job that you like, having the freedom to enjoy life, having opportunities to achieve excellence, perfecting your skills, earning name and fame, holding leadership positions of power and authority, enjoying a higher status in society, having a good net worth or assured income, and having fulfilling relationships with friends and family.

Generally, people are happy when they have opportunities to be themselves, express themselves and actualize their potentials, talents, dreams and aspirations. When they live in countries that provide them with such opportunities to reach their personal goals and earn recognition for their individual talents and skills, they experience greater fulfillment and inner happiness than when such conditions are absent or limited.

A world of scarcity is a world of misery. Movies and literature may glorify scarcity and poverty and demonize wealth in support of certain deluded agendas, but the human heart knows in which direction lies its happiness. This is the material aspect of success.

Spirituality and happiness

Now, as to the spiritual side of happiness, the general belief is that spiritual people are somewhat serious about life and not very fun loving. This is a fallacious belief. While material success brings us happiness, it can be cemented further with spiritual effort. Our scriptures suggest that happiness can be experienced as peace and stability by contentment, giving and remaining centered in our spiritual selves.

People who attend to their spiritual needs and cultivate a certain spiritual attitude early in their lives are generally happy and peaceful. We learn from our spiritual masters that more important than happiness, which is fleeting, is overcoming the afflictions and modifications of the mind, which is usually accomplished by practicing detachment, renunciation, moderation, balance, sameness, discretion, purity, restraint, discipline, honesty, non-covetousness, resolve, concentration, meditation and devotion. Spirituality demands sincere and austere effort. Not everyone can stand up to its challenges. People have to discover their own spirituality.

Some find peace in the company of Nature, some in helping others, some in saving the wild animals, some in providing shelter, some in volunteering, some in being themselves, some in yoga, some in the service to God and some in avoiding the company of the worldly. It depends upon the temperament of each individual, and whether you want to balance your material desires with spiritual aspirations or devote your attention and resources fully to your spiritual growth. This is the spiritual aspect of happiness.

Religions and happiness

Religions may make people either happy or miserable. It depends upon how they look to their religions, what they learn from it, where they focus their attention and how they use their knowledge and principles of religion for their growth and development.

Each religion has higher and lower aspects. Depending upon their beliefs and attitudes and the area of attention, religions may become a major source of happiness or misery. They may lead you to light and wisdom or to darkness, delusion, and ignorance. They may lead to misery and suffering if people use them to promote persecutions and discrimination of individuals, caste and class divisions or unjustly invest certain groups and individuals with moral and temporal authority to punish others in the name of God and divine justice. If history is any proof, religions might have provided solace to individuals who were predisposed to certain beliefs, but did not create conditions for lasting happiness of people upon earth.

Therefore, we can safely conclude that religions do not guarantee happiness, unless they are used for righteous and just purposes. With right knowledge and temperament, certain people can derive peace and happiness from their religions. Those who do not believe in organized religions may also achieve the same level of peace and happiness by developing a personal philosophy of their own according to their knowledge and experiences and use it to cushion themselves from disappointments and setbacks. Fear and anxiety are major obstacles to peace and happiness. People can deal with them with the help of their religious beliefs and personal philosophies.

Religions are also effective in creating happiness when you are willing to sacrifice your selfish happiness in the larger interests of common good and in the hope of achieving spiritual liberation. Both require, holistic vision and unflinching faith. In other words, when properly used and aligned to their nature and purpose, religions can improve the spiritual wellbeing of people and help them experience peace, solace and security. This is the religious aspect of happiness.

Happiness here and hereafter

The scriptures of various religions suggest that happiness is not possible here but only hereafter. They depict the earth, the mortal world, as the most miserable and sinful place in the creation of God where demons await at every turn to tempt the souls with evil desires. According to them, it is the preparatory ground, certainly not your final destiny or cherished place. You may even consider it a testing ground or slippery slope because it is not what it seems to be and everything in it is a potential trap, including your happiness.

What you consider material success by world standards may actually be a sinful compromise in the judgment of heaven since material success is hard to win without sacrificing moral values. The scriptures remind you constantly with monotonous regularity that living in such a miserable and depressing world, filled with sin and evil, you are entitled to experience here rare moments of divine rapture like the sunlight that glistens through dark clouds. You will find blissful happiness on a lasting basis only in the immortal heaven of Supreme God where everything is in perfect harmony and superfine condition. One of the Upanishads goes to the extent of explaining that the bliss of being in the company of God is a billion times more intense than that of the carnal pleasure experienced through sexual union.

Thus, in one way or another, every religion conveys the same implicit message that the purpose of your life here is to exercise restraint and prepare yourself for the life after death, dealing with the demons of your own mind and postponing your pleasures and natural urges until the end, rather than pursuing pleasures for pleasure sake. They warn you that trying to find happiness in this world is like chasing a mirage, because everything that you find here is impermanent, unstable, and fuels your desire for having more of the same.

Therefore, from a heavenly perspective, neither wealth nor success will guarantee true happiness in the next world, but detachment with them. True happiness hereafter comes only at the expense of an arduous effort, at the end of a long and grueling struggle when you have suffered enough and sacrificed enough. To qualify for the immortal life in the highest heaven you should have carried in your heart the embers of agony, learned the lessons of your life out of such suffering, and perfected yourself on the path to liberation, letting go of everything including your preference for comfort and happiness.

Circumstances and happiness

Recent researches in happiness suggest that certain conditions predispose people to happiness. For example people are found to be happiest when they are with their friends rather than with their spouses or children. Similarly, research indicates that money is not the most powerful factor in influencing people's sense of wellbeing.

Instead, there are other factors like a good night sleep, helping others, being appreciated, feeling useful, finding a purpose, which tend to make people feel good about themselves and their accomplishments. Abraham Maslow suggested that the satisfaction of needs leads to happiness, especially satisfaction of higher needs such as the self-actualization needs. They lead to "peak experiences" that are characterized by uplifting, empowering and ego-transcending emotions such as euphoria, bliss, feelings of self-worthiness and even the mystical experience of feeling oneness with the world or the universe. Studies also show that our happiness also depends upon how we frame our experiences or interpret them. For example, a person may feel happy in an unhappy situation if he perceives it as a learning experience or sees some clear advantages in it.

Love and happiness

Love and happiness do not necessarily go together. Those who are in love may experience happiness in the presence of their lovers.

However, they may also suffer from anxiety and depression if they are separated from them or if there are barriers which prevent them from seeing each other. The greatest love stories in human history are also the greatest human tragedies because in them the lovers do not meet in the end, which proves that for human beings love can be a source of pleasure or unhappiness.

Like other human emotions, love also deteriorates overtime. Romantic love creates suffering rather than happiness because it makes people vulnerable and puts enormous emotional burden upon each partner to adapt to their mutual expectations. Authentic happiness comes from being free rather than being bound. If you are seeking happiness out of love relationships, you must be prepared for disappointments and setbacks. If you can learn to lover others without expectations and without attachment, which is very difficult for ordinary people, then you will have better chances of experiencing happiness in your lover relationships. In other words, love can make people happy only if it is selfless and free from conditions and expectations.

Success and happiness

It is a common belief that you are happier if you are successful. The truth is the pursuit of success may not lead to your happiness unless you learn to balance both your success and personal wellbeing. Success demands change and change demands compromise and adjustment. Therefore, to achieve success you may have to make certain choices and sacrifices which may reduce your happiness.

For many, success means willingness to work for long hours, coping with professional jealousy and constant scrutiny, denying yourself that precious vacation opportunity or missing quality time with your friends and family. All of them can be potential happiness busters. Even if you manage to resolve them while striving for success, more problems may arise later when you achieve success. If achieving success is one part of the story, managing it is another. The peak of any pyramid is always sharply pointed. Just as standing on it is difficult and painful, standing on the peak of your success is more stressful and challenging than climbing and reaching it.

Thus, for the ill prepared and the unsteady, success may prove counterproductive. When you are successful, you have to deal with the attention and the responsibility that come with it. Many people break under the constant glare of publicity and media attention. Some succumb to self-destructive habits, and sabotage their own success and wellbeing. Therefore, if you are aiming for success and if you want to be happy, normal and peaceful, you have to cultivate a healthy mindset where you can remain in control of your life and actions and avoid the side effects of success.

Happiness is not the sole aim of human life

There is more to life than the mere pursuit of happiness because true happiness depends upon many factors. Human beings are not happy by just being happy. They want to achieve and accomplish more. Most of them want to lead meaningful lives, with pride and dignity, and be liked, loved and respected. They want to lead a life that defines them, elevates them in the esteem of others and contributes to their overall wellbeing. Such expectations demand immense effort and sacrifices on their part, including the sacrifice of happiness itself.

Therefore while happiness is important, it is not what human life is all about. Human beings regard life both as an opportunity to experience the richness and diversity of life as well as to accomplish certain important goals, which they cherish in their hearts as self-actualizing. The final result of all that accomplishment, they presume, would be happiness. Thus, people experience happiness for a variety of reasons, including even negative ones, like the defeat or the demise of an enemy or the incarceration of a serial killer.

Reasons for unhappiness

It is important to know that unhappiness is not the exact opposite of happiness. The absence of one may not trigger the other. Sometimes, they may also coexist. In most cases, people alternate between them according to their thoughts, attention and memories. Happiness and unhappiness are essentially different emotions experienced by humans under different circumstances.

However, knowing what makes you unhappy can be helpful. With the knowledge, you can develop effective strategies either to cope with your unhappiness or minimize its possibility. Some of the factors which lead to unhappiness are chronic physical and mental illness, comparison, negative self-talk, conflicts, abusive relationships, unhealthy habits, failure, criticism, disapproval, jealousy, hostile environment, fear and anxiety and lack of meaning and purpose in life. By knowing them and understanding them, you can learn to control your behavior and responses and improve your chances of experiencing happiness

Happiness in giving and serving

While happiness is an important component of life, we know from experience that we do not live by happiness alone. We have to accomplish other aims to experience fulfillment or inner satisfaction, for which we may have to temporarily sacrifice many things, even happiness.

Take for example people who go abroad for higher wages leaving behind their families, people who volunteer to live in economically backward countries to render community service, or people who choose to visit war torn areas to report about the conditions there. They sacrifice many comforts and personal happiness to achieve their goals and improve their circumstances. They transcend their own need for happiness and learn to make sacrifices for the welfare of the others. Research in the field of human happiness indicates that those who serve others derive more happiness and satisfaction in their lives than those who live solely for themselves.

Measuring happiness

About two hundred years ago, a British philosopher felt that it was possible to measure happiness and quantify it by taking into consideration certain factors such as its intensity, duration, speed, certainty, purity, consequences and so on. John Stuart Mill and Francis Edgeworth followed in his footsteps and tried to improve upon his methods of quantifying happiness.

While it may be possible today to measure the intensity of a feeling or emotion by studying brain impulses, and responses, we are still far away from devising universally acceptable methods of measuring happiness. We may intrinsically know how happy we are and by observing with certain sensitivity how happy others are and use that information to compare and contrast, but still that knowledge would be inadequate to quantify happiness on a measurable scale.

Our happiness may range from very unhappy states to very happy states, with several grades of happiness or unhappiness in between. We may use this information to devise questionnaires and survey forms and ask people to answer whether in a particular situation they are very happy, happy, somewhat happy, not happy and very unhappy. Based upon the answers, we may arrive at some logical conclusions. Using this approach, Ed Deiner devised a standard scale called the "Satisfaction with life Scale" to determine a person's satisfaction in subjective terms and identify areas of dissatisfaction.

In this method, each participant has to answer few simple questions, stating whether he or she strongly agrees, agrees, slightly agrees, neither agrees nor disagrees, disagrees or strongly disagrees with a particular statement concerning his or her life. Another scale, called the "Subjective Happiness Scale," follows a slightly different approach. As the name indicates, it uses a simple questionnaire form, asking the participants to rate themselves on a scale from one to seven to measure how they would regard themselves in terms of their happiness.

While such studies seem inadequate, they do establish that happiness is better measured by a person himself in a subjective state and in subjective terms rather than by an outsider in an objective state. Even with such limitations, these methods help therapists and behavioral scientists to identify chronically depressed patients and help them find meaning and purpose in their lives. Unhappy people tend to fall into deeper states of unhappiness if they are not helped in time to recover from their negative thinking. These methods help researchers and counselors gauge the emotional states of their patients and suggest suitable remedies. They also help ordinary individuals to become cognizant of their own psychological states and work for their emotional wellbeing.

Any study of happiness based upon certain criteria is useful only in a limited sense since it is not an exact science. Although happiness is too complex a mental state to fit into a definitive model of quantification and statistical analysis, it would be better if people use quantifiable methods to become aware of their own emotional states and hidden feelings and work on them.

Authentic happiness

Authentic happiness comes from within, not from the external conditions as many believe. It is an intrinsic quality that does not depend upon circumstances or favorable factors to sustain itself. It is also an elusive quality that many people never experience in their lives. The following points in this regard are worth reflecting.

1. Happiness is not the chief aim of human life. From the perspective of science, it is survival; from the perspective of philosophy it is finding purpose and meaning; and from the perspective of scriptures it is happiness in afterlife. Real and lasting happiness is an ideal that remains elusive for almost everyone.
2. Happiness is relative to your desires, expectations, and values. Therefore, there is no simple formula to know what makes everyone happy.
3. Happiness cannot be faked. We may keep smiling at people and situations with an artificial smile, but in weak moments we betray our true emotions through involuntary words and actions.
4. Depression is the most glaring problem of human life. By the time you have finished reading this article at least 10 people

would have committed suicide in various parts of the world and twice that number would have actually thought of ending their lives. According to the study done by World Health Organization, one person dies every 45 seconds because of suicide.
5. If you know anyone who is not happy, try to bring some cheer into that person's life with your generosity or kindness. Research shows that we become happier when we make others happy.

Six ways to boost happiness

In his book The Rough Guide to Psychology Dr. Christian Jarett suggests the following six research or "evidence based ways to boost your happiness."

1. **Smile**. Even an artificial smile seems to lead to happier mood in many people.
2. **Don't have kids**. Parents on average are less happy than non-parents.
3. **Become a political activist**. Activism of some kind seems to make students happier and energized.
4. **Be grateful**, counting your blessings, expressing thanks, showing gratitude and focusing on what is working for you and contributing to your happiness
5. **Engage in repeatedly enjoyable activities**. Engaging in activities that boost our happiness in small doses was found effective to achieve long lasting well-being.
6. **Mix with happy people**. Studies show that happiness increases when we frequently interact with people who are happy.

The principles of happiness

Psychologist Martin Seligman suggested that human beings are happier in certain conditions. He used the acronym PERMA to name the following five conditions that are conducive to human happiness.

- Pleasure
- Engagement
- Relationships
- Meaning
- Accomplishments.

In my experience and observation, I have noticed that the following 14 factors can potentially increase your happiness, or create opportunities for you to experience happiness.

1. **Self-knowledge**: Knowing what you need, what makes you happy, how to make yourself happy, etc.
2. **Acceptance**: Making peace with yourself, accepting who you are and what you are, your abilities and limitations.
3. **Adaptability**: Adapting yourself to your environment, adjusting your temperament, learning not to compare yourself with others, and learning from your failures and successes.
4. **Purpose**: Having a purpose in life that is worth living for
5. **Vision**: Having a vision that gives you the ability to view your problems and circumstances with right attitude and from right perspective.
6. **Control**: Being able to make decisions about your life and destiny that empower you and make you feel good about yourself, and staying in control of your thoughts and emotions.
7. **Belongingness**: Having people around you who care for you and stand by you when you need them the most. Letting others know that you need them and care for them.
8. **Attitude**: Readiness to adjust your expectations according to situations and focus on things that give you hope and happiness even in unfavorable circumstances.
9. **Discipline**: The ability to stay the course, sticking to the plan, remaining committed to your goals and principles.
10. **Balance**: Ability to control your passions, emotions, desires and expectations, your personal life and professional life etc.
11. **Health**: Making your health one of your long term priorities, with provision for adequate rest, exercise, proper diet etc.
12. **Environment**: Creating an environment that is conducive to your wellbeing.
13. **Family**: Knowing that your happiness depends largely upon the overall happiness of your family.
14. **Profession**: Knowing that your profession plays an important role in your life and happiness, and how you can make it a source of happiness and celebration, rather than stress and anxiety.

Proven Techniques to Make Money and Grow Rich

In his book Think and Grow Rich, Napoleon Hill proposed what he termed a "magic formula" which would help people to make a "stupendous fortune" by turning their dreams into riches and achieve, peace, prosperity and abundance. It was a revolutionary effort on his part as he interviewed 504 rich people of his times and garnered their secrets to know how they made their money. Since it was a research-based effort, his work is considered an authoritative and reliable source of information for people to follow his methods and achieve peace and prosperity.

Because of the foundational research he had done in the manifesting powers of the subconscious mind, his work is still considered important both for inspiration and practice. Napoleon Hill named his book, "Think and Grow Rich," thereby suggesting in the title itself the powerful connection between thinking and manifesting. He discovered a process through which one could make miracles happen, using thoughts, dreams and desires, in conjunction with positive emotions, and reinforcing them with clear vision and repeated affirmations. He declared in the opening chapter that "thoughts are things," and suggested that with "definiteness of purpose, persistence and a burning desire, "anyone could translate their thoughts into "riches and other material objects."

Most of the ideas presented by Napoleon Hill were well known to the sages and seers in the Oriental world for millenniums. They are reaffirmed in the Upanishads and many Hindu scriptures as internalized Vedic rituals and yoga practices to manifest the powers of the mind, connect to the universal consciousness, and unravel the transcendental truths hidden in creation and within oneself. The Jainas used them to conquer their minds and bodies and reach omniscience. The Buddha employed them to transform the human consciousness and arrest its modifications.

They are also suggested in Christianity and Islam to reach out to dreams and visions not of this earth. Before Napoleon Hill, many western philosophers, theosophists and writers referred to such powers. By relating them to business and commerce and to worldly success, Napoleon Hill clothed them in a language which most people understood. Therefore, although he was not a pioneer in this field, a lot of credit goes to him for making those ideas popular in the western world.

Thought is a powerful factor in shaping our lives. People may complain about not having this and that, but none can complain about the scarcity of thought. People may not know how to think correctly or effectively, but everyone has the potential to think and form ideas and opinions. Napoleon Hill stated that people were able to realize their dreams using their commonest asset, their own minds. It was not wealth which created wealth in the first place, but a mind enriched with the power of purpose, desire, emotion, determination and affirmation. To quote his famous words, "Whatever the mind of man can conceive and believe, it can achieve." Again, "There are no limitations to the mind, except those we acknowledge."

In the following discussion, I present, in my own way, a few factors identified by him which he believed would help people, irrespective of their present financial conditions, to achieve "money, fame, recognition and happiness." Ever since, he published the book, countless people read it and benefited from it. Most of the books written later about abundance and thought power are mere reassertions of what he originally stated. Therefore, here I decided not to reinvent the wheel, but rather present his ideas in my own words and according to my own understanding and interpretation. For a more detailed study, I would recommend his book.

Desire

Desires are common and universal to all living beings that possess some form of consciousness. They are especially pronounced and active in humans. They act as powerful motivating factors and draw us into the world of sense objects and sensual pleasures. In fact, it is very difficult for normal people not to have any desires. It is even more difficult to suppress them or control them. They play a vital role survival and continuity. However, not all desires are conducive to our Wellbeing. Some desires are positive and constructive, while some are negative and self-destructive. With the help of desires, we can either turn our dreams into great riches or succumb to temptations and fall down.

Therefore, we have to be careful about what desires we entertain in our minds and which desires we think mostly. We can turn our desires into dreams, and with sustained effort, purpose, determination, organized effort and precise goals, we can turn our dreams into riches and reality. According to Napoleon Hill, it is not sufficient to have a mere desire, but "a burning desire" to achieve what you intend to achieve. To achieve success, you must mix your desires with determination and turn them into "concrete action." It means you should have well-defined goals with clarity of purpose, and well laid out plans.

Once you identify your purpose and goals, you must put all your energy and effort into achieving them. Napoleon Hill proposed a six step method to turn your desires into gold. They hinged on the central idea that you should have a well-defined goal, coupled with a concrete plan of action to achieve it, and you should remember it frequently until it is firmly planted in your consciousness. With burning desires you can overcome insurmountable difficulties and achieve the impossible.

Faith

If desire is the initiating power, faith is the sustaining power. We may begin our actions because of desires, however, we may not continue in our effort unless we have faith and the conviction that we have chosen the right course of action and our actions would bear fruit. We need faith to adhere to a disciplined effort and implement our plans to fulfill our desires.

Napoleon Hill suggested that when we blended our thoughts (or desires) with faith and other positive emotions, our subconscious minds would pick up those vibrations, as in case of a prayer, and change them into their spiritual equivalents before transmitting them to the Infinite Intelligence, or the Universal Mind for their manifestation.

In other worlds, with faith you can transform your desires and dreams mixed with positive emotions into powerful prayers and infuse them with the tremendous power of the Almighty so that they would bear fruit almost miraculously. Napoleon Hill believed in the miraculous powers of the subconscious mind and its affinity with the Divine Mind. He proposed that when an idea was presented to the subconscious mind repeatedly along with powerful emotions, it would eventually accept it and materialize it into its physical counterpart.

The same principle holds true with regard to both positive and negative thoughts and emotions. Whatever thoughts and emotions people entertain in their minds and eventually accept them influence their behavior and destinies. What we call bad luck or misfortune is actually the result of negative thoughts and emotions we entertain in our minds repeatedly. If we focus upon the negative, we invite negative events into our lives and surround ourselves with negativity.

Therefore, Napoleon Hill suggested that it was important to entertain only positive thoughts and emotions and let them dominate our minds. Thoughts mixed with faith and positive emotions would become a magnetic force and great motivating factor. They gather strength by attracting similar thoughts, and when favorable circumstances are presented, they would materialize into reality.

Auto suggestions

The mind has its own way of thinking and framing each experience. The way our conscious minds work depends upon the mental habits we form out of our learning, knowledge, experiences and beliefs. Although we can control and regulate our conscious minds, in most cases we do not exercise proper control. Hence, most people "go through life in poverty." If we do not send proper thoughts to our subconscious, we will let destructive thoughts settle in our subconscious minds and interfere with our dreams and destinies.

Therefore, Napoleon Hill suggested that we should write down our intended goals or desires on paper and read them loudly and repeatedly, mixing them with positive emotions, until they were firmly implanted in our subconscious minds. To quote his own words, "Your ability to use the principle of autosuggestion will depend, very largely, upon your capacity to concentrate upon a given desire until that desire becomes a burning obsession."

It is important not only to think about your desires and goals frequently but also to use your imagination and visualize them as if they already happened. Using this trick you can persuade your subconscious mind to go into action and transform your desires into practical and actionable solutions, which you may perceive in your conscious mind as inspiration, creative ideas or intuition. When it happens, you must instantly begin to act on the idea until it becomes a reality.

Specialized knowledge

By specialized knowledge, we mean the specific knowledge that is required to achieve the desires and dreams or the specific goals a person aims to achieve. It refers to the knowledge acquired not only through education but also through experience, intelligence, observation and understanding. In the words of Napoleon Hill, "An educated man is not necessarily one who has abundance of general and specialized knowledge."

According to him an educated person develops the necessary skills and faculties to get whatever he wants, without violating the rights of others. As in case of Henry Ford, whom he quoted as an example, he may not have the necessary technical knowledge but he knows from where to get it and how to organize it into "definite plans of action." To achieve your goals, you need specialized and organized knowledge. You do not have to possess such knowledge, but you must know from where to get it and how to make use of it.

Therefore, you do not have to worry that you do not have the required education or technical qualifications to perform certain tasks that are vital to your success. You should apply commonsense and seek the help of those who posses such knowledge and make use of it. If possible, you may also acquire it through self-study, by going to an evening school or college, or through distance learning. You may use such knowledge to implement your plans or, if you do not have the wherewithal, you may sell your plans and ideas to others, who have similar goals.

Conclusion

Apart from these, Napoleon Hill mentioned other factors which contribute to our success and prosperity, namely imagination, organized planning, decisiveness, persistence, mastermind, transmutation of sexual energy, subconscious mind, the hidden potential of the human brain, sixth sense, and eliminating fear and doubt. He believed that armed with these principles anyone could realize their desires and goals. If you have not read the book "Think and Grow Rich," and if you want to unlock the secrets of your own mind, or at least for inspiration, you should find a copy and read it immediately. In this short discussion, you are merely introduced to the subject. There is a lot of useful information in the book, which needs to be assimilated and internalized for better results. It will open your eyes to many truths regarding the power of your subconscious mind and your potential to be the master of your life and destiny. If you try hard, you will realize and even know by experience how you may realize your dreams using the most powerful resources you have within yourself, namely your thoughts, desires, faith and determination.

Why People Avoid Having Goals

A lot of people dream about their lives and their future, but do not make an effort to set goals for their future and work for them. They just drift along, rather aimlessly, expecting the best, but not doing enough to improve their lives. For them having goals is rather a tedious affair, which requires effort, discipline and focus for which they are not mentally or emotionally prepared. Many people do entertain dreams and desires about their future. They wish for better lives and more success. However, dreams and desires are not goals. Only a few succeed in shaping them into meaningful, precise and well-written goals. Vague thinking about future does not qualify it as a goal or a plan. A goal is not just what you want to do in life in a wishful way. A goal is a dream with a theme, a picture with full details, and a purpose with a definite plan. Goals must be clear, specific, written, realistic and achievable. If you have clear goals, you will have greater focus, confidence, resolve and clarity.

In spiritual life goal oriented effort is not appreciated because it connotes ambition and desired-ridden actions, neither of which are helpful to overcome worldliness. On the spiritual path you have to live freely, without any encumbrances, practicing renunciation and detachment, and letting things happen on their own, rather than making them happen. Striving for particular goals by a spiritual person is deemed retrogressive, since it negates the very purpose for which renunciation is recommended. Ideally, a spiritual person flows with life, dealing with situations as they arise, without worrying about his survival or success or what may happen to him the next moment. In normal life, we cannot afford to live this way, although at times it may be good to let go of things and live without the thought of the next day or next year. A spiritual person may still have goals without being unduly attached to them, involved with them or particular about their outcome. What is important is having goals and pursuing them with certain resolve and sincerity, whether such goals are about your spiritual aspirations or your material needs.

There are reasons why common people do not prefer setting goals for themselves. Some of those reasons are internal and the others are external or circumstantial. Fear of failure, ignorance, prejudice, irrational beliefs, lack of discipline and focus, lack of drive and ambition, resource constraints are a few important reasons why most people do not prefer to have specific goals and work for them. Self-destructive or self-limiting thinking is another reason. Many people do not think that they deserve success because they suffer from low self-esteem, which prevents them from thinking big, as it lowers their self-image and confidence, besides creating self-doubts. These and other factors develop in them a certain rigid and defensive mindset which makes them averse to setting goals and taking risks.

Brian Tracy, in his book, the Maximum Achievement, identified the following seven reasons why people do not prefer having goals and thereby fail to unlock their hidden potential to succeed.

1. They are not serious about their success.
2. They do not take the responsibility of their lives.
3. They suffer from guilt and unworthiness.
4. They do not know the importance of goals.
5. They do not know how to set goals properly.
6. They suffer from fear of rejection or criticism.
7. They are afraid of failure.

People who do not keep goals in their lives for one reason of another can be divided into the following four main categories.

1. The ignorant ones: They do not know that goals are important and necessary for their success and happiness. This is a common problem among those who do not have proper education, who have not been exposed to any information about goals or their importance. It does not mean that they do not think about their future or improving it. They just do not know the mechanics of goal setting. They may do better if they are taught to improve their lives by choosing a few important goals and working for them.

2. **The unprepared ones**: They do not consider that goals are necessary or important. Such people may know vaguely the importance of goals, and may have seen, read or heard about it. However, they are not still convinced that goals can do them any good. They may even mistake having goals for lack of freedom and self-imposed restriction. Therefore, they prefer to live their lives without specific goals and aims. They may have their own values and principles, which they may put to work with faith and dedication, but they lack motivation to establish clear and specific goals. Such people can do better and exceed their own expectations, if they rethink about their attitude and choose a few specific goals that can transform their lives and destinies.

3. **The undisciplined ones**: Those who do not have the commitment and discipline to work for their goals fall into this category. They may have the knowledge of goals and may also choose a few goals to regulate their lives. However, they do not make adequate effort

because they do not want to lose their freedom or commit to the discipline which is required to pursue goals. They do not like the hard work, structure and discipline, which any goal oriented effort demands. They also lack patience and ambition that are required to achieve goals, or deal with the challenges one may face while reaching them. For them having goals and working for them is too stressful, intimidating, monotonous, mechanical to take any action.

4. The weak hearted ones: These are people having weak resolve to achieve anything worthy of honor and pride in their lives. They avoid having goals for fear of failure, criticism or public ridicule. People with self-doubt and low self-esteem generally fall in this category. They do not want to pursue goals because they do not want to fail or fall in their own esteem or that of others, and humiliate themselves in the process. They exaggerate their fears or indulge in irrational thinking to avoid having any goals at all. It is the flight response which prevents them from being effective in their lives. For some people failure is a learning experience because they have a growth mindset. Those with rigid mindset feel crushed by disappointments and failure and prefer avoiding it rather than deal with it. Therefore, they do not want to take any risks by setting goals and deal with the uncertainty arising from their actions.

If you are one of these, see what you can do to overcome whatever resistance you may have to set your goals and work for them. The lives of successful people show that they achieve success mainly through goals and goal-oriented effort. The most successful people are those who have written goals, who know where they want to go and in which direction they want to progress. We may not be able to predict future with certainty and we may never be sure whether we achieve our goals or not, but we can minimize uncertainty to some extent, by planning in advance, maximizing our potentials, working on our strengths, working around our weaknesses, learning from our failures, and keeping ourselves in a positive frame of mind.

How To Become An Expert In Any Field

This is the age of knowledge and information. It is also the age of expertise, innovation, and specialization. What would you prefer, a million dollars with no intelligence or a brilliant mind with a million hopes, ideas and aspirations? The Facebook founder received an offer for a billion dollars few years ago to sell his company. A billion dollars was a lot of money for a young man who did not have even a thousand dollars to start his company. Yet, he rejected the offer because he believed in himself, in his goals and in his vision which laid his path clearly before him.

If you have the vision, and if you have the willingness to make it real, you will eventually reach your goals and realize your dreams. You can be part of a little group of exceptional people who can make a difference to the world with their skills, knowledge and ideas. It does not matter in what area you specialize. If you have specialized knowledge or expertise in some professional field, you will increase your value and your chances of success.

Life upon earth is a great opportunity to expand your knowledge and enrich your experience. Many people do not make use of it. They spend their valuable time in cheap entertainment or frivolous matters. Few years ago, over two billion people, most of them outside U.K., watched the marriage of prince Williams and Kate Middleton. Collectively one fourth of the humanity spent 2-5 billion hours in watching the wedding of two people whom they would never meet in person. Perhaps they would have wasted another 100 billion hours in the next few weeks and months trying to know how the newly married royal couple were doing, what clothes they are wearing or how many kisses they have exchanged in public view.

People blindly follow celebrities on the social networks. If a film star posts a twitter message saying that her cat just woke up from sleep, a thousand people would respond to that message with comments and retweets. Perhaps a celebrity's cat or dog will have more followers and admirers on social networks than teachers, doctors, and professors. This is just an example of how people waste precious moments, opportunities and resources, without even knowing it. Your life, worth and value do not depend upon a film star or singer you admire and follow. It does not depend upon how you push your way through a raucous crowd into the first row during a concert and manage to shake hands with the singer, but upon what knowledge and intelligence you have and how you make use of them.

To succeed in any field you must stand out in a world of mediocre people. Your exceptional qualities must be clearly discernible. People must feel confident in the radiance of your knowledge. Your expertise does not arise from your family background or the name of your university. It comes from your effort, dedication, commitment and passion. You do not have to graduate from Harvard or Oxford to become an expert in any field. Let us not forget that the world's most renowned and knowledgeable people originally came from poor and middle class families and relatively unknown schools and colleges. Frankly, you do not even require university education to be successful in this world. Some of the world's greatest people were illiterate or semi literate. Akbar, the Mughal Emperor, for example, was an illiterate person, but he excelled as a king and administrator.

Have you ever noticed who are the most sought after people in society, in a work place or a profession? Apart from good looking people and celebrities, with whom society is always infatuated, it is usually the ones who are renowned for their knowledge and expertise in a particular field, and who have an exceptional ability to solve any problem or deal with any crisis.

People go to them because they are reliable and dependable in difficult times. They do not mind spending precious money or time to meet them or seek their advice. Organizations are willing to spend huge amounts of money to hire them or retain them because in a competitive environment they can make a huge difference. Here is how you can join this group of rare individuals and earn for yourself distinction and respect in your chosen field.

1. Choose your field: Identify the area in which you want to develop the expertise. In each field there are specific areas of expertise and each requires a specific set of skills and knowledge. Choose the one that appeals to you most or for which you think you have the passion. Think of the motivation or why you want to develop expertise in that particular area and make sure that your decision is not based on whim or the need to seek the approval of others. If you want to become an expert in some area, it must be to actualize your dreams and aspirations, not to win the approval of others.

2. Know what you need to do: Do research to find out what you have to do to develop necessary skills and become an expert. Spend time to know how you may reach that goal. If you are unsure, find people who are known experts in that area and meet them personally. If you cannot do it, read books and articles written by them or about them to know what makes them unique and how they developed their skills. Create a mental picture of the person you want to be. Write it down and make it your ideal image of the person you want to become through hard work and determination.

3. Prepare a clear action plan: Draw an action plan in writing, with tasks and schedules clearly specified according to your goals, to acquire knowledge and skills in your chosen field. State clearly in what timeframe you want to accomplish them and what specific actions you might need to reach them. If the knowledge is highly specialized and requires rare skills, you may have to take an academic course, study books, coach yourself, or seek training under the guidance of an expert. Think of all the possibilities and opportunities, how you can use of your strengths, and resolve the problems that may arise from your weaknesses.

4. Put your plan into action: Once you have drawn an action plan, you have to implement it with conviction and commitment. This is the heart of your whole endeavor. Here your motivation has to come entirely from within, for which you have to rely upon none but yourself, and reason with yourself in moments of self-doubt and negativity. If you ever have to face that situation, keep returning to the image you developed in step two to refocus and energize yourself. Depending upon how you deal with yourself and your thoughts, you can be your best friend or your worst enemy. You should not let your negative thoughts, doubts and fears, sabotage your effort or weaken your resolve. Do not rest until you feel comfortable with your knowledge and expertise and satisfied that you have reached your set standards. Seek others' opinions about the progress you are making. Join a professional club or association to see how your peers in the field are doing. Keep reading and improving your knowledge.

5. Have role models: Every field has its own role models and authority figures whose words and actions are followed by those who want to reach similar goals. Identify a few of them and study their methods. See what you can learn from them, where you can agree and disagree, and how you can improve upon them. If you can manage, network with a few people and see whether they can provide you with any guidance or mentoring. Join organizations and association related to your field, to connect with others, exchange ideas and establish rapport. You can also attend seminars and public events, where you can mingle with them or listen to them.

6. Improve your skills constantly: Some people stop studying and learning after they complete their academic education. It is a big mistake. Learning is a lifelong commitment. It never stops. There is no end to what you can learn or know, and no limit to the knowledge and expertise you can acquire. Studies have shown that age is not a constraint to learn, and although the pace of learning may slow down with age, people can acquire many soft skills and knowledge in old age also. Even if you think you have become an expert in some field, you cannot stop learning since have to stay competitive with the latest researches, findings and inventions in your field. Therefore, keep learning, improving, and practicing your skills with enthusiasm and curiosity. Learn from every possible source, without missing an opportunity, and keep your mind open and receptive to new ideas and thoughts. Push your limits to the extent possible by competing against yourself. The more you learn and practice, the more skillful you become.

7. Be a good person and help others: Your knowledge and expertise should help not only you but also others. Practice humility and virtue and keep your mind in balance. Knowledge, and the authority that comes with it, can have a corrupting influence upon you. Your knowledge and expertise should not make you an arrogant and conceited. Virtues such as integrity and honesty are as important as skills and expertise in any field. Use them for right purposes and right ends. Become a source of inspiration to others rather than a cause of frustration. The more you know, the more humble you should be. Do not feel discouraged if you are not immediately recognized or rewarded for your helping nature. If you keep hope and faith, you will be recognized soon, just as no one can stop the fragrance of a flower from spreading in the garden. When your time comes, they reveal themselves, despite the people who may not be happy to see you successful.

Mastering the skills

The simple formula to achieve success in any field is to know exactly what you want to achieve and do everything possible the right way to make it happen. Before you begin the journey, you must know the price you have to pay, the sacrifices you have to make, and the time and energy you have to invest to realize your goals. You should not expect to achieve excellence by chance. You must plan for it and work for it. At times, the price can be high. It may cost you peace of mind, relationships and valuable resources. If you keep your focus and effort, you will eventually succeed. Equally important to remember is how serious you are about your goals. If you are intent upon your goals, you have better chances of reaching them. You should also know what you want to do when you reach your goals, and your ultimate purpose. Is it to be happy, recognized and rewarded, outsmart others, feel good about yourself or express your deepest talents and aspirations? If you know the purpose, it will help you to keep your morale high and your mind focused.

Self-reliance, self-confidence, determination, positive mental attitude, courage, integrity, clarity of thought and purpose, specific goals, self-discipline are valuable resources which you can use in your life to acquire knowledge and skills and pursue your cherished goals. If you are intent upon a particular goal and work for it vigorously, you are bound to achieve it, no matter the obstacles and the difficulties. To reach your goals, you must be willing to change your thinking and attitude and invest enough time and energy to be where you want to be.

If you are determined to achieve excellence in your chosen area and willing to give your best, you are bound to achieve it. Find your passion and strengths, and integrate them into your life's essential purpose to achieve you goals. By doing it, you will not only realize your life's dreams but also serve as a role model to others to accomplish their dreams in the right manner. Therefore, decide to be the best in your profession, and become one.

Enjoying The Simple Pleasures Of Life

You do not have to be a rich person or possess riches to enjoy life. If you have riches, you will have better options and opportunities to use luxuries and enjoy a better life. However, it is not the only means by which you can bring cheer into your life. If it is untrue, only a few people in this world would have been really happy or able to enjoy their lives. Whether they are rich or poor, people can make themselves happy, and within their means they can learn to enjoy their lives. It is even said that people in poorer countries are often happier than those who live in rich countries because their needs are simple, and lives are less complicated, and they are in better harmony with their environment to which they adapt easily.

Your happiness and enjoyment arise from what you expect from your life, how you take your burdens and where you really focus. You may be a millionaire, but being so is not a one way ticket to enjoyment. If you are smart, you can enjoy life without being rich. This is not an excuse to choose poverty or settle for less. Life does not always happen according to your expectations. If you are forced by circumstances to live in unfavorable surroundings or circumstances and cannot afford luxurious vacations, you can still use your ingenuity to enjoy the simple pleasures of life, by cultivating the right mental attitude and devising suitable methods.

It is true that in life wealth matters. You can surely enjoy a better life and feel good about yourself and your accomplishments, if you have an abundance of resources at your disposal. Living a luxurious and comfortable life is the sweet reward of success. However, it does not always guarantee happiness or enjoyment. It is incorrect to assume that only rich people enjoy life or only they are happy. To enjoy anything, your thinking and attitude are equally important. You must be free from worries and anxieties or able to control your mind. You may go on an expensive vacation, but if your mind is occupied with problems and worries, you will not be able to focus on enjoyment. A person I know, after a separation battle, went on a long vacation to Italy to get over it. When she returned, she was even more depressed because she could not reconcile to the fact that her marriage was a failure and she was responsible for it. In Italy, she kept on thinking about her children whose custody she lost. Sometimes, people go on vacation to get over their problems. It may not always work because to enjoy life, attitude and state of mind are equally, if not more, important.

Up to a point, luxuries and other external factors may make people happy, even if they are not internally prepared well for the joys of life. However, it is difficult to say how long they can stay that way. Beyond a threshold the luxuries of life do not excite people at all or help them to deal with their gloom. The world cannot make you happy if you are not willing to be happy. This is the fundamental truth and the same principle applies to enjoyment also. Your internal condition is more important. If you are not internally happy, you cannot find happiness outside. Things may excite you, but not do not make you happy.

You need to be happy to enjoy life, and to be happy you must be in a positive state of mind. Again, it depends upon your expectations, and the way you interpret your life and experiences. It is difficult to argue whether the CEO of a business organization with the best amenities at his disposal enjoys life better than a monk who lives in a monastery in a remote mountain and eats only one meal a day. In both cases, it is their attitude, outlook, thinking, and perceptions, which determine their ability to enjoy life.

You can enjoy life wherever you are by finding reasons to be happy and contended, and focusing upon what you have rather than what you lack. If this not true, the world would be a depressing place to live because more that 95% of the people in the world live within limited means and cannot afford luxurious vacations or extravagant spending. Therefore, focus upon how you can enjoy your life within your means and circumstances. See what you can do to create your own moments of happiness. If you cannot afford expensive vacations and cruise trips, you can still use your creativity to explore other avenues to experience great moments. Whether you are rich or poor, two conditions are important to enjoy life and increase your potential for happiness.

1. An open mind free from prejudice and preconceived notions.
2. Present moment awareness or the ability to live in the present.

It is an illusion to think that you can enjoy life only when you are free from problems and responsibilities, or when you achieve certain goals. People expect to enjoy life when their children grow up, when they get a promotion or pay rise, or when they retire and become free from duties and family obligations. Unfortunately, when people reach those milestones they may get busy with other problems or do not even remember what they wanted to do before.

You do not have to fall into such a mental trap, and postpone you enjoyment to a future date when you have an ideal life or favorable circumstances. Life is a series of events from birth to death. The problems do not end and the journey does not stop until the end. Death and decay are the only certainties towards which life relentlessly moves. As you become older, it becomes increasingly difficult for you to perform certain physical tasks and get the best out of your life.

Therefore, if there is any good time to enjoy your life, it is here and now, wherever you are and in whatever circumstances you may live. Your enjoyment does not arise from the absence of problems and challenges, but from your mental attitude and perceptions.

Whether you are rich or poor, you can enjoy life by cultivating the right attitude and taking advantage of the numerous opportunities life offers to you to experience the simple pleasures of life. Here are a few ways to attune yourself mentally to enjoy your present life.

1. Break the monotony of life by occasionally breaking free from daily routine and doing things differently.
2. Spend quality time with your friends and family, and spare some time for yourself.
3. Learn to pause and relax with any recreational activity such as listening to music or watching a movie.
4. Learn a new hobby, skill, or art and express your creativity.
5. Read an interesting book or listen to audio tapes.
6. Call your friends and speak to them.
7. Go for a long walk in a nearby park.
8. Visit a museum, historic or scenic place and learn about local history.
9. Go on a long drive in the country side and enjoy the open spaces.
10. Join a voluntary organization where you can help others.
11. Mentor a child or a teenager who needs help.
12. Learn yoga or meditation techniques from a qualified teacher and practice them.
13. Join a prayer group or a laughter club.
14. Watch a sunset or sunrise, or an evening or night sky.
15. Visit any place where you lived before and see old friends.
16. Go to a nearby lake, river, canal, stream, or beach and spend some quiet time watching the scenery.
17. Help your children learn new skills.
18. Occasionally stay alone doing nothing.
19. Prepare a special meal and invite your friends to join you.
20. Clean your house and cupboards.
21. Visit local markets or village fairs to observe people and their lifestyles.

22. Write about your thoughts and experiences for a blog or a journal.
23. Learn to be yourself in the company of others.
24. Stay positive and make the best out of everything.

Using your creativity, you can devise many such activities on your own. The ultimate purpose of human life is enjoyment. Use the many opportunities it offers to explore and experience the richness and diversity of the world in which we live. The moments that you spend upon earth are precious, which cannot be valued in monetary or material terms. You must use them wisely to be consciously part of the existence that you perceive and hold as real, even though you may not fully grasp the mysteries about it or its ultimate purpose. You are here to experience life and let life happen to you, using whatever resources that are at your disposal, without being a burden to others or causing them inconvenience.

You are the witness, the observer, and the enjoyer of all that happens to you. Although you cannot avoid suffering, you are not here to suffer, as if you are a victim of circumstances. You are here to observe and experience life, and gather finest moments of harmony and happiness without becoming involved with it and without being caught in preferences, commitments and prejudices.

You are a traveler in the journey of life with an inherent capacity to consciously enjoy the diversity of existence and see the universe from inside. You have the right to enjoyment here and now, cultivating the right attitude and an open mind.

How to Develop Curiosity and Sustain it

Curiosity means eagerness to know something, or having an exceptional or excessive interest in knowing something. Curiosity is the main driving force in our exploration of things that we do not know or want to know. On the positive side, curiosity contributes to our knowledge and awareness. On the negative side, it leads to the invasion of privacy, gossip, and unnecessary interference.

Curiosity is responsible for our inventions, innovations and progress in various fields of knowledge. Without curiosity it is difficult to sustain your interest and enthusiasm to learn new knowledge or acquire new skills. Curiosity helps us to know ourselves, the world in which live, the people we meet, establish relationships with them, and enjoy our lives.

Since curiosity sustains our interest in acquiring knowledge and expanding our field of awareness, it is also important to our success and happiness. It is difficult to achieve success in any endeavor without having curiosity in what we do or pursue.

In life you may not like people who ask questions frequently or those who are not easily satisfied with simple answers. However, we have to admit that the progress of the world depends greatly upon such people only. Their curiosity is the fuel that drives the wheels of our civilization. They are responsible for exploring the unknown and the unfamiliar and starting new movements and trends in every field.

It is not true that only exceptional people have curiosity. Curiosity is a common human trait, found in all humans, and even in many animals. Whether rich or poor, literate or illiterate, all people have curiosity about something they like. However, there may be individual differences among people about what arouses their curiosity. Some people are curious about what others do or say in their private lives and how they live. Some are especially curious about what their friends, family, neighbors, colleagues and relations may be thinking or hiding.

Many people are habitually drawn to gossip columns and tabloid news. They watch television programs, or listen to talk-shows, and radio news, mainly out of curiosity, as they are driven by a strong desire to know the private lives of well-known people, writers, political leaders, film stars and other celebrities, how they live, what they do, with whom they have affairs, or how they are celebrating their success. In fact, a whole industry thrives upon this particular human behavior and fills the airwaves with 24/7 news stories and breaking news.

While a majority of people are drawn to famous people and their private lives, a few develop curiosity in the mysteries of life and existence. They become inquisitive about things and events that are currently beyond the grasp of human mind. They explore the unknown, the unfamiliar and the mysterious and seek answers to difficult questions, as they are dissatisfied with what they already know.

Therefore, they challenge themselves to explore the unknown and overcome their ignorance. The world owes a great deal to them because they are responsible for many major inventions and discoveries that move the world forward on the path of progress and innovation. Curiosity about life, our existence, the world and the universe in which we live is better than curiosity about private lives and secret affairs of people. The former elevates your thinking and vision while the latter constricts your view and degrades your thinking and character.

Curiosity is an inborn human trait. Some people put it to great use while some use it for ordinary purposes. Some use it to seek answers and find meaning in their lives and actions and expand their knowledge, while some use it to know the mundane aspects of life. We can use curiosity to develop skills, mastery, excellence and success in our professions and areas of interest. We can use it to improve our knowledge and understanding of the world, people, and things, and even to know ourselves better by probing into our own nature. Alternatively, we can live with the "know-it-all" attitude, with our heads buried in the sand.

Can curiosity be developed and improved?

The answer is affirmative. Like any other human trait, curiosity can be developed and sustained. To do it we have to understand what sustains and increases our curiosity. For example to develop curiosity, you need an open mind, fearlessness, hunger for knowledge, creative thinking and positive mental attitude. The following suggestions are useful in this regard.

1. Know your passions and dreams: You become curious when you are deeply interested in something, which incites your passions and dreams. Therefore, find out what interests you most, pursue it with dedication. As you become involved with it and drawn into it, you develop curiosity about it.

2. Keep an open and non-judgmental mind: Many people are afraid of the unknown and the unfamiliar. Therefore, they prefer staying in their comfort zones and avoiding taking risks. To cultivate curiosity, you must have an open mind, and you must be willing to explore the unknown, with an adventurous spirit, take risks and accept failure as a learning experience.

3. Transcend your fears: Free yourself from the fear of criticism, negative self-talk, and the disapproval of others. People may discourage you from pursuing goals about which they have no knowledge or in which they are disinterested. Therefore to pursue your curiosity, you must use your own judgment and disregard any criticism you may face in the process.

4. Develop an inclusive mind: To know about anything you must study it from various perspectives, for which you need to free your mind from preconceived notions and prejudices. You must consider all options and alternatives before you draw any conclusions or make decisions.

5. Practice inquisitiveness: Do not be afraid to ask questions and seek answers. As some said, there are no foolish questions, only foolish answers. Expand your knowledge and awareness by gathering information, seeking clarifications and questioning your own assumptions and beliefs. Contemplate upon the mysteries of life and the various perspective from which truth can be studied. Search for answers to those questions that intrigue you and perplex you.

6. Practice mindful observation: The more you observe things and life, the greater will be your curiosity. Many people do not observe life mindfully because they do not pay attention and do not live in the present. If you live in the present and observe carefully the happenings around you, you develop your own insight into things based upon your experience and perceptions rather than what you are told.

7. Stay positive and hopeful: A negative mind is a closed mind. Negative people do not seek answers because they do not see opportunities or possibilities. They lack curiosity because they do not believe in the possibility of knowing more. Even when they become curios, they may not show much interest to pursue it because they do not see positive outcomes or expect to gain any benefit. If you think there is nothing else to know or no possibility of gaining anything from knowing, you will not pursue knowledge or experience curiosity. However, if you keep faith and hope in the possibility of knowing further, and doing further, your curiosity stays alive.

Curiosity drives your success, ambition, knowledge and awareness. Curiosity makes you inquisitive and adventurous, prompting you to stretch your mind into the unknown and gather information about the strange and mysterious facts of life. It is therefore important that you cultivate this unique quality and make use of it for your betterment, knowledge and happiness.

Dealing with People and Relationships

Human relationships are fickle. Think of all the relationships you had in the past. Think of the people you met, the friendships you formed, the great moments you spent with them, and the time energy you invested in them or they in you. What happened to them and your relationship with them? How many of them are still in touch with you? Do you know where they live, or whether they are alive? Do you think of them at all? How many of them do you think still remember you? Do you know where, and what they might be doing right now?

One of the most challenging aspects of human life is how you can cope with the impermanence of human relationships and, how you can deal with the unpredictability of human behavior upon which such relationships depend. Both professionally and personally, managing relationships is challenging and time consuming, unless you prefer shunning society and living in isolation. If you are a sensitive person looking for satisfying relationships in a world that is driven mostly by self-interest, you are bound to feel hurt and disturbed and suffer from alienation and frustration. Many people are lonely even when they are in a crowd because they do not feel connected to the world and its ways. If you are a seeker of truth, who believes in certain values and beliefs, you will feel disappointed to see opportunism, deception, and falsehood upon which many relationships thrive.

Pragmatism teaches that human relationships thrive on tact and manipulation. However, your idealism may prevent you from using tact and diplomacy in your relationships since it means you are not honest with others and not presenting your true self to them. Any conscientious person faces this dilemma and experiences inconvenience if he or she has to use deceptive ways to build or sustain relationships and influence them.

If you are not happy with the people and relationships in your life, you do not have to feel disheartened. It may be comforting to know that most people experience problems in their relationships and do not succeed much in building genuine relationships. They may earn the appreciation of others, but it does not necessarily mean that their relationships are any better, because the appreciation itself may be part of the deception and manipulation. Even self-help experts, counselors, and spiritual people, who have the knowledge and wisdom to tell you how to live harmoniously and mange your relationships, may have great trouble putting the same principles into practice in their personal lives and find fulfillment in them. Mahatma Gandhi was loved by millions of people, but he had great trouble getting along with some of his children. Even well known spiritual gurus of modern times had trouble with their closest disciples and followers.

One of the intriguing facts of human behavior is that exceptional intelligence does not guarantee a successful life or a likable personality. Exceptional people may find it hard to relate to others or communicate with them. They may also show exceptional selectivity and individuality in their dealings with others and thereby alienate many. Socrates, one of the wisest philosophers of the ancient world, faced a lot of criticism from his contemporaries for his forthright approach in exposing people's ignorance and fallacious beliefs. He was constantly riled and ridiculed by his own wife for his lack of interest and incompetence in household matters. History is full of instances where the most intelligent, enlightened and extraordinarily talented people were criticized, ignored, ridiculed, insulted, misunderstood, imprisoned, abused, stoned, tortured, killed, skinned alive or crucified for their lack of human relationship skills, or "tact." This is not an exaggeration but a well-known historical fact, which is well documented by writers of all ages.

Human beings tend to glorify and romanticize exemplary relationships in fiction and mythology because they do not find such ideal relationships in real life. The idealism, which they desire to see in human relationships, they express in art and literature with their imagination and create lovable characters to exemplary and idealize human behavior that they do not normally find in real life. Sometimes, they also do it by fictionalizing real people and romanticizing their behavior. People indulge in such delusions because they need images and symbols of perfect relationships to keep their faith in humanity and aim for perfection.

It is true that exemplary people and adorable relationships hardly exist in the real world. If they exist, they do not last for long. Most relationships pass through a temporary phase of idealism, but somewhere along the course they deteriorate as the masks come off and the true nature of the people involved are betrayed in their behavior. In real life, people are prone to treat strangers with varying degrees of distrust, fear, suspicion, and intolerance. It is normal because our survival instinct teaches us to be defensive in an increasingly complex, violent, and scam-ridden world. If you have any doubt, ask yourself, whether you would readily stop your car in a lonely place during the night and assist any stranger who is stranded on the roadside and waves you for help.

The world is impermanent, where things and people keep changing and where you can take nothing for granted. If you remember it, you will not feel hurt or disturbed when mean people show their true colors, when genuine relationships become broken, or when you have to deal with difficult relationships. Selfishness is at the core of our relationships. People do not readily form relationships unless they see some apparent benefit in doing it. If you do not have much to offer to the world, as power, prestige, status, or wealth, you will find that not many people will be inclined to know you or become interested in you. It is how the world has been since the earliest times. If your fortune fades, your relationships also fade.

Fewer people are interested in the radiance of your thoughts or the purity of your heart, but only at the color of your face or the weight of your purse. If are in love, beware, because it can fade anytime once the initial enthusiasm wanes. People come to you when they need you. Once their last interest is served, they will show up only if there is a compulsion or a strong reason. Laila and Majnu or Romeo and Juliet were products of our idealism about the perfection we can bring to our relationships. Their creators made sure that they died young before the reality of marriage wore them down. Imagine what would have happened if they were alive and somehow succeeded in getting married. The part two of their famous love stories would have degenerated into a routine marriage life, characterized by intermittent quarrels, arguments, and misunderstandings.

However, it does not mean that you should avoid meeting people or feel worried and insecure about them. Surely, if you are not careful, relationships can potentially cause you a lot of stress. You cannot also ignore the impermanence and the uncertainty that dog many relationships. It means, you cannot be a passive spectator in your relationships. You have to cultivate people skills and social intelligence to manage them and avoid getting hurt or disturbed in the process.

A relationship is a social contract. It arises from your inherent desire to extend your consciousness and your identity into the world, and the things that you love and cherish. The best way to deal with your relationships is to be relationship-proof. You must be strong enough not to be hurt by them, and wise enough to absorb the shocks and surprises that arise from them. You must also be smart enough to get the best out of them and prepare for the worse, since anything can happen in relationships as people and circumstances change and you yourself may change. In life, we all need to pay a price for our relationships and we must be willing to pay it when the time comes, without feeling oppressed, wronged or disturbed. We must be realistic enough to admit that relationships are usually between two people who have their own minds, views, opinions, interests, preferences and prejudices. We cannot change others, control them, or coerce them without losing any of our own humanity or decency. Some relationships are so destructive that people who get into them eventually lose their balance and their sense of right and wrong.

Human nature is like a flickering flame. You can only go that much closer to a person. Beyond that, you will be burned. You should always be aware of the invisible barriers that exist between people, and the space you need to create and maintain, even if you think they are very close to you. If you cross those boundaries, you will be violating one of the cardinal principles of human relationships. People do not like you if they feel that you do not respect their right to privacy or their personal space. This is not cynicism. This is the truth.

Ask yourself. Who gives you maximum pain and suffering in the world? Usually it is your closest friends and relations, whom you love and think as your own. Why does it happen? It happens because in close relationships we tend to forget the personal barriers and overstep into the sensitive areas where people may feel hurt or vulnerable. While dealing with close relations, we also tend to lower our defenses and bare our hearts and souls to others. In the process, we show others our true feelings or the darker side of our basic human nature. No one is an exception to these situations. We lose our balance in close relationships, and in the process we hurt others or feel hurt by them. Human nature is a mixture of contradictions, most of which we try to conceal from the world, until we find our match. None should be blamed for this, because the problem is not with a particular individual, but the way we are created and molded by Nature and circumstances. Your emotions tend to overwhelm you when you are vulnerable, and you are very vulnerable in the company of your near and dear.

Some relationships last for a little time. Some may last longer, but in the end, all relationships tend to lose their initial appeal. Many religious traditions recognize this fact. The world is unstable. Hence, some call it a phenomenon, or a ripple in the cosmic ocean, and advise people to be aware of their desires and attachments and not to expect too much from it. Indeed, if you exercise detachment and restraint in your relationships, you will be better off. You will also do well if you bring out your best behavior and put into practice a few important principles such as the following.

Love: The starting point of love is yourself. When you love yourself, you will learn to love others naturally. You will not look to them for approval or attention. Instead, you will give it to them. If certain things in you are broken or out of alignment, it manifests in your life as conflicts, pain, and suffering. Therefore, to realign yourself, keep repeating in your mind these five affirmations, "I love you. I forgive you. I am complete. I am the source and the cause. Thank you."

Compassion: Do you care for anyone other than your closest family members or those who matter to you? See how you treat people in your life. Are you by nature respectful? Do you show compassion? You should have genuine sympathy for people, especially for those who are part of your life. They truly deserve your sympathy because they go through a lot of suffering in their search for peace and happiness. You can heal them with your thoughts, love and sympathy. If you are not happy with someone, it is better not to say it, unless there is a strong reason for it.

Understanding: Understanding comes from deeper awareness. When you know why people act in certain ways or what compels them to display certain behaviors, you will treat them differently. People are shaped by many factors and influences. Try to understand the motivation behind the behavior people display, so that you can deal with them with maturity and deeper awareness.

Harmony: You are happy when you are in harmony with the world and do not try to change it according to your desires and expectations. If you are self-centered, you will measure the world according to your standards and values and find much disharmony. Instead, you must accept people as they are and look for a common ground upon which you can build your relationships. Focus on the positive aspects in people you meet, what you like and what you can learn, and try to get along.

Forgiveness: What sets you free from your past, and your troubling relationships is forgiveness. You will be stuck in them when you hold grudges and keep thinking about the past injustices you suffered. It can also lead to many additional problems. For example, if you were disciplined heavily in childhood, you may have issues with authority figures and following instructions. Instead, try to forgive those who you think might have wronged you, clear the cobwebs of your past from your mind, and move on. Before you forgive anyone, you should also forgive yourself. It is important for your self-healing. Remember the five affirmations, which were stated before, "I love you. I forgive you. I am complete. I am the source. Thank you."

Relationships are not set in stone. They are fragile like the cutlery in your cupboard. Handle them with care when they last, but do not expect them to last forever. When they are broken, you have to decide whether to walk away from them without hurting yourself, or put the pieces together to rebuild them. When relationships are broken, you have many choices, depending upon your goals, personal philosophy, beliefs and convictions. You may either let them heal slowly or let them fade away. In any case, it is important to forgive yourself and others and move on. For a worldly person, a relationship is either a necessity or an obligation. However, for a spiritual person it is an opportunity to know himself and others, and cultivate deeper awareness, knowledge and detachment. Since he knows the impermanence of relationships, he is not troubled when people and relationships change or fade away.

When You Lose Your Job

You are successful to the extent you are willing to embrace failure and deal with it. If success assures you a certain position or status in life, failure leads you towards it, provided your determination and motivation are stronger than your fears and anxieties. There is no guarantee that you will always have the same job and you will always be as successful as before. If you are wise, you will be mentally prepared for all eventualities and safeguard your interests when circumstances are not in your favor.

Losing a job is just one form of adversity to which everyone is vulnerable in the present world economy. Its impact upon your life depends upon various factors such as your age, the number of dependents, marital status, qualifications, previous experience, your relationship with previous employers, reasons for losing the job, your network of friends and how much money you might have saved for the rainy day. If you live in affluent societies, you may have some protection under the constitution from government welfare programs. However, if you live in poor countries, you are your own security and solution, apart from any miracles you may materialize with your prayers and supplications.

In searching for a job, your age and circumstances are important. Nowadays, old people have a hard time finding jobs, as companies prefer recruiting younger people rather than older ones. If you are young and if you have taken up a temporary job to meet your current expenses, it does not matter much if you lose the job. With effort and persistence, you can surely find a job somewhere. However, if you invested a lot of time and energy in your career and if you lost your job at a crucial juncture in your life, when you are about to climb the ladder of success, it may leave you with a lot of pain, anger, fear, and insecurity

Whether you are young or old, when you are working for a business organization that operates upon profit motive and quarterly earnings it is always a good idea to stay cautious and not take anything for granted. In these difficult times, you should not only plan for your career but also for the contingencies. The earlier you start saving money for the rainy day, the better it will be for you in old age. Your savings must be sufficient to cover your expenses for at least a year, which includes any payments you may have to make on the loans you have taken and the credit card debt you have incurred. As you know, it is necessary to have a good credit score to secure a good job.

Therefore, when you are unemployed, you have to ensure that you credit score is not impaired. Depending upon your situation, you have to have a job even if it is less rewarding, until you find a better one and recover from the loss. The following are a few options you may explore to cope with situations that may arise, upon being fired, downsized, or forced to leave your current job.

1. Avoid harboring negative feelings towards those who are responsible for your predicament. Even if they were mean to you, there is no point in wasting your time and energy thinking about them.
2. Consider all the options that are available to you to recover from the situation and find gainful employment. Estimate the time you may need to do it and mentally prepare for the waiting.
3. Unless you are confident and planning for a longtime, you should not think of starting your own business. You must be careful when if you choose this option, because managing a small business requires a lot of initial effort and a different mindset.
4. Network, network and network. Keep contacting people even if they do not give you the same attention they were giving before
5. Reach out to people whom you might have helped in the past and ask for their help
6. Be willing to relocate. In adverse situations you must be willing to make difficult choices
7. Exercise regularly so that you may not gain weight or feel depressed
8. Find inexpensive ways to improve your skills and job knowledge
9. Maintain a positive mental attitude even if the situation is challenging
10. Have a few personal and professional goals and work for them
11. Go on a small trip to clear your mind
12. Keep yourself busy until you return to work
13. Dispute your irrational self-talk if you are prone to negative self-criticism.

Know that you are source of all that happens to you. You might have lost your job for various reasons. You cannot control all situations or foresee all possibilities, but you can control your thinking and responses. With an open mind, you can analyze and determine your role in the loss. Learn as many lessons as you can from your experience and use it to heal yourself. It is in such times that you have to come out with best solutions and remain confident and hopeful about your future and your ability to resolve the problem.

When Your are Criticized

People do not care about what you feel. They care about what they feel. If there is a conflict or disagreement, they are going to hurt you or say unkind things to you. Therefore, you should care about what you think and feel and how you respond to it. You are the most important person in your life. You should never forget it. - Jayaram V

When you are criticized, how do you feel? In the past when I was criticized, I used to feel bad about it. I would struggle a lot internally and keep thinking about it. My mind would engage in imaginary arguments to counter the criticism and build necessary defense. I knew that it was irrational and incorrect to keep brooding over an incident that already happened, and I should either accept the criticism or reject it and forget it. However, my low self-esteem would not let me forget the incident easily. I would keep thinking about it for a few days until a new issue cropped up, or life fell into routine again.

Indeed, over the years, I have improved and learned to accept criticism as a message from the world about myself or others. I have learned to deal with criticism rationally and objectively as a self-assessment review process. Now, I do not take any criticism personally as an attack against me, but as a measure of the other person and any relationship I may have with that person. Yes, I do learn from criticism not only about me but also about the other person who criticized me. Every time, someone criticizes you, know that it speaks a lot about the other person also. Criticism mirrors the critic, his knowledge, understanding and his character also.

Some people criticize you out of love and concern, and some out of envy and hatred. If you can trace the motive, you will respond with more maturity to any criticism. However, in real life you may not always be able to control your emotions when you are criticized. It is difficult because you cannot fight off the natural and instinctive reactions of primitive mind in you, which is always the first one to react to any threatening situation. It has only one mission in life, which is to protect its owner (you) from all possible and perceived dangers. Since your rational mind takes time to analyze the situation and assess the damage or the threat, your instinctive and initial response to any criticism is always emotional. For the primitive mind, any criticism is a form of attack and a perceived threat. Therefore, it will not just let it go. To protect you from the perceived threat, it responds promptly, releasing certain chemicals into your blood stream and provoking you into a state of self-defense.

Rationally speaking, you should not be angry at all about any criticism because it is nothing but an opinion of another person about you, which you do not have to accept and subject yourself to self-torture. You are pained by criticism because a part of you believes in it and accepts it as true. Even if it is true, you should objectively take it as useful information about you, your actions, intentions, behavior, circumstances, or the people you deal with. You can also consider it an opportunity rather than a threat and use it to know you, or those who criticize you.

Criticism should be treated in the same way that you would treat a weather bulletin or news from a weather channel. It is meant to forewarn you against the problems you may face and the actions you may have to take to safeguard your interests. If you are positive minded, you can use criticism to your advantage, without hurting yourself, perceiving in it an opportunity to know about you or your circumstances, and take a remedial action. You can also use it to protect yourself from toxic relationships, negative attitudes, and harmful consequences that may arise from them.

Unfortunately, ever after making good progress in controlling your responses, criticism may still occasionally cause you pain because a part of your behavior is always on auto-pilot and cannot be fully controlled. Whenever it happens, you have to keep remembering that the criticism is just an information process from which you can learn about you or the critic. As the sages declared, you have to change what you can, accept what you cannot, and get on with your life knowing the difference.

In these years, living in different environments, and having met numerous people, I have learned an important lesson. You cannot stop people from saying what they want to say. Their criticism speaks more about them rather than you. Their judgment is mostly a judgment about their personalities or a reflection of their knowledge and self-esteem. In their criticism, you may discern the desperation and dissatisfaction of their own inner critics who cannot be silenced easily with reason and facts.

You might have often heard people in power and position being criticized by their colleagues and associates for their actions and decisions. Most of the times it happens because of the differences in knowledge and perspective. When you are holding a position of authority, you will receive a lot of information which is not normally available to others. Hence, your thinking or perspective will be very different from that of others. When people criticize you, you may not respond or defend your actions, which may make others criticize you even more since they may perceive you as stubborn, indifferent, or arrogant. It may happen even in your personal life. Since you cannot disclose all information about your private life to others, you may be misunderstood or criticized for your actions.

If you want to make progress in your life, you should focus upon the criticism rather than the critic and value criticism as a feedback and nothing more. You should learn to take it in your stride as a learning opportunity, without beating yourself with negativity. It is not always necessary to talk to your critics and persuade them to win their approval, unless their opinion matters to you or your tasks.

Your feelings in response to any criticism leveled against you are also important. They speak a lot about you, your thinking, attitude, beliefs, and your self-esteem. Negative comments hurt us because we are conditioned to find approval from others and not draw attention to ourselves by being different or noticeable. It is a survival instinct embedded in our animal brains. Animals which live in packs know that if they are distinct or apart from the herd, they will easily become prey to their hunters. Therefore, they always try to mingle with the group and hide in it. Identifying with the herd helps them to remain safe from dangers.

We follow the same instinct in our lives and relationships. We prefer being part of a group rather than standing apart and become noticeable. The same attitude reflects in our response to criticism. If we are criticized we take that as being not appreciated, understood or recognized. For many people, criticism in any form is greatly demotivating and depressing, which prompts them instinctively to withdraw into their self-protective mental shells or seek desperately for physical or mental support and approval. In the long run, it does not help, because you will not find security in the approval of others and you cannot live forever seeking other people's approval.

Criticism is doubly hurtful when our attitude towards criticism is also regulated by our negative self-talk. We are criticized not only by others but also by ourselves. When we are awake, our inner critic keeps speaking to us and judging us continuously how we are doing and whether we are living according to our expectations and ideals. This self-talk has a lot to do with how we feel about our lives, our actions and relationships. In most cases when we are criticized by others, our inner critic also joins the chorus by lending a helping voice and making us feel even more oppressed and depressed. Thus, in the midst of criticism we have to deal with not one but two voices and two criticisms at the same time. In such situations, your inner critic may become too critical of you and others, and may complicate the matter even further, prompting you into a fight or flight response.

In ideal situations, you should not take any criticism personally. At the best, a criticism is a message or a feedback about yourself or your actions. It is like a piece of raw data coming from the world, giving you information about your life, actions, or personality. Instead of accepting it as a piece of data, if you personalize it, you will lose objectivity and fail to make use of it effectively as an opportunity to improve yourself.

You can use criticism to improve yourself or depress yourself. In any criticism, you always have this choice. You can perceive in it an opportunity to improve or a threat to lapse into self-pity and feelings of persecution. The best way to deal with it is to accept it as a possible feedback and act upon it rationally and analytically. For that you have to recognize that your happiness comes not from the approval you gain from others but from being yourself and knowing yourself. When others criticize you, you have to see whether their criticism is genuine and justified. If it is not, you may regard it as a reflection of the person who criticized you. If it is genuine, you may regard it as valuable information about your or your actions and use it effectively to improve yourself.

What Do you Think Success Means?

What is true success? People know what success is and who are successful, but they may not be able to tell you clearly who a successful person is and what constitutes success. You will know in the later part of our discussion why people have such difficulty in defining success. For now let us focus on what success means to different people.

Success is a relative term. If a person, who is making 10 dollars an hour, suddenly gets a new job and starts making 50 dollars an hour, that person will deem the exponential increase in the income a great success. Now let us turn our attention to another person who has been making two million dollars annually, except this particular year during which his income came down to just over a million. One million dollars is a large sum of money by any standards. Many people will not be able to save that much money during their entire lives. However, despite a million dollars of annual income, that person may still feel unhappy and unsuccessful.

So what made the difference here? It is the expectation. If your expectations are high, very likely you may feel disappointed with modest achievements, even if such achievements may be viewed by others as highly successful accomplishments. Sometimes, not only your expectations, but also the expectations of other people may influence your thinking about success. For example, if you have highly critical parents, who are difficult to please and who demand a great deal from you, you may be under constant pressure to please them through your achievements and may not feel happy at all, even if you have done well, if you have not met with their expectations.

There is another angle to success. Your concept of success is deeply connected to your values and beliefs. If your value system says having money is the most important thing in life, then you will deem that as success. On the contrary, if your value system says that apart from having money, peace, stability, integrity, happiness and contentment are also important, it presents an entirely different picture of success to you. Some people are extremely wealthy, but not happy. Some people are plain and ordinary, but are very happy and secure. Some people make lots of money, but do not save much. Some people do not make lots of money, but save a great deal of what they earn. Some people live with scarcity mentality even after they become rich. Some people spend with a generous heart, even if they have limited means. We do not know whether we should call one or the other successful because we are not sure how far their lifestyles and their individual habits contribute to their success or sense of well being. Let us now analyze some of the most common views about success.

1. Success means being happy.
2. Success means winning a game or a competition.
3. Success means acquiring something that you have been working for.
4. Success means getting a great job that is the envy of many.
5. Success means becoming rich, living in a large house, driving a luxury car and having all the comforts of life.
6. Success means becoming a celebrity.
7. Success means getting recognition, name and fame.
8. Success means having status, power, influence and control.
9. Success means freedom from want, fear and insecurity.
10. Success means being able to get whatever you want and whenever you want it.
11. Success means overcoming failures, disappointments and obstacles.

Now what is the commonest factor in all the above stated definitions of success? They view success in terms of achievement, accomplishment, fulfillment and attainment. They allude to having something, which you dearly wanted or which gives you an advantage over others or which adds to your status, power and prestige. In short, they tell you that success means realizing whatever goal or dream you set your mind upon, from which you derive a sense of accomplishment and fulfillment.

Many people are not sure whether they are successful or not because they do not have goals. When you do not have clearly defined goals, it is difficult for you to know whether you are successful or not. You may have vague expectations, but they do not give you a true measure of your success. Therefore, it is important that you set clearly defined goals for your life or your career and work for them.

There are a few more facts about success. First, success does not guarantee happiness or respect in society. Your happiness comes from within, and it is usually connected with your expectations. If you have low self-esteem, probably you may not be easily pleased with your achievements and still feel unhappy about any inadequacy or imperfection you perceive in yourself. Successful people, including some big celebrities, with low self-esteem may spend a great deal of their lives with the fear that people may ultimately find out their incompetence and think poorly about them. As for the respect, it depends upon how people perceive a successful person.

We live in a competitive world where many people, including our closest friends and relations, would be too happy to see us fail. Therefore, successful people know that success puts a great burden upon them to stand up to the expectations of society and frequently prove their merit. They also know that as role models of society, they are subject to extra scrutiny and harsh judgment. Secondly, a successful person need not always be successful and need not always feel confident about success. No one can take success for granted. However knowledgeable, capable, intelligent and skillful a person may be, past successes do not guarantee future successes.

If you want to be successful, what should you do?

1. First, you should have clearly defined, specific, measurable, and achievable goals.
2. You should remain focused on them day and night and think of them as frequently as you can.
3. You should make the best use of your resources to achieve them, such as your skills, your time, your intelligence, your knowledge and your social skills. Your resources are your investment. They actually constitute your wealth.
4. You should be perseverant and persistent until you reach your goals.
5. You should be flexible to change your plans, but not your goals.
6. You should learn from your mistakes. Each time you fail, ask yourself how you may do better next time. This "how can I do better" question is very important and has a tremendous value in your success. It is what creates people like Thomas Alva Edison, with tough minds.
7. You should never give up. If you are focused on "how" you will not easily give up until you reach your goals.
8. When you reach your goals, celebrate your success, broadcast it and rejoice in it.
9. Finally, share your success with others. Let them know what makes people successful. Help them gain from your experience.

On Writing Skills and Becoming a Writer

So you think you are not a good a writer because you tried a few times and thought it was not easy to translate your thoughts into words? If you do, you are not an exception. A lot of people think they are not good at writing. They can speak fluently in the same language and convey their thoughts, even when they are not thinking. Yet, when it comes to writing the same thoughts, they struggle. If they can speak instantly, you should wonder why they cannot write. Is it not a contradiction? Is it not strange that people have no problem speaking but suffer from a mental paralysis when it comes to writing? We can understand the reason in case of those who are illiterate, but what about those who have graduated from schools and colleges, and who might have written several essays and term papers to complete their education?

A friend of mine told me several years ago that he wanted to write an autobiography of his life, because he had gone through several interesting events and they would make an interesting reading. He was a spiritual person who experienced several moments of heightened awareness. He also met several yogis and sadhus, with whom he exchanged a lot of information. His own parents were very spiritual people, and they too narrated to him several interesting incidents from their lives. My friend said that he would write his autobiography so that people could learn from it. It was almost two decades ago he told me that. He never finished his book. I presume he did not go beyond a few chapters. He told me that he had a difficulty in putting his thoughts and ideas into writing and he was still working on improving his writing skills.

You may probably come across many people in your life who can speak fluently and impress everyone but cannot write with the same energy and erudition. I had a boss who was a brilliant speaker, but he had to depend upon his ghost writers to prepare his speeches. People cannot write as effectively as they speak because they do not practice enough. When you write anything, you have to be careful because your mistakes will be too obvious. Writing requires discipline, proper usage of words and their meaning, and knowledge of grammar, and syntax. It also requires mental clarity or the ability to think clearly and express your deepest thoughts in a language which people can understand. However, with effort and practice, you can overcome such hurdles and learn to write like anyone else. Here are a few points worth considering.

1. If you can speak, you can write.
2. If you can say few words about yourself, you can write.
3. If you can tell a joke, narrate to a friend what you did today or how you felt during a particular even, you can write.

It is now easier to write because rules of grammar and syntax have been considerably slackened. Literary writing is now confined to schools and academics. If you write in purely literary form, the younger generation will consider you outdated and old fashioned. You now have many platforms to write, and many opportunities to express your literary skills. If you are uncomfortable with long passages and complex sentences, you can express your thoughts in idiomatic or colloquial language, as most people do on social networks and pulp fiction. You do not have to worry if your writing sounds more like a conversation rather than a literary work as long as you can adequately convey the meaning and emotionally connect to your intended audience. In today's world, the distinction between good literature and bad literature has been slowly disappearing in people's esteem. Academicians may still worry about the niceties of expression, but common people connect to writers who can speak to them in their language. We also have integrated writing into our lives so much that perhaps presently we write more than we speak.

Some myths about writing

The following are a few important myths, which discourage many people from writing.

1. **Myth 1**: To be a good writer, you need to be creative. Creativity does not make good writers. Good writers make use of their creative skills. With effort anyone can be creative. If you learned in your childhood how to lie to your mom and dad, you were indeed creative.
2. **Myth 2**: You need to be well educated. Most teachers and faculty members of literature in any language end up being teachers and rarely earn any distinction in writing. On the other hand, many writers of great repute came from humble backgrounds, and were average students. Some of them did not even complete their graduation, but later learned the craft on their own.
3. **Myth 3**: Not everyone can write well. It is the biggest myth. Writing is a skill. If you can write a letter to your friend, send an email, you can as well write. If you have written essays in

your school and college, you have already developed the basis writing skills.
4. **Myth 4**: You need inspiration to write. Inspiration can help you to write well. However, writers do not depend upon only inspiration to write. They train their minds to write whenever they want. With discipline you can learn to write in different environments and circumstances.

Why should you write at all?

You may wonder, why writing is important and what good does it do to you. Well, writing is a skill, and like any other skill it has its own value. It can give you an edge in standing out, in making yourself clear, in making yourself known and understood, and most importantly in being yourself. Besides, there are other advantages.

1. Writing is therapeutic. It helps you relieve stress and pent up feelings.
2. Writing brings clarity. It helps you to organize your thoughts. As you begin to write, you will realize how difficult it is to express your deepest thoughts and feelings. However, if you persist, you will gradually learn to express your thoughts and emotions with great accuracy.
3. Writing helps you to discipline your mind. Writing requires both concentration and meditation. By nature, the human mind is fickle. When you write, you are forced to think with focus and attention, which helps you to see to things differently.
4. Writing increases your self-awareness. It helps you to know you better. Writing is a journey of self-discovery into your own heart and your deepest self. While writing, you bring out the hidden aspects of your personality and your forgotten memories and rediscover yourself anew. As you express your thoughts in writing, you uncover your deeper self, which you do not usually notice in normal circumstances.
5. Writing increases your awareness of the world. When you write, you have to be sure about your facts or you have to search for facts. Both of them lead to increased awareness of the world.
6. Writing is cathartic. It helps you to free yourself from the unwanted and negative thoughts, and repressed memories and emotions.
7. Writing makes you a good thinker. Writing forces you to think. Since as a writer you have to make yourself known and understood, and write clearly, you are automatically forced to improve your thinking skills.

8. Writers are well remembered for their work. If you are a writer, you have greater chances of being remembered and appreciated even after you leave the world as people may still find your work useful for their study and research.
9. Writing helps you to improve your creativity. When you write, you see more patterns and connections in the world around you that were not known to you before. You will also learn to see things from different and unusual perspectives, which improves your creativity.

Written words play a significant role in the progress of humanity. The world is able to remember only those people, whose words and writings remain in the conscious memory of their subsequent generations. The words of the Buddha, Jesus, Mahavira, and Guru Nanak influence our minds and thoughts even today because someone cared to record them for posterity. Imagine, how much knowledge and wisdom we might have lost in the past 10,000 years because people had no proper means to preserve their writings or their thoughts. I wish my forefathers of the last twenty generations left a record of their lives for their descendants. I wish we had many writers in the past who had a sense of history and left a detailed account of what happened in their times. The world would have been a better place, if writers of previous generations left biographical accounts of their own lives, what they saw and experienced and how they felt about their lives and relationships.

How can you become a good writer?

How can anyone develop good writing skills? The following suggestions may help you polish your writing skills and become a good writer in the process.

1. Write as if you are talking to someone.
2. Write from your heart.
3. Write a few words every day.
4. Write whatever you like.
5. Keep a journal.
6. Start a blog or a newsletter.
7. Read books on writing.
8. Have a few mentors who can guide you.
9. Join a writers club.
10. Attend a book fair.
11. Keep reading and expanding your knowledge.
12. Become a good observer.
13. Attend a writer's workshop.
14. Keep an open and inquisitive mind.

Techniques to improve your writing

Writing is a craft. It requires regular practice, effort and knowledge of certain techniques and practices, which facilitate precise expression, style and creativity. Here are few techniques that will help you improve your writing.

1. In your first draft, you should suspend all judgment and write whatever thoughts and ideas that cross your mind about the chosen subject, without fear or hesitation. You may edit it afterwards to your liking and organize the information according to the outlay, but when you begin writing, let your mind flow freely.
2. Take any passage, article, or a story written by a well-known writer and try to write it in your own words. Compare them both and see whether your writing has any merits or needs improvements.
3. Take any incident from your life and try to write about it in different ways and from different perspectives, shifting your emphasis from one topic to another.
4. Read the works of well-known writers of the current and previous generations to know how writing styles have changed overtime and how people expressed their thoughts then and now.
5. If you know more than one language, try to translate an existing piece of writing from one language to another, or pick any subject and write about it in all the languages you know.
6. Write a story for your kids or children, and ask them for their opinion. If you can write for children, you can write for everyone.
7. Learn to express the same idea in different ways with different age groups in your mind.
8. Take a poem and use its theme to create a story or an essay. Conversely take an essay and see whether you can write a poem with the ideas presented in it.

Everyone is unique. You have a message, or a story that is shaped by your unique experiences. As a writer, for you your life itself is a valuable resource, or a treasure chest of information from which you can constantly draw inspiration and material for your writing. Bring out your uniqueness, and your personal philosophy based upon your experience, and share it with others to the extent it does not hurt you or those who may be part of it. Cultivate the habit of writing on a regular basis. Write about anything, or at least keep a journal and note down the impressions of your daily life.

What Makes you Happy

There are many theories about happiness and many approaches to happiness. Happiness depends upon a number of factors. Some of them are universal and some are specific to each individual. What makes you happy, does not necessarily make others happy. Some are happy to be idle and do nothing, while some become unhappy if they are not active or busy. Some people are just happy without any specific reason, whereas some remain unhappy even after they achieve success and recognition. Sometimes the most successful people are also the most miserable. They become increasingly self-destructive and alienated from reality. Thus, a number of factors contribute to happiness.

Factors responsible for happiness

Studies in human behavior suggest that the following intrinsic and extrinsic factors may have a bearing upon our happiness in different degrees.

1. **Genetic factors**: We discussed elsewhere in this book that people are born with a set level of happiness, which cannot be changed except temporarily. Some emotional traits are inborn, and happiness may be genetically determined in some respects.
2. **Health**: There seems to be definite correlation between health and happiness. Healthier people are happy and happier people are healthy. Studies also show that people who experience positive emotions frequently require fewer hospitalizations and are less prone to stroke and heart attacks.
3. **Social life**: There is a significant correlation between happiness and eventful social life. Happy people are more likable. Hence, they tend to have successful friendships, happy marriage life, positive relationships, better social engagement, and better interpersonal skills. Happy people have better chances of getting married to positive partners than unhappy people. Studies also show that supportive relationships contribute to greater happiness.
4. **Work life**: Happier people are more likely to have better jobs and succeed better than unhappy people. The nature of one's work also determines the level of happiness. Those who are engaged in satisfying jobs experience positive emotions compared to those who do not like their jobs. Autonomy,

freedom to make decisions and sense of control greatly increase work related happiness.
5. **Social and Demographic factors**: Factors such as age, gender and ethnicity influence our happiness, but their impact seems to be limited. In the initial stages, old age may begin to bother us as we notice the decrease in our energy and enthusiasm levels. However, as we grow older we may learn to accept the inevitable and cope with it. Similarly social status and income levels also influence our happiness levels to some extent.
6. **Money**: Money seems to make people happy but only so long as they are motivated by the lure of money. At some point in our earning spree, money becomes secondary as the burden of managing it becomes more troublesome than keeping it and enjoying it. Studies show that in case of money perceptions influence our happiness more than the money itself. Thus, a person of average income who believes she has sufficient money is more likely happier than a person with better income status but believes his financial status is not good enough.
7. **Attitude**: Our thoughts, beliefs, expectations and attitudes have a direct bearing upon our happiness and well being. Happier people are more optimistic and more willing to push themselves and take their chances without feeling defeated or rejected. They learn from their experiences and adapt better to situations, balancing their expectations with pragmatism.
8. **Sense of control**: If you feel you are helpless, restricted and limited by people and circumstances you are not going to feel happier. Happiness comes from autonomy, freedom to make decisions, being in control, and having the freedom to mold your life according to your dreams and desires. Those who have the freedom to make decisions for themselves are generally happier than those who have to depend upon others to make decisions for themselves.
9. **Success**: In theory success seems to make people happy and happy people tend to be more successful. However, success brings in its own wake additional problems which may limit one's ability to enjoy success or experience happiness on a lasting basis.

Strategies to boost your happiness

From the above discussion, we can conclude that happiness is possible, attainable and a noble goal worth aiming for. Studies in positive psychology suggest that through simple strategies, we can learn to feel better about ourselves and increase our levels of happiness. According to Martin Seligman and others who have done research in this field, three factors are the key to happiness:

1. A pleasant mind,
2. Virtuous character
3. A purposeful and meaningful life.

While such efforts may not produce lasting results, they are the proven methods to improve happiness and general well being. The following suggestions are based on the information we have examined so far in this article, which contribute to your happiness by boosting your morale, wellbeing and positive state of mind.

1. **Focus on the positive**: Your happiness increases to the extent you focus on the brighter aspects of your life and fill your mind with pleasant memories and feelings. In short you have to find your own happiness, making use of the opportunities that come your way.
2. **Make happiness your main goal**: If you want something badly, you have to go for it and do the necessary to achieve it. Make happiness the chief aim of your life. Whether you are spiritual or not, subordinate all other goals to it, even your spiritual and religious ones. If you are serious about it, you will eventually come to it, finding your way.
3. **Bear the burden of happiness**: Like all good things in life, happiness demands its own price as discipline, self-control and austerities. For the sake of happiness you may have to bear with pain and suffering as a necessary preparation to change your thinking and behavior. Take for example your health. You cannot have good health, unless you do regular exercise and eat a balanced diet. It means you have to undergo pain and discomfort and lead disciplined life to overcome your initial inertia and reluctance.
4. **Manage expectations**: There are limits to what you can do. No technique is perfect and no method will ensure 100% guaranteed results. We have also noted that there is a set level of happiness to which everyone eventually returns after experiencing some emotional highs and lows. It means that beyond a point there is nothing much one can do about happiness. Therefore, temper your expectations without losing hope.
5. **Use your strengths**: You are happy to the extent you are in harmony with your deepest aims and aspirations, and make the best use of your talents, strengths and interests. Martin Seligman, who championed positive psychology, called them signature strengths. Using your signature strengths gives you

the sense of control, opportunities to experience fulfilling relationships, greater job satisfaction and even self-actualization.
6. **Build on virtue and character**: True happiness is built on a firm foundation of virtue and character. They provide meaning and purpose to your life and a valid reason to rejoice in your actions and accomplishments, besides boosting your morale and making you feel good about yourself, without negativity, shame and guilt. Knowledge, wisdom, justice, honesty, kindness, gratitude, fairness, forgiveness, self-control, courage are some of the universally recognized components of an ideally positive and virtuous life, which you can pursue to experience overall satisfaction with your life and increased happiness.
7. **Let go of your past**: Everything looks different in retrospect. Your past can be a hindrance to your happiness if you do not let it go. Mentally, it is difficult to do because a part of our thinking becomes frozen in time. The best and the most conventional way to deal with it is by cultivating detachment. With detachment you can move forward in your mental timeline and make peace with yourself. Detachment is the highest virtue and key to peace and happiness.
8. **Cultivate meaning and purpose**: Meaning and purpose are key components of your happiness. I have already suggested that happiness should be the chief aim of human life. You can expand this goal to include the happiness of others. With that, you can increase your potential for happiness substantially. You also gain the trust and support of others as you transcend your selfishness and show genuine concern for others. It leads to a greater sense of fulfillment and better opportunities to live for a greater purpose, as you engage in satisfying relationships and noble causes.

In conclusion, let us say that happiness of yours and others should be your main goal. It should rest firmly upon the foundation of virtue, duty and character. Your aim for happiness should not be a cause of disruption to the happiness and wellbeing of others. You should not also seek happiness at the expense of others. By filling your mind with positive emotions, making the best use of your natural and inborn strengths and imparting meaning and purpose to your life, you can increase your happiness, self-esteem and sense of belongingness. In the process, you will experience satisfaction and fulfillment that you have not lived in vain, even if you have to deal with the hardships of life, as part of your life's central purpose.

The Powers That Shape Your Life and Destiny

Your life and destiny, and your peace and happiness, primarily depend upon the following three important factors.

1. **Your disposition or essential nature (Your inner Self)**: This is what you make happen with your thoughts, abilities and actions
2. **External conditions (the world)**: This is what others may do to you by their thoughts and actions with or without your involvement.
3. **Acts of God (fate or providence)**: This is what happens to you because of fate, karma, or the actions of God, divinities and invisible forces.

Internal conditions

Most conditions in your life are self-created. External circumstances do play a role, but if you focus upon them solely, you are bound to frequently feel helpless and disappointed because they are difficult to control or change. Many people focus on their circumstances rather than their abilities and talents to change their lives and feel frustrated. The truth is you can make a difference to your life by your own thoughts and actions. You can learn to think differently and choose differently. You can use your strengths rather than focusing on your shortcomings.

You have adaptability and many other abilities, which you can use to deal with the problems and obstacles you face in your life. For example, your happiness, peace and wellbeing depend upon many internal factors such as the following. By paying attention to them and fine-tuning them to your nature, you can experience profound peace and happiness in your life. The yogis learn to be indifferent to everything by stabilizing their minds. You may not achieve that level of perfection leading a worldly life. However, you can exercise control over your thoughts and emotions by paying attention to the following and knowing more about yourself.

- **Thoughts**: What thoughts do dominate your mind mostly?
- **Desires**: What drives you and motivates you?
- **Beliefs**: Do your beliefs empower you or depress you?
- **Emotions**: What emotions dominate your mind and why?

- **Responses**: How do you respond to situations that provoke fear, anger, anxiety, greed, envy, love and pride.
- **Preferences**: What do you like, and what do you prefer doing in life?
- **Prejudices**: What makes you feel disturbed, angry or resentful, for no fault of others? What are your unverified beliefs and assumptions? What ideas and opinions do you automatically associate in your mind to race, gender, color, caste, creed, nationality, appearance, age and so on?
- **Resolve**: How strong is your resolve to accomplish your goals, and how often do you make a decision and implement it completely?
- **Virtues**: Do you believe in the importance of good conduct and virtues in human life? How often do you lie to and cheat your close friends and relations, business associates, customers or the government?
- **Discipline**: Can you stick to a plan until the end? Do you finish what you begin? Can you stick to a plan or a decision? Can you resist temptation?
- **Knowledge**: Do you have the right knowledge of the things and people you deal with? Are you sure that your knowledge will help succeed in life?
- **Skills**: Do you have the skills to perform your job and do you try to improve them continuously?
- **Actions**: Do you take responsibility for your life and those who depend upon you, and perform actions that are necessary for your and their welfare even if they are difficult to perform?

External circumstances

It is true that our happiness and success do not always depend upon internal conditions only. External factors play a role. We cannot live without the help of others, without interacting with others and without depending upon others. We are always part of something that is bigger than us, family, society, country, community or the world to which we belong. We cannot escape from their influence, or the conditioning they impose upon us. They shape your life, beliefs, thinking and values.

You may break away from your family, but a part of your family values and beliefs always live in you as your own. You may migrate to another country, but the memories of the country in which you were born remain in your consciousness for the rest of your life. We are intricately related to our environment as we are related to our own identities.

Countless people help you to become what you are today. Most of them you do not even know, Take for example the items you buy from a grocery store. Imagine how many people might have worked hard right from the raw material stage to make those items available to you in a finished packing.

Apart from family, country and society, the following are external factors also shape your life, namely teachers parents and grandparents, friends, relations, strangers, employers, books and films, role-models, government, professionals, hospitals, schools, technology, wars, religion, institutions, law and order, pets, nature, pathogens, manmade disasters, and geographical conditions.

Acts of God

Luck, fate, natural calamities and unexpected events also play a role in our lives. You may attribute them to your past actions (karma) or pure luck precipitated by invisible forces. Sometimes situations may develop in your life, for which you do not find obvious explanations. Every year, millions of people lose their homes and their near and dear in earthquakes, wild fires, floods, cyclones and hurricanes. Sometimes these events brush past you without harming you and sometimes they just ram right into the lives and homes of unfortunate people, destroying their hopes, dreams and all the hard work they put in.

Many events and coincidences happen in our lives for which we have no ready explanation such as chance meetings with complete strangers who may end up as our intimate friends or life partners, finding a dream job, a right solution to a nagging problem or a miracle cure one thought would never be possible. Some of the events make people happy while some give great distress. Logically we do not know why they happen. However, our scriptures suggest that they may happen because of the following:

- Past actions
- Thoughts and desires
- God
- Nature
- Divine or demonic forces
- Fate

A strategy for life

Since we know the three factors that guides our lives and destinies, we can use the knowledge wisely to our advantage and secure our lives. In all this, we must know our limitations, and what we can and cannot control. Our control over internal factors is much stronger than our control over external factors, while we may have little control over acts of God or fortuitous circumstances. We succeed to the extent we learn to control our minds and thoughts and discipline our lives. In this regard self-awareness is the key. We must become our own observers and guardians, and try to improve our thoughts and behavior.

With regard to external factors, although we have limited control over them, we can either change ourselves or change our environment and circumstances within the limitations and increase our sphere of influence and control. Networking, building relationships, improving communication skills, adaptability are few approaches by which we can extend ourselves into the external world and make our presence felt. In our dealings with people, we must aim for cooperation rather than exploitation or deceit. There is nothing much we can do about acts of God, because they cannot be predicted. However, we can be proactive and take preventive and precautionary measures to reduce their possibility, besides taking effective action when those conditions arise.

Three Rules for Peace and Stability

Our happiness depends greatly upon our ability to reach our goals and satisfy our desires. Alternatively we may find happiness by controlling our desires and cultivating detachment. Both approaches are effective and have their own consequences. One is the path by which one becomes increasingly involved with the world and Nature in pursuit of happiness and fulfillment and the other by following which one becomes disengaged from the world and lightens up both mentally and spiritually, leading to complete freedom from attachments.

Both approaches have their merits and demerits. In this article, I would like to touch upon the three fundamental ways in which you can reclaim control over your emotions and experience peace and happiness within the limitations to which you are subject. I am not saying that you will experience supreme and permanent bliss with these, but I am confident that if you implement them sincerely, you will remain in control of your life and manage your reactions and responses intelligently and appropriately according to the situation.

1. Take action to stay in control: When you are driving a vehicle, you cannot relax and leave the steering wheel to itself. You have to do your part to stay on the road and drive in the right direction. In life certain actions are imperative. You cannot sit idly and let life pass by. You have to do your part to stay in control of your life and keep yourself and your family free from harm and danger. It also means you have to perform your daily actions such as going to work, keeping your house clean, eating healthy food, doing exercise, improving your knowledge, educating your children, taking care of your job, spending quality time with your family, and keeping your morale high.

They are the core tasks or responsibilities that you cannot simply transfer to others or expect them to perform for you, unless you want to be led by them and become a burden to them. There are also certain aspects of your life or personality, which you cannot ignore such as your education, your academic achievements, your skills, mastery in a particular field, knowledge, intelligence, virtues, friends, reputation, honor, the help you have rendered, compassion you have shown, or the merit you have gained through your actions. You make them possible mainly through your personal effort. You may already have them or you can achieve them with effort, faith and confidence.

Therefore, take what you can from the vessel of abundance God has poured into this world. Reclaim your share. Take what you deserve and what you can, without ignoring the importance of virtue or the law of consequences in doing so. Take risks wherever necessary without harming others or damaging your future. This is the power zone, the zone of your influence, creativity, and control. Do whatever you can, honoring the rules of life and making the most out of it. Share your success, knowledge, and riches with others to the extent you can afford and believe necessary. You are the master in this zone of control. Do what it takes to be in control of your power zone, with an aim to extend it further.

2. Seek the help of others: Our lives coalesce and overlap those of others. We are interconnected to others and to the rest of the world. Many people contribute to our success, survival, and happiness, such as the teachers who educate us, friends who help us, critics who keep us in touch with reality, relations who remind us of our responsibilities, spiritual masters who teach us our true purpose, government bodies who protect us and society in general which facilitates our survival and identity. From experience you know that however able and skillful you may be, you cannot entirely live by yourself. There are tasks, which you cannot perform all by yourself. To complete them you need the help and cooperation of others.

No one has complete knowledge or all answers to solve every problem. Even if you are self-sufficient, you need help from others, the world and Nature. When you have complex problems, you may have to seek the guidance and help of experts. When you are unhappy, depressed, or demoralized, you may require the support and good will of those who matter to you such as your friends, family, partners and colleagues. When you are successful, you have to share your happiness and the rewards of your success with those who matter to you, and who might have helped you. Otherwise, you will not experience belongingness, or the feeling of being loved and wanted when you badly need it. From observation we learn that Nature intends us to seek help, when we need it. For actions that you cannot perform all by yourself, you should seek the help and cooperation of reliable and trustworthy people who can help you with their knowledge and skills.

Many people hesitate to ask for help, and thereby limit their success. Some take help, but do not acknowledge it or express gratitude. The truth is, however powerful and influential you may be, and whether you know it or not, you always depend upon others. Countless people help you all the time to live in comfort or fulfill your needs. They help you to earn money, keep your environment clean, protect you from crime and violence, save you from ill health, provide you with basic amenities, and make you feel safe and secure. You should acknowledge the help you receive from them, and express your gratitude. You should also reciprocate by being generous on your part in your dealings with others and helping them wherever possible.

3. Acknowledge your limitations: Knowing your boundaries is important. You should know your limitations and surrender to things that you cannot change. There are certain aspects of your life which you cannot change, however hard you may try. For example, you cannot change your parents, gender, race, your country of origin, height, physical features, mother-tongue, aging and sickness, and your blood relations. There is no point in resisting them or blaming God or others for the things that have been given to you by birth. Accept them with equanimity for what they are and get along with your life. Manage what you can and accept what you cannot. This simple philosophy will help you focus on the essential aspects of your life rather than worrying about things you cannot change.

Whatever you may do, there are certain things which will never change or which may never happen. There are also many things in life over which you have no control. For example, you cannot stop aging or death, prevent the gradual weakening of the body as you grow older, totally remove suffering from your life, reform this world, or put sense into the minds of those people who have determined to destroy themselves and others. Instead of feeling frustrated and resentful towards them or yourself, you should accept that you cannot control everything and everyone. Indeed, your happiness lies in letting them go. It is important to be realistic in your expectations and not to be delusional about your abilities and accomplishments.

It is equally important for your happiness to respect the laws of Nature. Many people refuse to accept truths about themselves and their circumstances, and live in a state of self-denial. In fact, we all do it to some degree, because our minds play tricks upon us and deceive us into believing what we want to believe in. There is no advantage in ignoring your natural limitations, indulging in self-deception and delusion, or trying to do humanly impossible things. Instead, you should focus on your strengths and opportunities, and see what you can do to make yourself live according to your highest vision. Think of what you can do, what strengths you have and what you can accomplish in the short span of your life, within the limitations to which you are subject. Knowing your limitations keeps you in control of your actions and grounds you in reality.

Adapting to your life

We do not have answers to all our problems. No one can live your life for you. At some time in your life you will realize that no one really cares whether you are alive or dead. If you happen to see your friends they greet you and if you do not appear for a while they will forget you and move on. It is life. You and the world grow apart as you age and enter into what people call the final phase of life.

In other words, you may spend your whole life in the externalities of the world, but eventually you have to return to yourself. Your life is your responsibility and the solutions that you work have to be specific to your situation. You may apply the principles of wisdom garnered by others through their experiences, but you have to devise your own specific ways based on them to find viable solutions to the problems in your life. If you do not own responsibility for your life, you are bound to feel unhappy and resentful towards others.

Everyone in this world carries certain baggage of woes and everyone to some extent lives in a state of delusion and self-denial. Your memories, your knowledge and reason conspire against you to keep you misinformed so that you will not harm yourself with depressing thoughts and stop enjoying life. They (your memories) let you write a story about you in such a manner that many facts are glossed over and only those that are pleasing to you and acceptable to your self-esteem remain in your active memory.

Therefore, do not trust your surface memory or the judgments you make based upon them. Do not give yourself away to emotions and impulsive thoughts since they may not be true but created by your mind to protect you from negativity and depression. You have to think deeply and challenge the underlying assumptions hidden in all the important decisions you make about your life.

It is said that in this world, you are your own friend and you are your own enemy. You are your friend when you work for your happiness and welfare, and become your enemy when you sabotage your life and your chances of happiness by holding depressing and self-destructive thoughts. Use the three formulas I have stated before to be true to yourself and take control of your life, thoughts, and emotions.

1. Do what is within your capacity and what you can control.
2. Take the help of others wherever possible.
3. Leave the rest to God with the firm belief that everything happens for a reason and for your good.

Duty, dependence and devotion are the three important practices and principles of your life. Give them priority as you fix your goals and engage in tasks to improve your chances of finding wealth, enjoyment, peace, stability, and freedom from want. Know that you are limited by your own self-limiting thoughts and fears, and if you want to move forward in your life, you must first become aware of them and find solutions to deal with them, without losing sight of reality.

How to Cope With Suicidal Thoughts

In India, where life can be tough and competitive, people commit suicide for various reasons. Sometimes, they do it for very frivolous reasons also, such as when they hear that their favorite leader passed away, or was arrested on corruption charges. It is possible that the news may be just a trigger for the suicide, while there may be deeper and hidden causes for taking that drastic step. According to a report that was recently published in some newspapers, it is said that in the last decade alone over a million farmers committed suicide in India, and the suicide rate in the country had been steadily going up among the younger ones.

Unfortunately, in a country of one billion plus people, some reach the unfortunate conclusion that the only way to make others listen to them or call attention to their problems is by committing suicide or threatening to commit suicide. During public agitations for social or political reasons, some activists go to the extent of committing suicide by setting themselves on fire in public view. Some are so depressed that when they hear the news of a leader or a film star passing away, they commit suicide, as if they are going to be together in the afterlife.

The rate of suicide is equally alarming in various parts of the world. According to a recent study, suicide rate has alarmingly gone up in the US in the last few years. About 38,000 people committed suicide in the USA in the year 2010. In the same year nearly 900,000 people committed suicide in various parts of the world. These are reported incidences of suicides. The number will be much higher if you add the unreported ones. Due to the social stigma attached, many suicide cases go unreported.

Causes and concerns

Most of the suicides happen when people feel helpless and come to the desperate conclusion that their lives are meaningless. Chronic depression, old age, ill health, and other issues also drive some people to end their lives. In all cases, the will to love and the longing for life, which usually keeps us in survival mode and life oriented, is gradually replaced by feelings of despair and loss of hope, until a threshold is reached.

Studies show that people commit suicide for various reasons such as health, age, economic and social factors, fear, helplessness and other psychological problems. Studies also prove that those who are accustomed to pain, violence and discomfort in their lives and those who have easy access to kill themselves are more vulnerable to feelings of suicide. It is also found that suicide rate is higher among younger people and those who suffer from chronic eating disorders. Many people think of committing suicide at some point in their lives, when they are going through severe adversity, but only a few actually commit the act. Illness, depression, pain and suffering, ill health, lack of love and affection, self-hatred, and guilt are a few aggravating factors.

We cannot be certain about future. However, based upon current trends we can make a few intelligent guesses about how life will be in the coming years and decades. When we analyze how our lives are becoming increasingly complex, one fact emerges very clearly. In future, life is not going to be any easier. With all the technological advances, it is definitely going to get even tougher and increasingly competitive as the population will increase, resources dwindle and nations become aggressive to promote their self-interest.

In the next few hundred years or so, if our civilization survives the madness and wickedness of a few, life is going to change radically for many. As new inventions and technologies come up, they require different skills and competence from the workforce. As lifestyles change according to the changing circumstances, there will be more demand for aggressive and competitive survival skills and strategic thinking. New ideologies may also surface as the older ones become outdated and inadequate. In a growingly complex materialistic society, people become more alienated and unwanted. As a result, unless adequate measures are taken by all governments to provide relief, there will be no shortage of people who want to end their lives.

The reason people resort to suicide is that under certain compelling conditions it presents itself as an easier option. It becomes the path of least resistance to those who want to escape from the agony and burdens of life without offering any fight. When a situation becomes hopeless and the person who is at the center of it reaches a certain threshold of tolerance when the fear of death prevails over the longing for life, it is difficult to stop that person from taking his or her life.

Suicidal feelings are induced and strengthened by negativity, hopelessness, and chronic depression. If such feelings are not resolved in time, a person becomes increasingly inclined to take his life. Life is a precious and wonderful opportunity to experience consciousness, self-awareness, relatedness, and be part of the existential phenomena we call Nature. On the other hand, suicide is a sheer waste of that opportunity. Taking one's own life is the desperate act committed by those who give up hope and see before them a no better solution. For obvious reasons, suicide is also an act of extreme self-denial by those who reach the desperate conclusion that dying is better than living. Suicide is not good because it does not solve any problem. It is a sacrilege against oneself and the loved ones, and most importantly, it is a selfish action with devastating influence upon those who are directly affected by it.

Coping with suicidal thoughts

Nothing can stop a person who is determined to end his life. If one has easier access to the means of self-destruction, it is even more difficult. The decision to live or not to live rests with each individual and individual alone. However, it is possible to help people who have suicidal thoughts to think differently and search for other possibilities and alternatives. They must be empowered to find enough reasons to hope for better and live. If you want to help those who suffer from suicidal thoughts, you can use the following suggestions.

1. Ask them to consider the moral, social, and spiritual consequences of committing suicide, and how their actions may affect the lives of others who love them or depend upon them.
2. Help them to find alternatives to keep themselves busy.
3. Engage them in an exploratory process to find a purpose to live, and reasons to continue their search for meaning and happiness.
4. Motivate them to consider the option of helping others, especially those who need help like themselves.
5. Create opportunities for them to express themselves without fear, guilt or shame.
6. Encourage them to be part of something bigger, nobler and higher, which will divert their attention from the negativity they experience and see a bigger picture of life.
7. Inspire them to look for opportunities to learn new skills and step out of their comfort zones to develop confidence, hope and courage.
8. Teach them methods and techniques to heal themselves or learn to bear pain and suffering with tolerance and awareness.

Changing the mindset

Most suicides are committed on an impulse. If you teach people to think rationally and dispute their suicidal thoughts during crucial, you can help them to control their depressing thoughts and suicidal tendencies. It can be done by teaching them to control thoughts and impulses by focusing upon the following aspects of life.

Hope: When life becomes hopeless, people begin to think about death. Teach people to look at the positive aspects of life and find every opportunity to increase their enthusiasm and happiness. Sometimes change of place or change of circumstances can help.

Expectations: Expectations are a major source of unhappiness, friction and frustration. Many people commit suicide when their expectations are belied. Therefore, it is important to teach people who suffer from chronic suicidal thoughts to manage their expectations by cultivating detachment and take life as it happens.

Purpose: If life is filled with purpose, the thoughts of suicide will not arise. Even if they do, people can control them and focus upon their purpose. If you ever have to help people who are going through a deep crisis, help them to find a purpose that is bigger than themselves and stick with it until the end.

Service: There are many people in the world who need help. Nothing is gained by a person who commits suicide. It is a totally selfish act, which leaves others who are closely related to them feeling devastated. You can help those who are prone to suicidal thoughts to think about others and find relief from their own feelings of depression and helplessness.

Reason: Most suicides are committed on an impulse. If you teach them to think rationally and learn to dispute their suicidal thoughts, you will help them to control their depressing thoughts and suicidal tendencies in crucial moments. Having an open and non-critical conversation, without being patronizing, is important to engage people in conversation and make them think.

Spirituality: Suffering is integral to human life. No one can avoid it. Those who suffer from suicidal thoughts need to be constantly reminded they have to accept and expect suffering and failure with a certain philosophical attitude, and they can use them to better themselves. Our scriptures and teachings of spiritual masters can be a great solace for people who are going through a lot of internal suffering. Spirituality and practices such as yoga and meditation can help people to deal with their negative and depressing thoughts and find solace in themselves.

Self-image: Those who suffer from suicidal thoughts experience self-doubt and low self-esteem. They look for approval from others and when they feel neglected or ignored, they suffer from depression. It is therefore, necessary to teach them to face others with courage and conviction and develop positive self-image.

Value of life: Suicide disrupts the progress of life and the smooth functioning of society. Human life is very precious and unique. Everyone who lives upon earth has a role and responsibility. Each of us is a point in a long chain of events. Each of us concludes or ends many tasks and processes that were started by the people of our previous generations. We also begin some on our own and pass them to our succeeding generations. For example, if I abort a child, I cut off a branch in my family tree. If I give birth to a child, I start a new branch. If I kill another living being, I cut off many branches of the family tree of that being. Anyone who commits suicide also commits the same damage. He ends not only his life but also the chances of any successors who may be born to him. Suicide thus disrupts the flow of life and creates chaos in the world. It leaves a small hole or a tear in the fabric of creation, which no one can mend.

Therefore, it important that people understand the implications of suicide, and why socially, morally and humanly it is not a good decision at all. They should remember that human life is a unique opportunity to live consciously and experience the wonders of existence. Those who want to end it through suicide must remember the scars they may leave upon earth and the unique opportunity they lose to live and experience life.

Understanding the Meaning and Mechanics of Success

We have discussed about success in a previous essay. We will add a few more thoughts about it here. Success is a vague term. You can define it and interpret it variously. Success can be as small as winning an argument or as big as becoming the President of a country. For a teenager, it can mean persuading her parents to let her go to her friend's place for a sleepover. For a child, it may mean managing to get attention and a warm hug from her busy mother.

Thus, for each person, each success in life has a specific context, meaning and purpose. Since success has many connotations and subtle nuances, many people find it hard to define it or understand what success truly means to them. Many develop their notions of success based upon films and television serials or by reading about celebrities and popular persons. Some confuse it with happiness and some with having something, such as a successful marriage, wealth, a big house, or power and influence.

How people understand, interpret, and experience success

People's response to success also varies. Some are successful, but do not know that they are. Some do not accomplish much of anything in their lives, yet may feel as if they are successful. In a majority of instances, people measure their success against expectations. While this is a useful criterion, it can also complicate our understanding and experience of success. If the expectations are high, moderate achievement may not make one happy. Conversely, if expectations are low, moderate achievement may look like a big success.

The same is true with comparison, and whom you consider your role model of success. A millionaire may not feel successful if she compares her achievement with that of a billionaire. A poor person may compare herself with a poorer neighbor and feel better. Thus, feelings, emotions and mental notions play an important role in the experience and feeling of success. Some begin with a lot of hope and enthusiasm on the path to success, but somewhere along the way lose their focus and zeal. Some achieve success but fail to manage their success and stay at the top.

Most people lack the will and energy to achieve success in their lives with dedicated effort and goal oriented approach. Some are haunted by their own internal demons of fear and lethargy and limit their expectations. They sabotage their chances of success with feelings of low self-esteem and negative self-talk, believing themselves to be unworthy of great achievement. They are too afraid to deal with success on their terms and venture out of their comfort zone to dream of success. It is also true that everyone experiences success on occasions and makes progress in some aspects of their lives. However, in most cases their successes do not radically alter their fortunes or lifestyles.

A simple formula for success

There is no magic formula for success. Success comes to you to the extent you want it and to the extent you are willing to work for it. However, you may also need luck at times, apart from right connections, right information, right resources, opportunities and facilitating factors. For that you must organize your life around your goals to secure the things that you need, want or enjoy. As you achieve goals, you lay the foundation for further success. The second part of this strategy is that you must learn from your experience, especially from your failures. It helps you become better and wiser in your actions, instead of becoming stuck and feeling frustrated. It also gives you courage and hope in the face of failure to persevere in your effort.

The third part of this strategy is that you must give it all. It means your dedication, concentration, and commitment must be complete and unconditional. Not many people are ready for success because every successful endeavor demands its own price. To achieve success, you must be willing to make necessary sacrifices and rise above your expectations. You must constantly stay ahead in the race for success, and outwit and outsmart those against whom you compete. It means you must prepare for the battle and do the battle, with readiness to embrace the consequences.

Lastly, but most importantly, you must know clearly what success means to you, why you want to achieve success and how you are going to make use of your success in your life. When you have clarity about your goals and purpose, it will save you from many problems and keep you focused and engaged in your tasks.

Building your philosophy of success

Success is thus not an end in itself. It is a way of life and part of a holistic vision in which you aim to secure the best joys and comforts that life can offer to you by effectively using your potentials, skills and resources. You can build your vision and philosophy of success by answering certain important questions such as the following.

- What does achieving success mean to you?
- Why you want to achieve success?
- Do you like to have goals and work for them?
- Do you have discipline, resolve, and commitment?
- Are you willing to accept failure as a learning process?
- Do you have the necessary resources?
- Are you willing to make necessary effort and sacrifice?
- Are you willing to face the consequences of winning against others?
- Do you trust you knowledge, abilities and talents?
- Is success going to change your character and behavior?
- Where would you like to see you after five or ten years?
- Do you have contingency plans?
- Are you going to enjoy your success?
- Are there anyone in your life with whom you can share your success?

Preparing for success

In simple terms, success means being able to accomplish what you want to accomplish. Therefore, knowing what you want and why you want are imperative for success any kind. There are four aspects to success: purpose, goals, plans and effort. There is no other better formula for success than following four-step strategy:

1. Having a purpose.
2. Having goals.
3. Having plans and strategies.
4. Having the commitment to persevere until the goals are realized.

For success in any venture, this is the simplest and the best formula. You must have goals and plans, and to reach them you must implement your plans with complete dedication. You should know clearly the purpose, or why you want to achieve success. Is it to make yourself feel good, or to achieve a greater cause that outlasts you? Do you want to achieve it alone or make other people partners in your success and share its fruit with them? Questions such as they are also important. Next to goals, come plans. In drawing your plans, you must know what you need, what you have and from where you can get whatever you may need but do not have. This is resource planning. Likewise, you may have to plan other aspects. In all this, the following points are also worth considering.

1. **Harmony**: Make sure that you are in harmony with your goals, and your skills and talents are perfectly suited to achieve them. You should also be mentally aligned to them. If you do not enjoy the effort and if you are not geared to accomplish the tasks that are essential to reach your goals, you may find it difficult to get going when situation becomes tough.
2. **Balance and stability**: In your zeal for success, you should not lose sight of the importance of having balance and stability in your life. Your goals for success should not cause problems in your personal relationships or family matters and should not affect your health and Wellbeing.
3. **Maturity and attitude**: You should have mental maturity and right attitude to absorb setbacks and failures, with enough common sense to make decisions, deal with ambiguity and uncertainty. You should also know when to take control and when to let things happen. Equally important is to know clearly what you can control and manage on your own and where you need outside help.
4. **Responsibility**: You should take responsibility for your actions. Whatever may be the path you choose and the decisions you make, you should not forget this simple rule: you cannot sleep walk through life, expecting others to take care of your life, do your work for you and drive you on the road to success.
5. **Humility and honesty**: When difficult situations arise, you must be willing to set your ego aside and deal with people and problems objectively. It is equally important to be honest with yourself, so that you will not be prone to denial and delusion.

When you take care of such issues, you greatly increase your chances of success. Success is a great blessing for those who know how to work for it, embrace it, manage it and survive it. With success arise many additional burdens and responsibilities. As someone said, success is not just a goal or an end in itself. It is a journey filled with adventure, excitement, responsibility and enjoyment. If you build your character while you work for success, you will not be burned by your ambition and desires. However, if you are careless, you may unwittingly become a victim of your own success. You should know not only how to achieve success, but also what success truly means to you and how you will make use of it for your greater good.

Coping With Stress in Daily Life

Stress is a major and one of the most common problems in life. Everyone suffers from stress to some extent, from small babies to grown-ups. The very process of living is stressful. As part of our survival mechanism we are hardwired to experience stress whenever we perceive threat to our wellbeing. Even dogs and cats do suffer from stress.

Symptoms of stress

Much of the stress we experience arises from the demands of life. A host of problems contribute to it. As society advances and grows in complexity, as expectations grow, and as the demands of life increase, our stress levels also increase proportionately. Deadlines, failures, setbacks, problems, fear, uncertainty, competition make our lives more stressful. Stress symptoms arise differently in different people. Some well-known symptoms arising from prolonged stress are fatigue, headaches, nausea, memory problems, attention problems, anxiety, worry, anger, irritability, introversion, withdrawal, depression, sleeping problems, eating problems and so on.

Causes of stress

Stress can arise due to external or internal causes. External causes are environment related. They may be under you control or beyond your control. You may deal with them by changing them or avoiding them or changing your attitude or thinking towards them. Internal causes may be either physical or mental or behavioral. You can either change them if it is within your capacity or accept them if they are beyond your control. Some of these problems can also be dealt with through medication.

Coping with stress

We cannot completely remove stress from our lives; nor can we avoid stressful situations. However, we can cope with it and manage it with effective and intelligent strategies. There are healthy ways to cope with stress and unhealthy ways. Drinking, smoking, overeating, avoiding problems, withdrawing, becoming angry, aggressive or violent are a few unhealthy ways in which people try to cope with their stress. To deal with stress, you need to understand and identify the causes of stress. Once you identify the causes either through introspection or with the help of a specialist, you can devise suitable strategies.

Four strategies to deal with stress

Basically, you have to deal with stress with the help of these four broad strategies.

1. Change stressful situations that are within your control.
2. Adapt to stressful situations which you cannot change.
3. Avoid stressful situations you can neither change nor control.
4. Accept stressful situations which you cannot change, to which you cannot adapt, which you cannot avoid and which are beyond your control by changing your thinking and attitude and developing proper outlook and philosophy.

Simple relaxation techniques

You can apply the above stated four strategies creatively and intelligently in your daily life to deal with stressful situations. As part of it, you can use the following simple relaxation techniques to reduce stress in your life.

1. Pause in between your busy moments.
2. Breathe consciously, when you find time.
3. Think when you have problems, instead of worrying.
4. Practice meditation to calm your mind.
5. Stay in the present when you are dealing with people and problems.
6. Set your priorities.
7. Become assertive.
8. Be expressive.
9. Learn to laugh.
10. Let go.
11. Sleep enough.
12. Eat healthy food.
13. Exercise.

Remember that some stress is normal and unavoidable. Stress becomes a problem, when it begins to interfere with your thinking and actions, and when it affects your health. If the symptoms are there, then effective and remedial action is immediately required.

How to Avoid Stereotyping

Many people do not practice yoga because they believe it belongs to a different religion. A hundred years ago many people in Europe and USA believed that the practice of yoga was harmful to mental health. Sometimes, you may come across people who may not even hide their resentment if you do not look like them or give them the impression that you are from a foreign country.

Many people in the USA have a problem pronouncing foreign names and laugh at them because they have a mental blockage to accept racial diversity or pronounce any name that does sound like a Christian name. I often face the problem when I speak to customer service people on the phone or visit local institutions. I have to repeat my name several times, even though my first name is not very difficult to pronounce. And then I have to deal with the strange looks people throw at me, as I came from some alien planet.

Every day, my first name is pronounced by millions of people, including illiterate ones, in several countries from all wakes of life. It is part of Indian literature, culture, poetry, and songs for over 2000 years. In many parts of India it is used as a greeting word or a common expression like hello, good morning, or hi. Yet, many educated people in the USA cannot pronounce it. It is equally true that when white Americans visit foreign countries in Asia or Middle East they face similar problems, not only with their names and cultural traits but also with their nationality. Especially, women who are accustomed to certain freedom of expression and dress habits find it very hard when they visit some countries to cope with sexist attitude and lewd behavior of men who live there.

Few years ago, when I was working at a call center, some elderly people would refuse to talk to me. When they heard my voice, they would ask me to connect them to a manager because they thought that I was speaking from India or far east and they did not want to discuss with me their financial problems. Fortunately, such customers were few. Most people I called preferred talking to me and would even tell me that in future they would like to speak to me only.

Prejudice and stereotyping are not particular to any race, creed or nation. People indulge in it almost everywhere. When I was In India, I had a similar problem. I was working in a north Indian state, whereas I was from South. Although my first name was Jayaram, people would call me Jayaraman because that was a popular south Indian name. Since I was from South, many people assumed that I was a southerner, who ate staple south Indian food, wore traditional south Indian dresses at home, and belonged to an orthodox Hindu family. It was a different matter that I had a mixed background. Since my parents lived in the North, I grew up both in both north and south and learned to speak fluent Hindi and even local dialects.

You cannot say that such behavior arises from ignorance or lack of education. I have seen even film stars, politicians, well-educated people, university professors, and celebrities showing it in their public utterances. Prejudice and stereotype thinking have been a part of Indian culture for centuries. Caste system and linguistic chauvinism, for which India is notorious, are the result of stereotyping only. In one of the social gatherings, a teenager even asked me curiously why south Indians did not wear shoes and other footwear in their houses and wondered whether it was a cultural thing because people ate their meals sitting on the ground instead of at the dinner tables.

Obviously, that girl never visited south India and saw how people lived there. She probably picked up those prejudices from her parents, friends, or relations. She also did not seem to visit any villages in the North to know that eating habits and lifestyles were influenced more by economic conditions and literacy levels rather than cultural and geographic factors. She was also unaware that many Indians would not allow people to walk into their homes wearing footwear, because they were usually made of animal skins and were deemed unclean and inauspicious.

Such prejudices are universal and common in most cultures. Sometime ago, in Soviet Russia there was an attempt to ban the Bhagavadgita because a section of people believed that the scripture promoted violence. The real reason was of course different. In countries like U.K., Germany, Greece, Soviet Russia and Australia, racial tensions are on the increase as the local demographics have been undergoing rapid transformation. They get worse when these countries go through economic recession, as the locals attribute their economic plight to the immigrants.

Few years ago I watched a video about Soviet Russia, in which the local youth would pick on immigrants walking on the sidewalks and beat them violently to drive home the message that they were unwanted. In Europe, few years ago a Norwegian extremist belonging to a fascist group gunned down 77 people because he thought they did not deserve to live in his country. You can see a similar trend in other places too. Many Muslim fanatics target Hindus and Christians in Islamic states because they are prejudiced against the minority communities who practice a different religion and preserve their traditions.

Prejudice has played an important role in the history of human civilization since the earliest times. Wars were fought because of the irrational beliefs and prejudices people held against one another. We know that, apart from other reasons, the second World War was caused by many racial and ideological prejudices. It was not that such prejudices prevailed only in Germany or Italy. Hitler had many sympathizes and secret admirers all over Europe and in many parts of the USA. In the end, although the Allies won and lessons were learned, the War bred newer prejudices and racial tensions in various parts of the world. Swastika, an auspicious Hindu symbol and the Sanskrit word Arya, which originally meant a person of noble origin, became tainted forever as symbols of fascism and oppression.

I believe even the animals practice group loyalty and prefer staying with their kind. Put a turkey in a flock of peacocks and the turkey would die of hunger and loneliness. Stereotyping helps the animals in their survival to find their prey and sense their rivals. It helps them to live in groups and communities, hunt in packs, and find better protection from other animals.

Stereotyping is common to all nations and peoples. It helps us to deal with the complexities of life and put some of our physical and mental functions on autopilot. However, when it is used for wrong purposes, it becomes a social malady, which makes people either victims or victimizers. From boardrooms to dinner tables, and from the most powerful and advanced nations in the world to the most underdeveloped ones, you will find groups holding against groups, tribe holding against tribes, nations fighting nations, and people staying divided based on religion, race or political ideology due to the irrational beliefs and prejudices they hold despite contrary evidence. Thousands of people die every year in various parts of the world due to communal, caste and tribal conflicts. People lose jobs or find it difficult to find jobs because of it. We can trace many problems and conflicts of the world today to the prejudices that people entertain in their minds.

Stereotyping means

Stereotyping means holding a general or fixed belief or notion about others without proof or validity. We are all familiar with it, even though some might not have heard the word. The habit of stereotyping is not particular to a group, nation or race. Human beings tend to stereotype and generalize their perceptions and experiences in dealing with the complexity of human life. They do it almost mechanically to make sense of the unfamiliar and the unknown and minimize the anxiety, fear and insecurity arising from facing the unfamiliar and the unknown. They rely upon stereotyping to make sense of the world and people, measure themselves, or to find security and social comfort in a group identity.

In other words, stereotyping is a natural tendency of the human mind to minimize effort and find mental shortcuts to process information and draw quick conclusions. Over generalization, over simplification, selective perception, irrational beliefs, ignorance, faulty learning, immaturity are some of the reasons why people tend to stereotype.

Stereotyping helps us to minimize the effort involved in decision making and problem solving and relate to others in specific ways. We stereotype not only those who are different from us, but also those who are similar to us. We assume certain personality types are either superior or inferior, friendly or hostile, intelligence or ignorant, reliable or unreliable, aggressive or docile.

We form both positive and negative opinions about people based upon it, and both may equally affect our ability to think and act rationally. Some conclusions arising from stereotyping may be right and even helpful to deal with the complexity of the world. However, in most cases, stereotyping and prejudiced thinking lead to irrational behavior, and logical fallacies. It also limits our ability to deal with people and situations effectively, with maturity and insight

Suggestions to avoid stereotyping

The following suggestions are helpful to guard ourselves against stereotype thinking.

1. **Respect individuals**: Treat each person as an individual rather than as part of a group. Do not assume that people will have certain traits or behavior simply because they belong to certain groups or nationalities.
2. **Respect their individuality**: Each person is unique. He may share some features with others, but his life and behavior are uniquely shaped by circumstances. Therefore focus upon the individuality of each person you meet, and what distinguishes him or her from the rest.
3. **Respect the humanity**: All people, irrespective of their color or creed, belong to the same human race. Our destinies are deeply

intertwined. We are the only intelligent beings in the known universe. Therefore, treat people with respect as the children of God or of the earth.
4. **Be rational**: Think and act rationally with objectivity when you deal with people or judge their behavior.
5. **Avoid assumptions**: Do not jump to conclusions or make assumption when you do not know people well. Avoid the temptation to make up information based upon your feelings rather than facts.
6. **Appreciate the diversity**: Imagine a world, where everyone looks alike and thinks alike. You will have no chance of being recognized or asserting your individuality. You are able to leave a mark upon the world and establish your identity because of the diversity that prevails in our world. Therefore, appreciate the diversity you find in the world and people around you. Contemplate upon how it enriches your life and contributes to your welfare. Appreciate and the role they played by different people and diverse cultures in shaping the human civilization.
7. **Gather more information**: Try to know more about people whom you tend to stereotype. Study their history, social and cultural background and examine rationally whether you prejudices are justified.
8. **See yourself in others**: Although people may belong to different social and cultural backgrounds and speak different languages, they share many common features and behaviors, and experience the same emotions. They are also driven by the same desires and concerns. Therefore, look for areas of agreement with others, and treat them the way you would like to be treated.
9. **Cleanse your thinking**: Make a list of your irrational beliefs and prejudices and examine them according to your personal experience and observation. See how far they are true and valid. Also, analyze your past to know how developed certain beliefs and prejudices and how you were influenced by your parents and peers in your childhood.
10. **Learn from others**: Prejudices and stereotyping prevent many people from learning from others. You can learn a lot from others, even if they are not as educated or knowledgeable as you are. The world offers you innumerable opportunities to learn from others, and you should wisely make use of them.
11. **Expand your self-awareness**: When you know more about you, you will develop better insight into human behavior and appreciate others with greater tolerance and understanding.
12. **Practice compassion**: All people deserve sympathy because they all suffer in their own individual ways. Whether they are rich or

poor, young or old, everyone who lives upon earth is vulnerable to innumerable hardships. Therefore, treat everyone with compassion, tolerance, and understanding.

13. **Know your boundaries**: You may protect your interests, and act with social responsibility, but you must know that neither the country nor the community with which you may identify belongs to you. You are just one of the billions of people who live upon earth for a short item and disappear forever. You may enrich them with your actions and service, but you cannot assume any special privileges for yourself based upon your birth or background. You can stand for yourself and defend your rights and actions, without infringing upon the rights of others to live their lives according to their vision and values.

14. **Identities do not matter**: In the end identities do not matter. They may help you to compartmentalize your life and perform various duties. They may also help you to define yourself to the world or establish and strengthen your relationship. However, know that beneath all those identities and layers of duality, you are but a human being who is expected to possess certain virtues and express them through your actions and attitudes. If you achieve balance and treat everyone the way you would like to be treated, with respect and consideration, you fulfill the expectations your religion and your humanity teaches you to uphold.

Seven Simple Techniques to Peace and Happiness

Babies learn the value of noise soon after they are born. They realize that they can get instant attention from the people nearby by raising their voice and making noise. They continue to do it until they learn to communicate in other ways. In some, this simple logic of survival becomes a basic strategy even when they grow up. They keep making different kinds of noises to get attention and according to their level of desperation become louder and louder. They use noise of various types to mark their territory, declare their superiority, establish their authority, control others or manipulate them.

Some become so good at it that they manage to remain in news and attract a lot of attention from those who become part of their lives. However, in some cases when the strategy fails, they may retreat into depressing silence and experience fear, despair, frustration, and negativity.

The noise that babies make to attract attention and secure help assumes many forms in a civilized society as people grow and become adults. You can not only hear that noise, but feel, it or see it in numerous forms as actions, words, dress and appearance, tastes, habits, skills, relationships, achievements, status, status symbols, profession, friendship, enmity, love, anger. They and many others are but expressions of the same primal noise only, whose sole purpose is to attract attention, create impression and secure approval, support, recognition and such other benefits.

Not all the noise we create in our lives is bad. We cannot live without making noise. Even to comfort others and help them, we need to use words and engage in actions. However, problems arise when we have to deal with people who value personal achievement and material success more than inner peace and spiritual Wellbeing. When it happens for a long time, many will become tired of it and yearn for peace and silence.

It is true that inner silence, or complete control over the movements of your mind and body, comes after a long effort, since it requires years of spiritual practice and persistence. However, as a beginning step, you can practice silence in limited ways and reinvigorate yourself. The following suggestions are helpful in this regard.

1. Know when to speak and when not to speak.

2. Speak only when necessary.
3. Learn to listen and observe more.
4. Practice economy of words.
5. Avoid critical, abusive and negative speech.
6. Keep a few hours every week to practice total silence.
7. When you are silent, keep smiling and remain positive.
8. Take deep breaths whenever you have time.
9. Protect your health with good nutrition and clean habits.
10. Avoid arguments with negative people.

It is possible to experience silence intermittently even when you are busy. You just need to take your attention away from whatever you are doing and focus upon the center of silence that always exists in you. You can remain centered in it for sometime before you return to your work and continue your routine. Drawing strength and inspiration from the inner silence of your heart will help you to cope with the stress that you experience in your daily life.

How to Deal With Unpleasant Situations

You can learn from both the pleasant and unpleasant aspects of life. Discretion is important in both cases.

You cannot always choose what is best for you. Sometimes life makes decisions for you.

An unpleasant situation is any situation that makes you feel uncomfortable, creates conflicts, causes you pain and suffering, takes away your freedom, subjects you to doubt and despair, or contributes to unpleasant memories and traumas. Life being what it is, no one can fully escape from unpleasant situations in their lives. You may deal with them successfully and take preventive measures, but you cannot completely avoid them. No insurance policy on earth can guarantee you freedom from unpleasant experiences. Sometimes it is the price you pay to find happiness and fulfillment in your life. Examples of unpleasant situations include marital discards, job related conflicts, enmity or hostilities, financial or material loss, loss of name or status, social unrest, family disputes, loss of near and dear, natural calamities, illness, and so on.

Leann was a graphic designer who worked for a fashion design company. When her department was merged with another, she had to report to a new supervisor. Her new boss did not like Leann as she thought she was rather overconfident and overambitious. She frequently started finding fault with her and undermining her importance in the team, until Leann found it too stressful to work with her and began looking for a new job. For Leann talking to her new supervisor about her work or the progress she was making became rather unpleasant and dreadful.

Menon was the owner of a bar and restaurant in a small town on the east coast. His business was running smoothly, until a competitor opened another restaurant in the same street and began offering a variety of food items. Menon did not realize the extent of damage caused by the new development until he noticed that he was losing a lot of revenue and many customers who were regularly visiting his restaurant before were not coming anymore. To make matters worse, he began seeing an increasing number of negative reviews about his menu items and service on the message forums. Menon had no clue what was going on, but he suspected that his competitor and his own manager whom he helped previously on several occasions were colluding and causing him trouble. For Menon the very thought of his failing business became a source of anxiety and depression.

Alex was recently promoted as a project lead in his department and given a very important assignment, which was sponsored by a top ranking official in the company. His boss told him that a lot was expected of him and his future growth in the company would depend upon how well he managed the project. Alex was given a team of six developers and two analysts to complete the project. The analysts were envious of Alex's popularity and growing influence. They were not happy to work with him as they felt he was their junior. They began talking on his back and delaying the project by raising unnecessary concerns. One of the analysts even tampered with the servers and brought them down to delay the project and put Alex in a vulnerable position. Alex knew what was going on, but he was unwilling to confront the analysts or complain against them because he was worried that his superiors might consider him a weak leader.

Radha had a happy marriage life or so she thought until her husband began coming home late and started telling all kinds of excuses. He also started drawing more cash from the bank to hide the details of his spending, and where he was going. She did not know what to do because she was a housewife who depended upon her husband for everything. She had no working experience and no college education. When she realized that her husband was cheating on her, she did not know what to do or where to go. For Radha living in the house and being ignored by her husband became an extremely painful situation and resulted in a nervous breakdown.

Daniel worked as a freelance reporter for a local newspaper. He had no family. His parents died long back, and he was divorced twice. Both his ex wives remarried and left him for good. Due to his erratic working habits, his employer did not hire him for a full-time job but paid him compensation for each assignment he completed. When there was not enough money, Daniel lived in the shelters and applied for food stamps. One day, he was diagnosed with a liver problem, which required surgery and an ongoing treatment. He had no insurance and no savings. He did not know how to raise the money and pay for the treatment. He found himself in a difficult situation where he had no control whatsoever on his life or his future. He found himself alone, depressed, hopeless and helpless.

Why unpleasant situations arise

The above are few examples of difficult or unpleasant situations which people face in their lives. They arise due to various external and internal reasons or a combination of factors. In most cases, they are caused by either your actions or the actions of others or acts of God, chance, or providence. Whether they are caused by external or internal factors, by you or others, you are primarily responsible for what happens in your life. The situations that arise in your life are mostly caused by your thinking, actions, and inactions, or by your explicit or implicit involvement. It may apply to even situations where you seemed to have played no role. An unpleasant situation is a bad karma, arising from your thoughts, actions or your past. You need to resolve it by understanding its root cause and finding suitable solutions.

The following factors, whether caused by you or others, are mostly responsible for unpleasant situations in your life.

1. Negligence or carelessness.
2. Ignorance or lack of right knowledge.
3. Lack of discipline.
4. Selfishness.
5. Bad habits.
6. Lack of values.
7. Lack of flexibility and adaptability.
8. Immoral and evil conduct.
9. Lack of trust.
10. Envy, pride, anger, fear and greed.
11. Wrong priorities.
12. Conflicts and misunderstandings.
13. Self-destructive behavior.
14. Desires and expectations.
15. Interference from other people.

Spiritually speaking, problem situations arise in our lives because of our imperfections, weaknesses, and mistakes. If we are wise enough we can learn from them and improve skills, actions, decisions, thinking and behavior. In other words, we do not have to always look at them as problems but as learning opportunities. A difficult situation means any of the following.

1. You are not in harmony with yourself.
2. You have not made right choices.
3. You are not optimizing your talents or potentials.
4. You are not listening to yourself.
5. You are not in alignment with your purpose.
6. You are not learning from your mistakes.

How to deal with unpleasant situations

It is difficult to generalize and say that a particular approach or solution will apply to all problem situations. Each problem situation requires a specific approach or solution. You can arrive at it by the following commonsense approach.

1. Analyze the problem.
2. Ascertain the causes.
3. Find alternative solutions.
4. Weigh the options.
5. Choose the best option and follow it.

While dealing with unpleasant situations, you have to remember the following.

1. Be completely honest with yourself and objective. Many people live in denial and do not acknowledge their problems or effectively address them.
2. Examine you role in each situation and whether there is any scope to resolve the problems on your own.
3. Try to be open, flexible and adaptable.
4. Give others the benefit of doubt.
5. Do not ignore any problem. Remember that when problems are ignored they become crises.
6. Have a strategy to tackle the problem, and ensure that whatever method you choose must be according to the strategy you have chosen. For example if your strategy is to find an amicable solution with minimum friction, you should not waste your energy upon fixing the blame or settling scores.

In problem situations people generally resort to two basic approaches or responses, namely the fight and the flight responses. You can use both approaches according to your need and circumstances. Sometimes you have to delay or avoid confrontation with the problem or the person who is causing it, but at other times you have to confront them. In either case, your decision should not be guided by fear but by the facts and the situation. Confrontation does not mean you use aggression or intimidation. It can also mean that you acknowledge the problem and actively deal with it on a priority basis.

The Roots of Unhappiness

It is difficult to accept life unconditionally when you have a mind of your own and when you are attached to things that you believe will make you happy. You will not easily accept conditions to which you are averse because of the unpleasantness you experienced when they were present. During your growing and maturing, you develop likes and dislikes, which condition your behavior and influence your thoughts and actions. Under their influence, you begin to choose and discard what you need or do not need according to your wisdom, hoping to live peacefully and experience the joys and pleasures of life. In this choosing and preferring you become subject to the duality of happiness and unhappiness.

The quality of your life depends greatly upon how to deal with the dualities of your life. At every turn in your life, you have to choose consciously what is good for you and avoid its opposite, rather than embracing life and accepting the conditions that present themselves to you. In making those worldly decisions you become vulnerable to the dualities of emotions, feelings and behavior, and experience anxiety, doubt, conflict and uncertainty. Thus, your unhappiness is mostly your creation, caused by your own choices and actions.

You may become unhappy for valid reasons or for no reason at all. Sometimes, you may not even know why you are unhappy. When life becomes oppressive, suffering may become so routine and common that people may not even notice their suffering and accept it as a normal condition of life. In the following discussion, we explore a few factors that are primarily responsible for suffering and unhappiness in the lives of many. If you want to resolve them, you should focus upon them, understand them, and analyze their role in your life.

Loss of freedom

We are the happiest when we have freedom to pursue our goals, dreams and desires, and live according to our chosen ideals. However, unfortunately, much of our freedom is taken away by society and circumstances. You may think that you are free, but you have to consider the number of invisible strings that pull you in different directions and keep you under control. It is true whether you live in a democracy or under a dictatorship, and whether you are rich or poor. Your freedom is always relative to your circumstances. People have to trade their freedom and individuality to be part of the world and enjoy acceptance and approval. It means as part of your social contract with the world, at times you have to live against your will and natural inclinations, which by itself is problematic and a major source of unhappiness for many people.

Lack of trust

The world is ever changing, impermanent, and unstable. You cannot even fully trust your own instincts, knowledge and abilities. Even after living with yourself for decades and knowing yourself well, you cannot feel secure because life is uncertain and you cannot take anything for granted, except perhaps the uncertainty itself. When you know that your powers and abilities are limited, and when you see that people can hurt you and harm you, you realize that you cannot trust anyone, including your own judgment. The lack of trust is a major source of anxiety and unhappiness. It makes people take control of other people's lives, infringe upon their freedom, or build walls of security around themselves. Lack of trust also prevents them from being open and honest and establish healthy relationships with others. Being careful, watchful, anxious, defensive, this is part of our basic instinct. We avoid unpleasant and threatening situations, which is perfectly normal, natural and truly human. However, when we overdo it, we limit ourselves and become imprisoned in the walls of our own fears and anxieties. It is difficult to enjoy life, if one has to weigh and watch every step as if one is walking in a mine field.

Your critical nature

Have you ever noticed how you create your own unhappiness and depression by your thoughts and judgments? It is because a relentless critic lives inside you, who constantly evaluates your actions and abilities and makes you feel inadequate and imperfect. He is a product of your past who is shaped by your beliefs, values, ideals, and parental instructions. By constantly drawing your attention to the negative aspects of your personality and achievements, he prevents you from experiencing harmony and happiness and from relating realistically to the problems and situations in your life. He is particularly trained to do this job and is exceptionally good in doing it. He is responsible for low self-esteem and self-destructive behavior. Comparing and contrasting, drawing conclusions and inferences, and reinforcing your past experiences, perceptions, beliefs, opinions and prejudices that make up your consciousness, he keeps you conflicted, unsure and unhappy. You can call him your unhappy self.

Desires and expectations

Your desires and expectations reduce your ability to perceive the world with an open mind and accept the conditions life offers to you. You cannot embrace life freely, if you are constantly driven to act according to your desires and expectations. As a wise person once said, "Expectations reduce you joy." In the journey of our lives, we rarely enjoy the present moment, because we are driven by the urge to fulfill our needs or live in the expectation of fulfilling them, which we believe are vital to our peace and happiness. Our sense of freedom is curtailed to the extent we live in the expectation of fulfilling them for comfort, security, money, belongingness, achievement and so on. For example, if you are expecting to earn a million dollars for the year but earn only half a million, you will be saddened by your under achievement. In contrast, if your expectation was only a hundred thousand, you will be extremely elated even though the amount you earned was the same. You should be therefore aware of how you can undermine your happiness by your own expectations. You can have expectations, because they fuel your actions and achievements, but they should not be the cause of your unhappiness.

Relationships

Relationships can give you a lot of trouble. They add drama to your life, but also make you vulnerable to suffering and trauma. I would put relationships in two categories: those that come to you by birth and those that you create out of your actions, desires and choices. You cannot do much about the former, other than making compromises or avoiding them. In the latter case you have ample choices. Human beings are unpredictable. Everyone who lives upon earth has desires, expectations, individuality, beliefs and interests. You must be good at understanding people, anticipating their behavior, and adapting yourself to their needs and expectations. Every relationship is a compromise of sorts, where you have to choose how far you are willing to bear the pain, suffering, and discomfort to get on with the other person. If you lack discretion or your own individuality, you may become a victim of other people's expectations.

Attachments

Relationships become even more painful, when you develop dependency and attachment to people and objects that form part of your life. Attachments arise due to desires and the expectation that having or not having certain things and people make you happy or unhappy. They are responsible for your likes and dislikes, which are traditionally known as attraction and aversion, and the duality you experience in relation to things and phenomena. You are happy when you are with what you like or separated from what you dislike, and vice versa. It is considered a major source of unhappiness and suffering in all cultures.

The spiritual approach to the problem of unhappiness

In spiritual life, accepting the world and yourself unconditionally is the highest virtue. It is part of an exalted wisdom and the mark of an enlightened mind. In materialistic life, you are mostly driven by your desires and expectations as you try to find happiness in selectively choosing things and having them. Spiritual people, on the other hand, embrace life by surrendering to God, or to the unknown and the uncertain, and let things happen, without resistance and without fear or anger so that they can learn from them and improve themselves. This attitude is well reflected in the lives of several saintly people, who renounce their worldly desires and live under the will of God with detachment, equanimity and indifference. They live life as it happens, renouncing their desires, accepting all dualities with sameness.

Of course, living with an attitude of dispassion and disinterest is not easy. It requires a lot of effort and prior practice to control our unstable minds and wandering senses. Your personality is an accumulation of things you have gathered in your life. It reminds you constantly that you are part of the world and never separate from it and that you may ignore the world, but the world does not ignore you. Even if you try to live like a lotus plant in the waters of life, some water anyhow will stick to the vulnerable parts of yourself. Hence, even spiritual gurus often succumb to mental and emotional disturbances and prove that they are human.

Strive for balance

However, you can apply the wisdom of this approach to increase your potential for happiness. You can use your discretion to know when to control things and when to let go of them. You can use your mind as well as your heart to open yourself to the immense possibilities that the world offers to you to enjoy the joys of living without becoming attached to them. Taking calculated risks, you can step out of your comfort zone and experience things that you normally avoid or ignore out of prejudice, fear or anxiety. By developing faith in your abilities or in a higher power, you can embrace life and live responsively, creatively and joyously.

Therefore, reduce your expectations. Cultivate detachment, equanimity and tolerance. Learn to speak without the need to impress or dominate. Respond to situations, without the need to control. Accept things as they are without the need to change them, and learn to say "YES" to what life offers to you. Let the light of God flow into your life. Watch the grand spectacle of life as it unfolds, as a spectator, without becoming overly involved. Once in a while let your heart follow its course, and let your emotions show up and color your life. Let the winds of fate blow, and the doors of life open. Once in a while let yourself stray into the pathless land of dreams and possibilities or travel without a map and without a destination. Improve your relationships and build trust and honesty. Removing the masks you wear in the presence of your dear ones, dare to be yourself.

Learn to say YES

You are conditioned to deal with people and situations according to certain norms, beliefs, and values. They color your perceptions and interfere with your thinking and reasoning, whereby you view life in a rather limited way and approach it with abundant caution. They prevent you from saying "YES" to the conditions and circumstances that arise in your life and remain positive about life, and equal to dualities. To enjoy the present moment, you can occasionally let go of your desires and attachments. You can let the beauty of silence or the profundity of a situation flow into your consciousness and fill you with peace and wisdom. Freeing your mind from the prison walls of your own fears and anxieties, you can choose situations to let the power of YES manifest itself. This is neither impossible nor impractical. With courage and determination, you can learn to loosen your defensive attitude and open yourself to the opportunities that you may have been missing because of your attachments and expectations. You can free yourself from habitual thought patterns and increase your opportunities to find happiness and fulfillment in the daily events of life.

Saying "YES" to life's numerous experiences and possibilities needs effort, an expansive vision, courage, conviction, faith, and an open mind that has learned to tolerate and accept what cannot be controlled or changed. To live our lives, we do not have to always say "YES," but we must be willing to accept life and the conflicting situations that may arise in our lives, especially those over which we do not have much control, or which we can neither avoid nor ignore.

Cultivating such an attitude is helpful in both spiritual and materialistic aspects of our lives. Therefore, once in a while learn to say "YES." Once in a while let the light of God flow into your life. Once in a while let your heart test the power of "YES." Once in a while let your heart take control and make the decisions. Once in a while let life happen to you. Once in a while let the winds of fate blow and let the doors of life open. Once in a while let yourself stray into the pathless land and see how emerge out of it.

What Success Truly Means

There is nothing personal about success or failure although many people take them personally. For many, failure is especially more hurtful and even shameful. The truth is, there is really no success or failure outside your awareness. From an existential perspective, there is only the right way or the wrong way of doing things, and the secret to reach your goals is to know the difference between them as quickly and efficiently as possible. To be successful, you need to perform right actions the right way and, sometimes, at the right time. Truly, success means using the right means to achieve the right ends, or perfect execution of your plans to reach your set goals. It means you need to know what gets you to your desired ends, and executing your plans with precision, discipline and perseverance.

Imagine what happens if you drive a vehicle in a wrong direction. First, you will not reach your destination. Secondly you will be delayed. Thirdly, you will be forced to find the right direction again. Now imagine what happens if you not only drive in a wrong direction but also in an opposite lane, against the incoming traffic. This will probably cost you a lot more than you can even imagine. You will encounter the incoming traffic every step of the way and may end up injuring others and yourself, besides causing a lot of property damage.

Life is similar or perhaps even worse than the roads upon which we drive. In life every road that you come across is just a one-way road. You cannot reverse or turn back. If you find yourself in the wrong direction or on a wrong lane, you have to keep moving in the same direction until you find a safe exit in the right direction to return to your previous lane again. For example, lot of youngsters join colleges without thinking seriously about their specialization. After spending a year or so they will realize that they made a mistake and try to correct it by switching their main courses. Considering how expensive college education in the USA is, you can imagine how much money and time it will cost them because of it.

Remember this. There is no failure or success on the path of life, but only the right way of doing things and the wrong way of doing things. There is only a right direction, and there is a wrong direction. You have to know the right way and the right direction, if you want to achieve success in any endeavor. Therefore, learning is important for achieving success. Successful people learn from their failures, and avoid the mistakes they committed before. Sometimes, you just do not know the right way and to find it you may have to test your methods and plans.

Therefore, if you are not successful in any venture, do not beat yourself with negative self-talk, or personally attribute your failure to any deficiency or inefficiency on your part. Accept it as the result of wrong actions or decisions made by you. Analyze what happened, and in future try to do it the right way. You can improve your actions and knowledge in various ways such as the following.

1. See what others have done and learn from them.
2. Know what the experts in the field have to say about it.
3. Read help manuals and information left by others about their experiences.
4. Work out different alternatives, without losing focus on your goals.
5. Keep doing and keep trying till you are on the right lane.
6. Focus on the "how" of doing so that eventually you will find the right method.

When depressing and deprecating thoughts enter your mind about your effort or failure, remember the following.

1. Do not blame God or your friends, or family for your failures. They are not responsible for what happens in your life.
2. Accept self-responsibility for the events in your life. You make things happen through your actions and decisions.
3. Know that there is neither success nor failure. There is a right way and wrong way, and there is a right direction and a wrong direction.
4. When things go wrong, try to find the right way and the right direction. Gather information. Analyze what had happened before. Think of alternatives and keep implementing them till you find the right method and right direction. If you persevere, you will find the right way and the right direction.

A Brief Guide to Relationships

Unless you have renounced life and become a monk, you have to manage your relationships and avoid being a source of pain and unhappiness to others. Indeed, even if you renounce life, you have to still manage your relationships in a monastery or a retreat to ensure that you are not breaking rules or disturbing the atmosphere there. From the time you are awake, until you go to bed, you have to deal with several people as you make your way through a labyrinth of problems and relationships. Your own happiness and peace of mind depend greatly upon how to relate to the world and to different people. Commonsense suggests that relationships succeed and strengthen when you practice the following

1. When you respect the boundaries of your relationships, and know your limits. It means that you should not make promises, which you cannot fulfill, expect too much from your relationships or take others for granted. It also means you will abide by the norms and standards society approves in matters of propriety.
2. When you keep space in a relationship. It means that you mind your own business and let others mind theirs, you will not invade the privacy of others, and you will recognize the rights and freedom of others to be themselves just as you recognize yours.
3. When you share information and responsibility. It means you will not take unilateral decisions, and when your decisions affect other people, you will consider their opinions before arriving at your own. It also means, you will not expect other people to take responsibility for your life, and you will not interfere with their right to make decisions and take care of their lives.
4. When you empower each other. It means you recognize that each relationship is a two way process in which each side plays a supportive role and empower each other to realize their goals and dreams. It means that you will be loyal to the people, whom you love and trust, stand by them in difficult times, and give them moral and mental support when needed.
5. When you are able to manage conflicts effectively. It means you will allow the other person in the relationship to have a say in resolving the differences and negotiate your way through the conflict resolution process, rather than indulging

in aggressive tactics to enforce your will. In other words, you must act with maturity, and an open mind rather than venting out your emotions.

Factors that are critical to a relationship

Relationships fail when they are not established on sound values and principles. The following factors or values contribute to healthy and strong relationships.

1. **Honesty**: Both sides must be honest in their dealings with each other and do not hide any information from the other person that may affect their relationship. Lack of honesty is the root cause of many broken marriages and failed relationships. Once the trust is broken, it is very difficult to rebuild a relationship.
2. **Loyalty**: Loyalty implies commitment, and how serious you are about the relationship. Sometimes, you may form relationships out of impulse, but for the relationship to continue there must be commitment on both sides. Both sides must remain loyal to each other through ups and downs, and not betray themselves to others or indulge in deceptive actions under temptation. When it is lacking, the relationship will deteriorate or degenerate.
3. **Open communication**: Both sides should regularly and effectively communicate with each other to avoid misunderstanding, miscommunication, suspicion, doubt and distrust. Relationships thrive when there is frequent and open communication between the two and when they are not afraid to speak their minds. It happens only when both sides are less judgmental and more forgiving.
4. **Love and caring**: It is not sufficient just to have positive feelings. They must be expressed and reflected in the actions and behavior of each partner. Both parties must express them through words and deeds, and find opportunities to nurture and invigorate their relationship.
5. **Respect**: Genuine respect shows itself through actions and attitude rather than mere words and gestures. Many relationships crumble when respect is lacking in them.
6. **Attention**: Attention is to a relationship what breathing is to a person. It means you acknowledge the presence of the other person in the relationship, respect that person's opinion, give consideration to his or her feelings and words, and participate in the moment with your heart and mind.
7. **Empathy**: There are many layers to a relationship in which feelings have an important role. With empathy you connect to

the other person's emotions and feelings and establish a deeper relationship.
8. **Compassion and forgiveness**: No human being is perfect. Just as you make mistakes, others also make mistakes. When you recognize human fallibility and willingly forgive others and yourself, you strengthen your relationships with them and give yourself and them a chance to move forward.
9. **Common interests**: Relationships thrive if both sides have identical interests in areas that touch their lives. While opposites may attract, research shows that in the long run having some similarities and identical interests strengthens the bonds of a relationship.
10. **Values**: Both sides must share some common moral, social and religious values for the relationship to survive and strengthen.

Intimate relationships

In case of love relationships the following factors are also important

1. **Intimacy**, which must exist both at the physical and mental level.
2. **Passion**, which must be expressed as well as expressed
3. **Sex**, which must be as per the mutual needs and expectations
4. **Fidelity**, which has to be genuine and unconditional
5. **Commitment**, which must be shown through actions and feelings
6. **Financial stability**, which means living within the means and planning your financial future
7. **Age**, which can be a problem if there a wide age disparity or if the relationship is solely based upon physical attraction.
8. **Health**, which is important because health issues such as stress and weight problems may create physical and emotional barriers between a couple and break their relationship.
9. **Sharing of intimacy**, time, resources, love, information and other factors, which are necessary to keep the relationship going
10. **Support**, which should be physical, mental, and emotional and which serves as the backbone of the relationship

Conflict resolution

The following suggestions are useful to resolve differences and conflicts that may arise in relationships.

1. Focus on resolving the differences rather than having your way.
2. Listen and understand the other point of view rather than speaking uninterruptedly to make your point.
3. Attack the problem, not the person.
4. Focus on the specific action or behavior that caused the conflict rather than the entire character of the person.
5. Avoid dwelling upon the past, and focus upon the present.
6. Respect the other person's feelings and right to express.
7. Focus upon solutions rather than the problem.
8. Give the benefit of doubt to the other person instead of making assumptions.
9. Avoid mind-reading and making presumptive judgments about the other person based upon your past, without adequate information or proof.
10. Accept responsibility for your faults and actions.
11. Do not expect the other person to read your mind and know your thoughts without you trying to explain.
12. Wait for the right time if the situation is too difficult to resolve.

Finally, remember that each relationship is a responsibility. Your relationship with others is part of an unwritten social contract, which you enter with society to fulfill your need for belongingness and to improve your chances of survival and happiness. Relationships may also help you to fulfill you material and spiritual needs. Depending upon several internal and external factors, they may also cause you a lot of problems. Therefore, you should exercise caution and not take any relationship for granted.

How to Survive in a Recession Economy

Going by the way the world has been progressing, you can expect to have at least three or four recessions in your lifetime. Present day world is so interconnected that recession in one part of the world affects the other parts. So even if the country in which live you is recession free, expect that if there is recession in one country, its ripples will touch many including yours too.

If there is a recession, what can you do? Recession, as you know, is a macroeconomic condition, which is entirely beyond your control. You cannot determine its progress or when it ends, but you can be sure that it is bound to have an impact on your life and your future in numerous and very hurtful ways. Recession, coupled with a stock market crash, can be more devastating especially for those who have retired or who are on the verge of retirement. Many Americans and residents of the USA became victims of a nasty recession that hit the country in recent times.

Although the stock market is currently booming, the economy is still in a recovery mode and many people who were affected by it have not yet fully recovered from its impact. Some are still looking for jobs or living under government welfare. The recession was caused by a host of factors including greed and complacency, and a workforce that did not adapt well to the emerging technological changes in the information age. It is appalling but true that millions of people lost their jobs and savings because of the reckless investments made by some very big financial companies and their not so diligent executives who thought that they were taking advantage of a market weakness.

As a result of the recession, housing prices stagnated in many states for years, while the income levels of many middle-class families declined. The salaries of many employees did not rise in proportion to the prices of many commodities or to the decline of dollar value. While the average annual income of people increased in countries like India and China, in the USA it went down.

Many Americans are now depending upon welfare programs to make their ends meet. Students and elders have alike been put through a lot of inconvenience due to these developments with little prospects of appreciable improvement soon. In such a scenario when things are not going well and a situation like recession is completely beyond your control, what can you do? How can you protect yourself from the short term as well as long term effects? How can you ensure that you can provide for your family and at the same time plan for your retirement? Here are few commonsense solutions which you can use in your personal capacity to deal with situations that may arise from economic recessions.

1. Make sure you protect your job: You cannot survive in the current job market, unless you stay competitive, keep learning, if necessary by going to school, and improving your job skills. You should not just stay in the job. You have to add value to the people you work for. Most importantly, you have to maintain good relations with people whose support is vital to your success and survival in the company such as your peers, colleagues, and those who have the decision-making power. If you are not getting an expected pay raise or promotion, do not complain. Keep working and wait for the right time either to ask for a pay raise or to look for a new job. It is better to work for big companies that are recession-proof and where you will have more opportunities to move horizontally into another department or vertically into a higher assignment, if your current working environment is worrisome.

2. Develop specialized skills in specific areas of your profession: You are lucky if you have specialized in a particular area which is vital to your company's operations. Specialization, nowadays, is a a form of job security by itself. If it is not possible, try to acquire skills in multiple areas and make yourself valuable and exceptional. Remember that in a recession you cannot take your job for granted. In today's world, since organizations follow a profit driven culture to keep their stakeholders happy, they can spring a surprise on you any day. Many companies also use recession as an opportunity to get rid of deadwood. Therefore, make sure that you add value to the team in which you work or you develop skills in multitasking and leadership.

3. Protect your operational base: If you are an independent professional or a small business owner, you have to find avenues to retain your customers and go the extra mile to keep them satisfied. Since in difficult times you may be forced to reduce your charges and thereby your income, you may have to double your marketing effort to secure new customers and additional business. At the same time, you have to minimize your expenses by eliminating the wasteful expenditure. If you have an office in an expensive area and location is not important to your business, you may consider inexpensive alternatives, including the option of having a virtual office instead of a real one. You may also need to engage a good tax consultant or a financial expert to plug all the leaks and minimize your tax burden. In a recession, as a small business operator your main task should be to survive and for that you have to use every opportunity.

4. Save much to the extent possible: In difficult times it is better to have foresight. To better prepare for future, you should save some income every month and invest it wisely in 401K or other tax exempted alternatives. Maintain a list of monthly expenses, and explore ways and means to cut down the expenditure. Try to keep yourself in good health so that you can avoid unnecessary medical bills. Keep fewer credit cards and use cash where possible. Besides, when you pay in cash, you will be helping many businesses as they do not have to pay the credit card charges. You should also negotiate with your credit card company for better terms, lower interest rates, and money-back options for the purchases you make. Use coupons wherever possible when you make purchases to save money. If you are in the habit of frequenting hotels and restaurants, you can learn to stay at home and enjoy home cooked meals.

5. Choose your leaders wisely: Of course, your one vote will not make any difference. However, in a democracy as a citizen you have to play your dutiful role. No country can afford leaders who have grandiose plans and extravagant spending habits at the expense of the public. Consider whether your love for a particular politician or political party is more important than your retirement and the future of your children. History proves amply that bad leaders are a sign of bad times and vice versa. A country will decline in every way when it has a succession of bad leaders.

6. Help others by doing voluntary work: This may not help you much financially, but it will help you absorb your own pain. In difficult times, you can help those who may be looking for a job or for moral support by lending them a sympathetic ear or helping them to network. It will not only make you feel good, but also will help you in the long run to expand your network of connections. Besides, you can also learn from others how to cope with your own problems.

7. Have faith in your destiny and in God: Trust that your current situation will eventually improve and life will return to normal. Live with the conviction that suffering is an important part of human life and you can always learn from your mistakes and difficulties. A recession, such as the one we witnessed in the USA few years ago, shakes up everyone and makes them realize the importance of financial planning and the need to achieve positive net worth. Those who learn from it will have a happy ending. Others may find the going tougher even when the situation improves.

Problems and Problem Solving

Problems are part of life. Problems can be big or small, and they can have an impact on our lives and minds in various ways. People react differently to the problems they face, some with courage and confidence, some with fear and anxiety, and some with knowledge and intelligence. Some ignore their problems and pretend as if they do not exist. Some take it more seriously than they should. Some read the problems differently according to their own state of mind and perceptions and try to resolve them accordingly without considering the facts and the reality of the situation. Politicians excel in using problems to blame their opponents or make a political case out of it. Just as people differ in their inherent nature, they also differ in their ability to understand and react to problems and crises they face in their lives.

Why do people not resolve their problems?

Following are a few reasons why people may not take their problems seriously or ignore them.

1. No threat is perceived: People who lack foresight do not perceive a problem until it is too close or too late. Those who are in denial also do not perceive their problems. For example, parents who ignore the wayward behavior of their children do not consider it a problem until it is too late.

2. The problem is too complex to resolve: When problems are caused by complex issues and multiple factors, it is difficult to determine their causes and find suitable remedies. Sometimes people who have a vested interest in the problem may deliberately complicate problem to delay solutions.

3. Lack or resources and ability: Some technical problems require specialized knowledge. Some problems require money and resources. For example, when recession hit the USA few years ago, many people were unable to save their homes as they lacked resources.

4. The problem is unknown: When a problem remains undetected it cannot be solved, even if you have the resources and the ability.

5. There may be other problems that need immediate attention: When a company or a person has too many problems, they need to be prioritized according to their importance or severity. When problems are interrelated, you have to focus upon the primary problems before resolving the secondary or dependent ones. For example if a computer crashes due to a virus, you have to first remove the virus before you can reinstall the operating system and all the applications.

6. Negligence and carelessness: Some people allow situations to deteriorate or their problems remain unattended because they are reluctant to make necessary effort or sacrifice. It happens when people are demotivated, depressed, and lack discipline or focus.

7. Fear and anxiety: When people are afraid of consequences, or when they are unsure of the outcome of their actions, they hesitate to take action. Fear and anxiety prevent many people from taking effective action to solve their problems. Fear of the unknown and unfamiliar, lack of self-esteem or self-confidence are major demotivating factors which force people to live with their problems rather than confront them and deal with them.

Points to remember about problem solving

What do you do when you have a problem? Would you just let it simmer or take effective action? A lot depends upon how you perceive the problem, how secure you feel about yourself and your own personal philosophy that dictates your basic approach and thinking about you and your life. The following are a few important facts about problems, and problem solving that are worth remembering.

1. Find the causes and fix it: This is useful both as a long term and a short term approach to problem solving. To solve a problem, you have to find its cause or causes, which, however, is not easy. The causes may be one or more, hidden or apparent, easy or difficult to identify, simple or complex, and may be within or beyond your control. If a problem is recurring in nature, its causes may be deeper than you think and difficult to resolve.

Finding the causes is important, because without finding them and addressing them you cannot make much progress in solving your problems. When problems arise, you cannot ignore them or avoid them, hoping that they will resolve themselves on their own. You cannot delay the solution or expect miracles, since experience shows that a problem becomes a crisis when it is not resolved in time.

Once you find the causes, it will be easier to find alternatives and solutions to resolve it. It is where you have a chance to shine and where you can use your knowledge, intelligence, reason and experience rather than your emotions to overcome the problem.

In understanding a problem and fixing it, you should always remember this golden principle. Do not assume anything, underestimate the consequences, or take things for granted. Treat the problems with the seriousness they deserve, keeping your emotions under control, and ascertaining facts related to it.

2. Focus on the problem and solution: Emotions make a lot of difference in your problem solving effort. In problem situations you give in to your emotions, which happens in case of many people, because you tend to focus more on the consequences and outcome rather than the problem and its solutions. When you have problems, it is easier to become distracted by your exaggerated fear of what may happen rather than what can be done about the problem itself. Feeling helpless is the last worst thing that you can do in a problem or crisis. The outcome of it may be even worse than the outcome of the problem itself.

The best way to avoid emotional vulnerability in a problem situation is to focus on the problem and the solution. If you think the problem is too big to resolve or beyond your control, still you should not lose your heart. In your mind and imagination, you should set aside all limitations, and use that freedom to empower yourself to think of all possibilities and solutions.

If necessary, talk to the people whom you trust and take their help. People are more willing to help you than you imagine. It is the best way to acknowledge them in your life and convey to them how much they matter to you and how you hold them in your esteem. Over dependence upon others is not good, but depending upon others in times of problems and crises, strengthens and cements your relationship with them. It brings you closer to their hearts and minds, besides making you humble and humane.

3. Have a plan: There should be one or more plans to resolve your problems. Plans are not solutions. Plans are the intelligent way by which you intend to implement your solutions to reach certain goals in your life, which in this case is problem solving. Your plan must be clear, precise, and time specific. That is, you should know in advance in what timeframe and what specific manner you want to complete your plan.

Your plan does not always have to be written. For simple problems, you can conceive a plan in your mind and execute it; but for serious and complex problems, you may need clearly written, specific and executable plans in which you can objectively and precisely identify your actions and measure their progress.

Your plan should also be flexible so that you can alter it suitably as the situation develops. At least in the back of your mind you should have more than one plan to deal with the unknowns and the variables that may exist in a problem situation or with the contingencies that may arise out of your actions. Flexibility is the key in planning and its execution.

4. Focus on the effort: This is the most important step. Any plan is useless unless it is well executed. You cannot afford to delay your responses to serious problems that arise in your life. Procrastination is not the right solution to any problem. Some problems may disappear automatically on their own, with the passing of time, as the conditions that produce them change. However, you have to be exceptionally intelligent to know when to delay a problem and when to act promptly.

Most problems do not go away until you resolve them or someone else resolves them for you. When you want to resolve a problem after finding a solution, you should focus upon the effort, the technique, or the method, rather than the result. If you focus upon the effort, the solution and the result will take care of itself. You have to focus on every step until you reach the goal, leaving nothing to chance, use your intelligence and your resources until the problem is fully resolved.

Therefore, when problems arise, always think, "What can I do now? What options do I have, or how can I move forward in this situation?" When you do such introspection, your mind will prepare you to focus upon effort rather worry and anxiety. You can envision how your actions will yield results. It will also help you to control your emotions, avoid wishful thinking, and plan realistically. Effort gives you hope, a sense of control and an opportunity to learn and improve from your own actions.

The antidote to any problem is not any action, but timely, intelligent and realistic action, which means you have to think rationally and practically, setting aside your emotions and doing what is necessary. Whether the problem is big or small, you have to remember that you can resolve it by an intelligent and realistic action only. Problems cannot be wished away, but they can be pushed away with intelligent and adequate effort.

5. Learn from your problems and move on: Life is never easy for anyone. Even a month old baby has her own problems. The little birds that build nests in trees near your house, those large pythons that roam in the swamps of the Everglades, the bears in Alaska, the white whales that swim in deep oceans, the lions in Africa and the tigers and elephants in the forests of central India, they all have problems. They have to deal with Nature, predators and poachers, friends and family, and harsh living conditions.

You may find God, but not a life without problems. Existence means struggle. When we come into this world, we enter into an unwritten agreement with Nature that we are willing to undergo whatever it takes to survive upon earth in all the conditions and circumstances life and Nature impose upon us. We cannot walk away from this agreement unless we want to die prematurely and unhappily.

However, dying is not a solution to any problem. No one can escape from the harsh realities of life with drugs and intoxicants to stay away from problems. We cannot blame others and feel justified by wallowing in self-pity, helplessness and inactivity. We have to face life boldly and spend our precious little time upon earth in pursuit of happiness and fulfillment. We have to overcome the problems and challenges we face by taking responsibility for them.

Living with vitality and enthusiasm is the best solution to the problem of suffering we face in our lives as long as we exist upon earth and remain bound to Nature. Until we depart from here, we have to accept life as a challenge and keep on resolving our problems with courage, confidence and even indifference.

Wise men learn from their problems, and minimize the possibilities of their recurring. With each problem, they increase their knowledge, awareness and intelligence. From each experience they distill wisdom and grow wiser. No matter what happens to you, if you do not lose courage and if you keep learning, you will make progress in the school of life.

Principles of problem solving

Finally, here are a few more golden principles of problems solving.

1. Problems arise because of you or in spite of you.
2. Problems are not always in your control, but your solutions are.
3. Problems are Nature's way of learning and perfecting.
4. Fear is not a solution but a response.
5. Problems test your will to live and survive.
6. Each problem tells you something about yourself.
7. Sometimes, a problem may be an opportunity.
8. When there is a problem, focus on the solutions and its resolution.

Two Success Factors Used by Successful People

What does distinguish a successful person from a not so successful one?

Why some people are more successful than others, and why some achieve success quickly while others do not reach even half the mark during their lifetimes?

Why do hard work and dedication not always yield the same type of results for everyone?

Again, why do some people seem to achieve success almost miraculously while some keep toiling their whole lives without appreciable result?

There are instances where many people started their businesses with an investment of a few hundred dollars and became billionaires, while some unfortunate ones invested millions, or their life savings, and ended up bankrupt?

There are many reasons why people achieve or do not achieve success in their lives or in their actions.

Many factors come into play to shape a person's life, including family status, genetics, education, health, emotions and even luck.

It is also true that luck favors a few, but not all.

In fact, success has a lot to do with individual effort.

With right attitude and a flexible mindset you can cross the hurdles created by chance or circumstances.

With regard to success, there are two fundamental factors, which makes all the difference between success and failure.

One is making use of the opportunities and the other is flexibility.

Both are important.

I have a friend, Marc, who is very successful. His secret, he never wastes an opportunity.

He invests a lot of time and energy in making use of the opportunities that come his way, which sometimes means days and weeks of preparation and hard work. He would not let them go even if it means he has to work hard and put in extra effort. He says that if you let go of an opportunity, it might never come back. For him success is all about focus, attention, hard work, and perseverance.

He is not an extraordinarily smart person, but smart enough to recognize opportunities when they come and seize them in time or before others recognize them.

He knows that no one gives you success on a platter. You have to earn it.

According to him timing is important. You have to recognize them in time and promptly make use of them. Since opportunities come in various guises, you have to be always on the lookout.

It is as if you are the guard at the gates of your own life and success. You cannot afford to sleep when you are on duty and you cannot let anyone or anything enter or escape without your knowledge.

Sometimes you will have an opportunity to say something to someone at the right time or help someone who needs your help badly. If you do not act in time, you will miss those opportunities and you never get them again.

Therefore, he cashes in on every opportunity that comes his way.

He keeps an open mind, free from preconceived notions and rigid expectations. It helps him to see opportunities which others are likely to miss.

If you are like him, chances are that you are already successful or you are on your way to achieve success. It means you are using your opportunities to create a life of your dreams.

In life you will have many opportunities to use your talents or overcome your weaknesses to realize your goals and dreams.

When they come, you must be ready to make use of them.

You must be wide awake to see them coming and be prepared to use them according to the goals and priorities you have chosen.

At least, you must try them before you decide to let them go.

It is true that your success and even happiness depend a great deal upon how you make use of the opportunities that come to you.

Successful people achieve their enviable positions because they make use of them, and waste no opportunity.

They seize opportunities in time and make use of them proactively. In this regard, what helps them is their optimism and open-mindedness. With flexible and adaptable attitude they improve their chances of success and see opportunities which others do not.

Rigid people do not see them with the same success because their minds remain closed. When opportunities come to them, they either remain ignorant or unprepared.

If success is your aim, you have to keep these two factors in mind.

- Make use of every opportunity that comes your way.
- Remain flexible with an open mind.

Interfering factors

Because of mental blocks and filters, many people do not see opportunities that may help them to succeed in their lives. The following are a few important ones in this regard.

1. Judgment.
2. Preconceived notions.
3. Mental rigidity.
4. Prejudice.
5. Fear and anxiety.
6. Lack of attention.
7. Lack of goals, purpose and motivation.
8. Social and cultural factors.
9. Ignorance

How to see opportunities that others do not

Each opportunity is a potential turning point in the journey of your life towards success and fulfillment. You cannot afford to be sleeping or careless when they come. You must be able to see opportunities in as many situations as possible to further your goals, realize your dreams and fulfill your desires that are in harmony with your values. Successful people are also innovative because they cultivate possibility thinking and use their creativity to see opportunities where others do not. The following suggestions are useful in this regard.

1. Act as if every opportunity is a once in lifetime opportunity.
2. Review your life and see how opportunities arose in the past, how they helped you make progress in life, and whether you missed any opportunities that might have made a difference to you. Let go of any negativity that may arise in the process.
3. Prepare a list of your important goals and examine your current situation to see what opportunities you may currently have to reach them and whether you can do anything about them.

4. See how others, who you think are your role models or your competitors, may use them or respond to them in similar circumstances.
5. Examine your motives, assumptions, beliefs, expectations, prejudices, habits and priorities that may be preventing you from seeing opportunities and achieving success and happiness. See what you can do to free your mind from those mental blocks and learn to see opportunities and possibilities.
6. Do not feel discouraged if you have missed some opportunities, failed to make use of them, or if things did not turn out as expected. Keep trying and adapting yourself creatively until you achieve your goals.
7. Principles and values matter. You will have many opportunities in your life to achieve success through wrongful means, by exploiting others, misleading them, harming them or deceiving them. You should remember the consequences of using such means, and stay free from any that will leave a blot on your soul.

Success is all about opportunities and how you make use of them. Smart people make full use of their opportunities for right purposes and just ends. They do not take anything for granted and always look for avenues to promote their causes and work for their goals.

Intention, Attention and Manifestation

Before we go into the main discussion, let us focus upon the meaning of these words.

- **Intention**: What you desire, hope for, expect, or intend to happen, achieve or attain in your life. It can be an idea, reality, object, state or a condition that dominate your thinking and motivate your action.
- **Attention**: It is where your mind goes repeatedly and persistently, and which engages you both physically and mentally in sustained action because of your passions, emotions, feelings, and desires. It depends greatly upon your intentions, desires, and expectations.
- **Manifestation**: It is what you create, materialize, or demonstrate in a visible and tangible form in your life through your actions, and with your knowledge and skills. Every manifestation is a transformation of energy.

Planets use their gravitational force to keep things together and stay in equilibrium. In life we use the power of love to attract things and hold on to them. It is an awesome power, which we all possess in equal degree. We can use it positively and unconditionally to achieve our goals and dreams. We can use it regularly to empower our thoughts and emotions and move towards our goals. This is an effortless way, and the way of the wise and the higher. It is also an ancient practice with a proven track record. You can call it moving with the flow, enriching your life, or manifesting your destiny.

The human mind has many latent faculties. One such faculty, which many do not use, or do not know how to use, is the power of manifestation. It harnesses this power with the help of belief or faith, intention and attention. In this world, you are but the sum of what you attract with your thoughts, beliefs, emotions, hopes and fears. Some of your thoughts and desires manifest instantly, some take time, and some may never materialize because you do not yet have the power to manifest them. You exercise this power regularly in your dream world where you create instantly whatever you desire and wish. It is your latent power, which dissipates considerably when you enter the wakeful world, where you are subject to many limitations and where your power to manifest your desires is greatly reduced by your own imperfections, fears and ignorance.

While you may not be able to instantly materialize reality in your wakeful state, you still have the power to attract what you think, desire, believe and want. You also attract what you fear and want to avoid. Hidden deep within the layers of your mind is a deeper reality, or a superior consciousness, which can manifest your thoughts and desires. You can call it by any name you want, God, super mind, angel, guardian angel, subconscious mind, alpha mind, hidden self, over mind, real self or whatever. For better clarity, let us call it here the higher mind.

Your higher mind has the wisdom to see things clearly and intuitively know the truth of things. It manifests your reality based on unconditional love. Which means it works for you unconditionally and tries to materialize whatever dominant thoughts prevail in your conscious mind. In proportion to the intensity of your thoughts and emotions, it creates results for you. If you entertain positive and empowering thoughts, it will try to create a positive and promising future for you. If you waver and lack conviction, or if you are driven by anger, envy, fear and such other negative emotions, your subconscious mind will manifest the same confusion and negativity in your life.

Such is the nature of your higher mind. It is love unlimited. It does not question you, judge you, or use any standards of its own to evaluate your thoughts and actions. Other than your conscious guilt, it does not know of any guilt. Since it has no will of its own, it neither filters your thoughts not tries to change them on its own. It accepts your conscious mind as it is, and tries to shape its thoughts. Purely and entirely, higher and beyond all categorization and classification, and without discriminating between the positive and negative, it acknowledges your wishes as its commands, and tries to manifest them with unquestionable loyalty.

Since human mind is seldom free from negativity and limited thinking, many people find it difficult to harness its true potential. A lot of training and mental discipline is required to overcome doubt, despair, negativity and conflicting thoughts before expecting positive results from your higher mind. The following suggestions may help you to harness the power of your higher mind.

1. **Use positive affirmations** to clean your conscious mind of any negativity and allow your higher mind to know exactly what you truly desire.
2. **Have faith in your higher mind's ability** to manifest reality. If you think it cannot do it, it will not do it. If you have doubts, it will manifest your doubts. It simply agrees with

you in whatever you think and do consciously. Hence, you have to be very positive about your higher mind, and not let any negativity paralyze its functions.
3. **Begin your day with positive thoughts** and images, and so also before you go to sleep.
4. **Be grateful for whatever that happens** to you. Even for those happenings that are seemingly undesirable, express your gratitude for the lessons you have learned and the progress you have made.
5. **Make your goals clear and precise**. With specific goals, you have better chances of creating right conditions and using the right methods to manifest your goals.
6. **Free your mind from fear**, hesitation, guilt, shame and such negative feelings. Remove the inner mental blockages when you use affirmations, images, worlds, emotions and visualization to send powerful subliminal impressions into your mind to communicate your intentions. Visualize your goals clearly and precisely every day.
7. **Focus on your strengths** and what you are good at. Your inherent potentials, skills and talents are your natural resources. They constitute your true wealth, and your God given gifts. You can rightfully use them to manifest various types of abundance in your life.
8. **Finally, have patience** and relax. Let your higher mind do the work, as you relax with positive thoughts. Do not instruct how and when it should manifest your desires. Your higher mind knows what to do, how to do and when to manifest your desires. It does it usually at its own pace and according to its wisdom. Therefore, relax, make your intentions known to your higher mind, and let it do the work secretly and quietly in mysterious ways.

The Basis of Happiness

Note: Some of the information presented in this article has also been previously discussed in another article on happiness. However, the information is somewhat different. Hence, we retailed both articles.

Many theories, philosophies, scientific discoveries and books focus on the problem of suffering and its resolution. They approach the subject of happiness with the assumption that your life will be better off if you are free from sorrow and if somehow you learn to cope with it and deal with it. In this, there is an implicit belief that happiness is the absence of sorrow. A person may not have any worries, but still may feel unhappy about some aspects of his life or behavior. Similarly, a person who has been going through a difficult phase in his or her life may experience a temporary relief by forgetting his or her sorrows, problems and worries, but it is doubtful whether it will lead to happiness on a sustaining basis.

Suffering is universal. We know it. What is universally common to all of is that we are vulnerable to the suffering that life inflicts upon us. Nature has not been able to mold our minds and bodies, or our skills, abilities and potentials, according to our vision, desires, and ambition. It has put an extremely limitless mind in a tiny, puny little body, which is vulnerable to death, disease, and destruction.

We are, therefore, destined to suffer from limitations, disappointments, setbacks and failures. Not a day passes without you having some problem or the other, and without you experiencing anxiety or fear in some form. However, in this drama what gives you the ability and the strength to cope with your suffering is the hope and the possibility of experiencing peace and happiness through intelligent effort. The hope or the expectation of happiness and fulfillment pushes most people forward and makes their lives worth living for. It also keeps them from losing focus or going crazy.

The strategy for happiness

The promise of happiness is this. You can heal yourself and establish conditions for a positive and meaningful life. Dealing with pain and suffering is important because we frequently experience negative emotions, which interfere with our happiness and Wellbeing and fill our lives with despair and frustration. However, we cannot resolve our suffering or secure happiness by merely dealing with our suffering. At the most, it is a partial solution. For lasting improvement or for sustained happiness, you need a wider strategy that will focus not only upon your suffering but also upon your happiness and positive emotions. In other words you should not only reduce your suffering, but also fill your life with happy moments, meaning and purpose.

In your preoccupation with the problem of suffering, you do not have to sacrifice your happiness or live selfishly. You do not have to live in perpetual agony, worry and anxiety. If the cause of the suffering cannot be fully resolved, you can develop alternatives to stay mentally strong, resilient and hopeful. It may not be even wise to expect a life that is completely free from worry. You must have a positive state of mind and a meaningful purpose which can help you to weather through the storms. Overall, you must feel good about what you do and how you live, with the satisfaction that you can manage your problems and actualize your thoughts to the best of your ability. That is all there to your essential happiness.

If you can secure these key components of success, you are on the road to a happy and fulfilling life. This is the theme of this discussion. It is meant to help you in this journey and come to terms with your happiness. It aims to let you know what great minds and recent developments in psychology have to say about happiness and what you can and cannot do to increase your happiness levels without losing sight of the essential purpose of your life.

What is happiness?

If you want to increase your happiness, you need to know what happiness is. Ask your friends what happiness means and they will most likely find it difficult to give a straightforward answer. I have seen that a lot of people struggle to answer this simple question. It made me wonder whether people think of happiness at all. If you do not know what you are searching for, how are you going to find it?

The Webster Dictionary defines happiness as a state of well-being and contentment or a pleasurable and satisfying experience. Bliss, rapture, joy, elation, exultation, ecstasy, euphoria, delight, enjoyment, exuberance, glee, jubilation, gratification are some of the synonyms associated with it. They suggest that happiness is a state of mind characterized by positive emotions.

The word 'happiness' said to have originated in the 14th century from the root word, 'hap,' meaning chance, fortune, or luck. Etymologically, its opposite is hapless, meaning misfortune or not having luck. Happiness may be difficult to define, but we experience it generally as a positive state of mind or as positive emotions, characterized as being happy, contended, satisfied, curious, enthusiastic, excited, elated, interested, hopeful, joyous, friendly, romantic, thrilled, pleased, appreciated, accepted, proud or successful.

If you are feeling good, it is pure and simple happiness. If you are smiling or laughing genuinely, it is pure happiness. It is happiness, if you are full of hope and inspiration, and if you are feeling connected to or related to someone or something. These are various positive emotions we experience during our lives, recurrently and frequently. You may call happiness any positive state of mind, which is characterized by any or all these positive emotions. It includes the overall satisfaction that you may feel about you and your life.

Your happiness manifests both physically and mentally. When you are happy, people around you know it and feel it. The language of happiness is universal. People may not understand you or the language you speak, but they will understand your happiness and can relate to it. The emotions associated with happiness may arise momentarily for a short time, or they may remain for long and become part of your core nature or what some call chronic happiness. Your aim should be to prolong your positive emotional states so that you will experience happiness consistently on an ongoing basis. When you are dealing with the world, you are bound to experience both positive and negative emotions.

Life teaches us that it is not always possible to remain intensely happy or spend every ounce of our energies in the pursuit of it. However, since happiness is important to your overall wellbeing, you should do everything possible to stay happy and maximize your positive feelings. If not, you should aim to remain, at least, moderately happy and contended most of the time. It is better if you frequently experience positive emotions for longer periods than if you them occasionally, followed by long periods of negativity and depressing feelings.

Happiness should be your ultimate goal. It should be the sum and the purpose of why you are here. It is much better if you can develop happiness as a natural state of mind, without making it a product of your expectations and achievements. You do not know why you are born, but you should know why you live and what you can do to fill the empty cup of your life. Unfortunately, most people do not think or live that way. Hence, you have a world full of miserable and unhappy people who do not know what they can do about it or how they can bring happiness into their lives.

The purpose of happiness

What is the need for happiness? This seems to be such a silly question that you may wonder whether it needs an answer at all. Frankly, it is an important question, which everyone needs to ask and look for answers. If you do not know the value of happiness, you are not going to look for it or work for it. To improve the quality of your life and the level of your happiness, you need to think about it and find an answer to it. When you have the answer, you will have the solutions also.

Many people think that they value happiness in their lives, but their actions and lifestyles tell a different story. To those who want to smoke, drink and take drugs for fun and enjoyment, here is an important message. What is experienced on such occasions is not true happiness, but a delusion of it. At the end of the road, you will meet only suffering, pain, loneliness and days and nights filled with remorse and guilt. You cannot call it enjoyment, except in a limited or a temporary sense.

In the long term, it is worse than hurting yourself with pins and needles. Unless there is a severe chronic pain or health problem, which cannot be cured by any medical treatment, one should not resort to the use of drugs or pain relievers to alleviate pain and suffering. Happiness and wellness go together. You will not travel far on the path of self-destruction before you realize that you left behind happiness where you began. It is commonsense that happiness is important to your wellbeing, and to feeling good and doing good. It is equally important that your happiness should not diminish the happiness of others or yours, or become the cause of it. Your happiness should rest on the firm foundation of virtue and values and arise from responsible living. It should be part of a broader vision, meaningful life, and righteous purpose.

One of the lessons that become self-evident as we grow is that if there is anything worth living for, it should be happiness. Unfortunately, when we examine our lives, behavior, and actions, we realize that we do not always follow it in our real lives. For one reason or another, people engage in actions which are sometimes self-destructive and which lead to pain and suffering. For various reasons they act against their own wellbeing and happiness. If this is not so, most people would be happy most of the time.

Many people sabotage their own happiness by being self-destructive. They pursue harmful habits and goals, even after knowing that it would lead to pain and suffering, and remain stuck in unhealthy relationships, negativity, and professions that continue to give them pain and suffering. It is as if they have chosen to suffer and placed a curse upon themselves.

For your own good, you should know how important happiness is for your survival and success, and what you need to do to experience it, with your long term interests in clear sight. In truth, you should not seek happiness in response or as an answer to your suffering. It has to be pursued to experience a positive life and to discover and actualize your true purpose and talent.

Happiness is a teacher. It serves an important function in your life. It lets you know what you are doing with your life, and whether you are living correctly making right choices and progressing in the right direction or not. If you are happy, it means you are doing well and in good shape. Otherwise, it is an indication that something needs to be changed or improved about you or your life. Happiness has its own intrinsic rewards. It increases your confidence and self-esteem and your engagement with the world. When you are happy, you feel encouraged to transcend your limits, seek new goals and pursue better rewards.

You need happiness for good health also. Studies clearly show that health and happiness are interrelated. It is difficult to say which comes first. Good health leads to happiness and happiness leads to better health. Studies also show that prolonged states of happiness means infrequent visits to hospitals and consultations with physicians. Happiness adds certain glow and aura to your personality, which no expensive plastic surgery can.

There is a direct correlation between happiness and the quality of life. According to a study done by Sonja Lyubomirsky, Laura King and Ed Diener in 2005, happy people possess adaptive and positive traits such as optimism and resilience which help them to stay on course in reaching their goals. In turn they lead to a better social engagement, coping skills and emotionally satisfying and rewarding personal relationships.

Happy people also tend to be people oriented and manage their marriage and family relationships well. Studies show that happy people are more likely to get married, have more friends, lead a busy social life and raise a family. A fifteen-year study in Australia by Gary Marks and Nicole Fleming indicated that happy people were more likely to marry in the following years than those who were not.

Since happy people also tend to be more positive, they are more likely to succeed in their professions, earn higher income and show greater initiative and enthusiasm in accomplishing their tasks or resolving problems and conflicts. In short you need happiness to feel good about yourself, succeed in life, gain better health, relate to the world well, live for right purposes and causes, seek fulfillment, and experience the inner satisfaction of leading a meaningful and purposeful life.

Philosophers on happiness

Everyone needs a philosophy of life. You need it even if you do not believe in God. That philosophy is going to be your shield and savior, which you need to protect yourself from the bumps on the road and the harsh realities of life that you run into. As part of your worldview, you also need a philosophy of happiness of your own, based on your beliefs and values. You should not only have it, but also know why you need it, what purpose it should serve and how you should pursue it. Having your own views about life and happiness helps you to live with clarity and pursue your goals with purpose and vision.

From the earliest times mankind has been grappling with the problem of happiness and how to pursue it without fear or guilt and without risking their lives. Philosophers and religious teachers alike dwelt upon this subject and provided their own answers. In the following discussion, we will examine some of the conclusions they arrived at in their search for happiness and purpose in life.

The subject of happiness attracted the attention of ancient Greek philosophers. Just as the Indian ascetics believed that true happiness came from within but not from the external things, the Greek philosophers also held similar beliefs. Foremost among them was Socrates, who was forthright in his opinions. His views on happiness are preserved in the form of three dialogues recorded by Plato, the Euthydemus, the Symposium and the Republic. In them Socrates argued that all people desired happiness and true happiness came not from external things but on how they used them. Happiness came from good use of things and suffering from their wrong use.

Aristotle believed that happiness was the ultimate purpose of human life. It should be the ultimate goal of all human actions. However, he felt that to experience happiness one must live virtuously and all actions must lead to the perfection of human nature. It meant happiness and good character went together and for the sake of happiness and well being and to perfect human nature, sometimes painful choices were necessary.

Epicurus, another Greek philosopher, believed that pleasure was the starting point of happiness. Those who pursued pleasure without fear and guilt experienced greater happiness. In pursuing pleasure one should use discretion to know which pains and pleasures were conducive to happiness. To put it simply, Epicurus believed in uninhibited pursuit of pleasure. A somewhat similar aim was proposed by the Carvakas, the materialists of ancient India. Both the approaches assume that pleasure and happiness are synonymous and through increased pleasure seeking activity you can enhance happiness.

Epictetus believed that interpretations of perceptions played an important role in creating emotional states. Positive and negative emotions would arise in response to external things and situations. However, the power to create them was not in the things themselves but in the attitude and perceptions with which they were held. In other words, your happiness or suffering was your mental creation based on what you felt about your experiences rather than what really happened. Epictetus also believed that true happiness stemmed from virtue and from the things and situations where we had the power to exercise control. To be happy, we must cease to worry about things that are beyond our control.

In the history of the world, countless philosophers spoke about happiness. The scope of this article would not permit me to include all their opinions. Hence, I picked a few representative opinions, which I believe are relevant to our discussion.

Do our religions promote depression?

There are many people in the world today who have reservations against world religions because they feel that religions are meant to make people unhappy and limit their ability and choices to enjoy life or pursue happiness. Unfortunately, somehow this belief has come to stay.

Religions are not meant to take away your happiness, but to enhance it. They point to a perfect state of existence characterized by pure happiness in which there is no scope for suffering. In projecting an ideal life which is conducive to the highest good, they may emphasize the need for an austere and disciplined life to deal with our vulnerabilities and imperfections. However, in doing so, they do not ignore the importance of happiness in our lives or our dependence upon it.

Religions believe that suffering is the small price you pay to reach the highest and eternal heavenly life. According to most of them, heaven represents the highest and the purest state of happiness, which humans can aspire for, while hell represents the worst of suffering. In other words, our religions want you to enjoy supreme happiness not only temporarily here but also eternally hereafter. However, such a goal requires effort, sacrifice and suffering.

Thus, your aspiration for heavenly life is actually a reflection of your longing for eternal happiness here and hereafter, which most religions promise to deliver under the condition that you abide by righteous conduct and exemplify certain virtues. The essential purpose of any religion is to alleviate human suffering and suggest a meaningful human conduct so that we may live our lives responsibly and secure maximum peace and happiness for ourselves and others. Our prayers and rituals are meant to seek divine help and secure these noble goals only. From a religious perspective, happiness refers to the state of complete freedom from want, dependence, conditioning, fear, death, and impermanence. When you reach this state, happiness comes without your seeking it or wanting it.

Is your happiness level predetermined?

It is generally held that external factors largely determine our happiness and given the same circumstances everyone can experience happiness. Research proves that it is not true. Both extrinsic and intrinsic factors influence our happiness. Recent research in this field places more importance on the intrinsic factors.

They suggest that our happiness has a lot to do with what happens in us and how we are conditioned, and our happiness level is largely and genetically predetermined. Happiness level means up to what extent or intensity you can feel happiness and sustain it. It seems it is not only specific to each individual but also remains approximately constant throughout the individual's life. It also means beyond a certain limit, you cannot greatly increase it or decrease it, or influence it.

Positive and negative events in our lives may slightly increase or decrease our levels of happiness, but once they pass we revert to our normal levels. In other words, up to a certain limit, people are hardwired to experience happiness, and there is nothing much they can do about it other than trying to keep it above the set level, like the way a pilot keeps his helicopter at a certain altitude during a rescue mission. To explain happiness levels, Phillip Brickman and Donald Campbell (1978) coined a new term, "the happiness set point," which suggests that our happiness has a lot to do with the way we are born, not the way we are raised. It is as if the karmas of our past actions are at play.

If it is true, it is an incredible finding, with far reaching ramifications in psychotherapy and behavioral sciences because if happiness is genetically determined we need to know what other aspects of our personality and behavior are also prewired, because in the natural order of things it cannot happen with just one emotion or mental state.

The conclusions of Phillip Brickman and colleagues are based upon their study of people who experienced significant positive and negative events such as wining a lottery, losing near and dear, or suffering from debilitating accidents. Their study showed that in both instances the events did not significantly alter the happiness levels of individuals in the long term to the upside or downside. After the initial euphoria or depression, people reverted to their normal set levels of happiness.

There seems to be a balancing mechanism at work in each of us, as part of our self-preservation instinct, to protect us from the excesses of our own emotional reactions. This may happen even with our anger or fear. After we go through some churning internally, we become normal again.

A recent study done by Sonja Lyubormirsky, Kennon Sheldom and David Schakade (2005) in this regards shows that genetic factors may contribute up to 50% of our general level of happiness. According to another study done by them, extrinsic factors such as income, social status, gender, ethnicity, etc., may contribute to a mere 10 to 20% only.

While further research may be required to validate these findings and expand its scope, it appears that the theory of happiness set point is justified on several grounds. In this regard, we are reminded of Epictetus, the Greek philosopher, who suggested that in triggering emotions, external events were not as important as internal reactions.

While external events seem to have a bearing upon our happiness levels, our emotions and wellbeing actually arise from our inherent nature and the way we interpret our perceptions. Commonsense also agrees with this observation. We know from experience that our happiness quotient is predetermined to some extent at birth. Some people and even families have a predisposition for happiness, while some seem to suffer from chronic negativity and even depression.

Studies consistently show that happiness arising from reaching difficult goals or accomplishing a significant gain remains short lived. For example, people who attend therapy sessions and show improvement in their happiness levels eventually return to their normal predisposition after some time. Each time you try to rise above the level, nature brings you down and keeps you in the zone. People in war torn countries or those who suffer from major life altering events, get on with their lives once the initial shock is absorbed and they come to terms with them.

These findings further suggest that we cannot take our happiness for granted, and we cannot sustain it beyond a point unless we keep working at it. While we may try to improve and influence our happiness levels, we have to accept with philosophical attitude that whatever we may accomplish in the process may be short-lived.

How to create favorable conditions for happiness

From the above discussion we can conclude that even though all factors are not within our complete control, we can create happiness by knowing what makes us happy and creating those conditions that increase and sustain our happiness. In this regard the following suggestions are useful.

1. **Find a purpose**. Purpose brings a noticeable change in your thinking, awareness, and attitude and makes you feel that your life is worth living and your aims are worth fighting for. It not only gives you opportunities to experience happiness and fulfillment, but also the strength to withstand suffering and hardship.
2. **Know what makes you happy and pursue it**. You can pursue your desires, but makes sure that in the process you use discretion and do not make yourself unhappy.
3. **Organize your life in every possible way**, including your home and surrounding. It makes your life easier, and increases your sense of control, order and regularity.
4. **Develop your own philosophy of life and happiness** which can help you to find happiness without feeling guilty or conflicted. It can also help you to withstand the rigors of life and the suffering it brings.
5. **Aim for happiness here and hereafter**. While you may practice your religion and spirituality either for liberation or for a place in heaven, you should not ignore the importance of happiness in this life. Both are necessary for you physical, mental and spiritual Wellbeing.

The Art and Science of Persuasion

People have their own beliefs and values, which they form over time and make them part of their identities and belief system. Hence, it is difficult to change their thinking and perception, and make them see your point of view or agree with you. However, with some effort you can persuade them to see your point of view or think like you, at least partially.

Research in human behavior and social psychology proves that in specific circumstances people change their opinions and responses, even if they seem to contradict their inner conditioning, and established patterns of behavior. By knowing it, you can improve your effectiveness and likability, and persuade people to see your point of view or understand what you want to say.

People do not have to agree with you, but they need to understand your point of view, and know at least that you think differently and hold certain opinions with which they disagree. Opening a dialogue and letting others know your point of view in a nonthreatening, gentle, and friendly manner is the first step in persuasion. People need time and information to change their thinking and perception. Those who work in marketing, publicity, or commercial advertising know it well.

The following suggestions are based on the actual research that has been done in this field and referenced by Noah J. Goldstein, Steve J. Martin, and Robert B. Cialdini in their book, "Yes! 50 Scientifically Proven Ways to Be Persuasive." You can use them to improve your persuasive skills and your chances of influencing people and changing their thinking and perceptions. They are especially useful if you are working in a service industry and if you have to regularly deal with people and their expectations.

1. Let them know how popular it is and how it is liked by others: Why do film stars and celebrities have millions of followers on the social networks, whereas your intelligent and witty posts, and unique quotations do not attract even a few hundred? It is because most people accept what others find acceptable. They follow those who are well known, popular or famous in the esteem of others. Therefore, let your audience know how your ideas and products worked in the past and how people found them useful or effective in their lives or in similar circumstances. Research shows that people tend to follow others or find their behavior agreeable if they are more like them. We are conditioned to accept the majority opinion and follow what others find useful, convenient, profitable and beneficial. This herd mentality is very noticeable in what people do, the products they purchase, the clothes they wear, the movies they watch and the trends they follow.

2. Limit the options: When you are trying to resolve a problem or conflict through persuasion or negotiations, you should not offer too many choices or options because it can be counterproductive. Research shows that when people are offered more options, it tends to have a negative effect upon them, as it creates confusion, anxiety, and indecision. Too many options mean people need more time to process the information and choose the right alternative or come to a definite conclusion. Too many choices overwhelm people and delay their decisions, as they cannot easily make up their minds.

3. Be careful about what you give away as free: Offering free products and services is a normal marketing strategy, which is practiced by many. However, research shows that it may not be a good idea if it is done carelessly without letting the customers know the value of what they are getting for free. It seems anything that has been offered for free loses its value and appeal in the esteem of others, as they may doubt the intentions of the offer and question its value and utility. It is also true that many times what you get for free is worthless, incomplete, or useless, and leaves you feeling cheated or disappointed. Therefore, if you want to give away any product or service for free to others for whatever reason, make sure that you let them clearly and precisely know its value or price, and the benefits they derive.

4. Offer the more expensive or difficult option first: In any persuasive effort, your aim should be to overcome resistance and clear any doubts and objections others may have about the proposal you offered them. Hence, it is better to start with the most difficult choices first where you may experience increased resistance, and depending upon the situation move towards the less objectionable ones. For example, if you want to sell your customers a television set, you may start by showing them the expensive models first and test the reaction. Depending upon their reaction, you can decide whether to show them the less expensive ones that fit their budget or expectations. Research shows that an option looks more attractive and economical, even if it is expensive, when it is juxtaposed with a more expensive or difficult one, and people tend to feel comfortable choosing the less expensive one as a compromise even if it is somewhat overpriced.

5. Avoid invoking fear and anxiety: Do not invoke fear to persuade anyone unless there is a compelling reason. If at all you have to invoke fear, make sure that the threat is real and the solution you offer is going to address it. Research proves that people block out fear producing messages if they have not been provided with effective remedial measures or specific plans to deal with them. In other words, if you want to warn others about an imminent threat or danger in doing or not doing something, you must combine your message with a specific action plan to deal with it. Otherwise, your message will be ignored or repudiated, as people may block out the message altogether or act as if it may not happen.

6. Cultivate the helping attitude: Helping others is the best way to expand your zone of influence. When you help others, you generate goodwill and favorable impressions in their minds about you. They begin to trust you because they have seen your good side. In the long run, your generous and helpful nature brings you rich rewards and cement your relationship with others. People tend to reciprocate the good you have done to them. It rarely goes unnoticed and unappreciated. Some people hesitate to show their generous side, or shy away from helping others even when they have an opportunity. By helping people, especially those who make a difference to you or your business, you increase your zone of influence and create more favorable opinions about yourself and your business in their minds.

In the present day world, persuasive skills are important since you have to deal with people and seek their help and cooperation in various aspects of your life. If you are in business or leadership positions, you need these skills even more. You cannot influence everyone that you meet in your life, or change their opinions. However, with effort and following useful suggestions such as the abovementioned ones, you can make your way through the maze of human relationships and interactions.

Cultivating the Virtue of Patience

If you walk slowly, you will have an opportunity to see many wonderful things on the way. However, if you run or jog, all that you see will be like a blur in your memory. Those who go on rollercoaster rides know how stressful the experience can be. When they are on the ride, they remember nothing except the rush of adrenaline, fear, and anxiety. Life is also very much like a journey. If you travel slowly, you will enjoy the journey, but if you rush through it, you will experience stress and a lot of anxiety. This is very much true in case of those who are always in a hurry to finish their deadlines and spend little time to relax and look around. What they see in their lives mostly becomes a blur and settles in their minds as vague impressions that are difficult to recall. In their eagerness to accomplish their goals and outsmart others, they lose the larger picture and miss the richness and wholeness of their lives.

Being alive and aware in an otherwise empty and inanimate universe is in itself a rare blessing and a great opportunity. We do not experience more life, or more of anything, if we live in haste. We may experience achievement, but not stability, and we may accomplish goals, but not fulfillment. Once you are born, you are forced to participate in the great competition called life and race forward. Most people live like comets, although they want to shine like stars. In fact, in a fast paced world like ours it is difficult to be patient. If you have any doubt, try to drive slowly on a highway and see how angry glares pass you by and how impatient drivers tailgate you and try to nudge you forward. For many people, living itself is a chore just as driving is. They want to hurry through it. Their impatience is well reflected in many aspects of their lives. It is well evident in the way people use the Internet, post their messages, or read the information with complete disregard to its source or authenticity. Most people browse the websites in a hurry. The average time they spend on a web page is usually less than a minute.

In the real world, many times people do not even remember what they have done during the day or the previous days. Since they have a lot of choices in making their selections, they do not appreciate anything easily and keep looking for more excitement and entertainment. If they do not like friends, they look for new ones. Many want instant results, and look for instant gratification. Whether it is watching television, eating or walking, they bring their restlessness into their actions. In a need driven society, where you are judged by what you accomplish and what you have, how can anyone practice patience? How can you be sure that if you wait for long, you will not lose some relationships and advantages? Most importantly, how can you fall behind in a fast paced world, when you have to deal with people who are themselves impatient and want to accomplish tasks ahead of others?

It may not be prudent to be always patient. Sometimes you need to push things, or care for those who matter to you with timely actions. You must have the discretion to know when to slowdown and when to move fast because certain things in life do not wait for you. Besides, events and situations are not always under your control, and you do not always enjoy the privilege of making decisions for you and others. Since your time is valuable and your opportunities are limited, you have to act in time to meet your deadlines and move forward with the world.

Discretion is important to know when you need patience, and when you can take liberties. In certain important matters that influence your survival and success you may have to wait for long until you get desired results. In such cases you must show patience. When situations are beyond your control and when you require the help and cooperation of others, you may require even more patience. There is a time for everything. In certain tasks that are time bound or consequential, you cannot do much until all the conditions are met. Patience is also required when you are in a learning mode, when you fail or stumble, or when you are experimenting, or when you are trying to change or improve people and situations. Since there are limitations to what you can accomplish, you must have patience towards yourself. In all these, you must know when to patiently wait and when to move on. Patience is certainly necessary in case of the following:

1. When you are in negotiations.
2. When you are working for your goals.
3. In maintaining and improving relationships.
4. When you are teaching or learning.
5. When you are perfecting your skills.
6. In dealing with situations that are beyond your control.
7. When you manage processes that require time and effort.

The following are a few important areas where patience is a virtue.

Contracts and agreements: You need a lot of patience in financial matters. When you apply for a loan or a credit card, or when you join any service plans, you are required to sign an agreement that will bind you to the terms of the service until the end of the contract.

Once you agree to the terms, most companies do not easily let you cancel any contract. Some impose heavy penalties. Some may even take you to court. You must be, therefore, very careful when you sign any document, because once you put your signature on any contract, your options become limited. If you have any doubt, please search the Internet for information against companies. You will find plenty of complaints that are posted by people who have signed up in a hurry, only to realize that they made a mistake, or they had been ripped off.

Financial issues: Patience is also required when you are investing your money in stocks. Investing in stock market requires a lot of patience and study. Just as you cannot hit every ball that is thrown at you in a game, you cannot blindly invest in any stock that you find on the Internet or in the stock market. You cannot also go by other people's advice without proper study. For each investment in stocks, you have to do a lot of research and wait for the right opportunity. When you buy and sell stocks, you must exercise great patience and caution. Many times, the stocks and the stock market do not move according to your expectations. Therefore, you have to keep your emotions under control and stick to your original plan and trading strategy.

Family matters: Patience is required in marital relationships and in your dealings with children and family relations. Marriage is a responsibility. It is where your patience is tested to the core. When you speak or act impulsively, which usually happens in close relationships, especially between married couples, you may create discard and make any reconciliation difficult. Same is the case with children, who are growing up and developing their own individuality. They may not like to trust you as much as they did when they were small, or find your advice and your words as interesting and comforting as before. Unless you give them space and allow them to return to you in their own time, after going through their own eye opening experiences, you will probably lose them forever.

A spiritual approach to cultivating patience

Patience is considered an important virtue in all religions, especially in spiritual practice. Spiritual life is full of challenges. It may take years before you achieve the required purity and perfection. In many eastern religions, one is expected to practice patience as part of one's transformation. They are advised to practice it by focusing upon the following.

1. In thinking and behavior.

2. In dealing with problems and suffering.
3. In accepting daily events and perceptions as they are.

Thinking and behavior: If you want to cultivate patience, you must begin with your thinking and how you respond to the situations that arise in your life. For example, what will you do when you are ill treated by negative people, or when you face disturbing and hurtful situations? Do you rush to judgment and react rashly, or patiently review the whole situation with detachment and let your higher mind prevail? If you patiently control your thoughts, and examine it from various perspectives, you will be less troubled by negative events and experiences in your life. If you have control over your thoughts, in troubling situations you will realize that they are good opportunities to learn important lessons and cultivate patience.

Response to suffering: Patience improves your ability to deal with hardship and suffering and overcome them. Many people wilt in the face of problems and consider their suffering unbearable. It happens because they respond to their suffering rather emotionally, instead of finding rational and effective solutions. You should know that in an impermanent world everything has a beginning and an end, and someday your suffering too will eventually resolve itself. If it is incurable, or it appears that it may last forever or for a long time, you can learn to deal with it patiently by cultivating a philosophical attitude and inner strength to bear with it. You can also respond to your own suffering with compassion, and express it when you see others sufferings.

Acceptance: This is closely related to the above two. It is how you embrace the world, its dualities and conflicting realities, without judgment, and without being attracted or repelled by them. It also means you do not condemn or criticize those you dislike or whose actions may not be to your liking. The world is a transient place. There is nothing here which you can take for granted, except perhaps change itself. The best way to live in such a world is to let go of your attachments and expectations and accept the world, its people and things for what they are, without judgment, ill will and resentment. It happens when you cultivate patience and remain in harmony with the world.

Fear, What Can you Do about it?

Fear is the most dominant emotion in humans as well as animals. It is also the most powerful motivating factor. It is even suggested that most of the emotions that we experience are variations of fear only since they are caused by the presence or absence of fear. For example, anger and aggression may arise because of fear only. Fear is again the basis of worry and anxiety. It is part of our self-preservation instinct. Therefore, whenever we perceive threat, either real or imaginary, we experience fear.

The psychosomatic nature of fear

When we perceive threat, our bodies undergo physiological changes to prepare us either to face the threat or to escape from it. It is known to psychologists and behavioral scientists as the fight or flight response. All living beings need extra energy in both situations, to face the threat or escape from it, and fear stimulates their bodies to meet with those energy needs.

The fight and flight response is a primitive mechanism, which is primarily under the control of your autonomous nervous system. What it means is that you cannot control the mechanism that triggers fear, and whatever control you may want to exercise upon it will be limited and happens later as a delayed response. At the most, you will gain control over fear, only after your body's initial response is complete and the initial surge of adrenaline has done its job.

In a threat situation, your autonomous nervous system puts you in a state of high alert, by increasing your heart rate, blood pressure, breathing, and helps your brain to cope with it by releasing more oxygen and glucose into the blood stream. These mechanisms are meant to wake you up rather rudely from whatever task or routine you are engaged in, and draw your attention to the threat. Other noticeable physical symptom one experiences during fear are stated below. Together they precipitate what we call the state of arousal.

- Sweating, which helps the body cool the heat generated by the muscles.
- Increased flow of adrenaline.
- Release of extra blood platelets into the blood to facilitate clotting.
- Release of endorphins to block any possibility of pain.
- Slowing down of digestion to conserve glucose.

The difficulty in controlling fear

Thus, fear has both physical and emotional components. Since it is deeply connected to your survival and autonomous nervous system, it is very difficult to control it or avoid it. Many people who are unaware of this aspect of fear blame themselves for their failure to control fear. Fear is a biological and physiological response to the threats created by the mind and body. Hence, there is no shame in having fears, or experiencing them. Indeed, if you do not fear at all, it should be a cause of concern because it is not only unnatural and abnormal but also indicative of some hidden problem. Fear is experienced by all. Even courageous people experience fear, although they may deal with it differently. Courage is not the absence of fear, but willingness to deal with fear from a point of strength.

Imaginary fears are worse

While the physical or biological aspect of fear is a common survival response to perceived threats, the emotional aspect of fear is where individuals show a wide range of behavioral responses that are induced mostly by internal factors. Your mind can produce fear, even without real threats, because after you experience fear, you may keep thinking about it, remember it, or visualize the event that triggered it. You may also think about the consequences and visualize the end, playing out different scenarios, according to your expectations, experience, and state of mind. All this activity, keeps your fear alive and even fuel it. In other words, your fears are psychosomatic in nature. Both your mind and the body play their parts in producing, sustaining and aggravating them. Your body has an inseparable connection with your mind and influences its functions, and your mind in turn affects your bodily functions and its overall condition. Most emotions that you experience are also psychosomatic and have a direct bearing upon your mental and physical health.

Your mind can aggravate your fear by keeping the threat fresh in your memory and not letting you think of anything else. As you keep thinking about it and keep envisioning different outcomes of the same situation, you may continuously experience fear, worry and anxiety, long after the incident has passed. The situation become even more complicated if the threat is imaginary rather than real. You can deal with real threats by either facing them with right solutions or completely avoiding them, but you cannot use the same strategy with imaginary threats or mentally exaggerated ones that linger in your mind and make it difficult for you to think rationally or act realistically. It is where you need effective coping methods to free your mind from your filters and mental constructs to see the reality.

Coping with fear

Fear manifests in us in various forms. Some common and frequent fears are, fear of death, fear of change, fear of failure, fear of rejection, fear of disapproval, fear of loss, fear of the unknown, fear of strangers, fear of separation, etc. Since we have seen how fears arise and how they affect our minds and bodies, the following suggestion may prove helpful to deal with your fears.

1. **Stay strong**: Regular exercise helps your build a strong body and mind and deal with the stress and anxiety that is induced by fear and worry. Studies show that regular exercise helps people to remain steady and strong in fearful situations.
2. **Keep good health**: Sickness and ill health are major causes of worry and anxiety. Hence, try to keep your health in good condition.
3. **Deal with irrational and exaggerated fears**: We have previously discussed how your imagination and exaggerated thinking can aggravate your fears, and keep you worried. You must, therefore, learn to dispute your irrational thoughts and ground yourself in reality.
4. **Face your fears**: Sometimes the best solution to deal with your fears is to face them rather than avoid them. It is the best way to break the illusions of your mind and know yourself better.
5. **Know when you should fear**: The purpose of fear is to protect you from possible harm. Hence, when there is a genuine cause to be afraid, you must respect it and avoid any situation that may endanger your life or your safety.
6. **Learn from your fears**: You can learn a lot about you from your fears. Hence, when you are afraid, you should not try to suppress your fear, or consider yourself weak because of it, but learn from it and adapt yourself accordingly. You should try to understand how your fears are triggered, what goes on in your mind and how you respond to them. As you become aware of your fears, you will get to know their causes and learn to deal with them with awareness and understanding.
7. **Stay away from violent people**: Some people use fear, threats and abuse to control others. Avoid them by all means.

Don't Look for Happiness at the End of the Journey

There are essentially two approaches to life and enjoyment. One is the thinking that I will keep working and toiling until the end and live a disciplined life so that when I die I will go to heaven and enjoy the pleasures of heavenly life. It is the same mentality which says, I will keep on working until my retirement so that when I retire and settle down well, I will go on a world trip, enjoy my savings, and a lead a leisurely life.

The second approach is that I will make the most out of my life here and now, even when I am engaged in actions to reach my goals and secure success and happiness. I may not currently have all the luxuries of life, but I know how to keep myself happy and contended and enjoy whatever blessing and comfort I have. The first approach is based on the value of having, and the second on being. You must have seen both approaches and both types of people in your life, and you yourself may fall into one of the two categories.

If you believe that someday somewhere at the end of reaching your goals and realizing your dreams you will find happiness, think again. You may be probably missing a whole lot of fun. In fact, you may be enduring more pain and suffering than experiencing any happiness, because your aim is not enjoyment but reaching your goals or expectations. You might have seen some workaholics. They keep working day and night, ignoring their own comforts and family needs to realize in the end that organizations treat all people working for them with the same set of rulers and seldom make exceptions.

The moral of this is that you must enjoy your life as it happens, while pursuing your goals and dreams with hope and determination. In this regard the following points are self-evident.

- Happiness has to be found here and now. Not just at the end a tiring and exhausting journey and effort.
- Tomorrow is a mere dream, or a mental concept. In reality, there is no tomorrow, until it comes.
- You can always plan and execute your actions to complete those plans. You have to in fact, if you want to find comfort and happiness and if you want to experience fulfillment and the satisfaction of having led a worthwhile life.

- However, there is a lot of fun in doing things and in accomplishing goals.
- The journey of life is as thrilling, fulfilled and adventurous as arriving at a cherished goal.
- That journey does not have to be exceptionally great. Every journey of life is unique and worth enjoying and remembering.
- You are the enjoyer. You must always remember it.

You are born to enjoy the experience of life. Your life is a rare opportunity for you to be aware and to become your dreams and aspirations. You were born not because you willed it or wanted it to happen. It happened for reasons beyond your knowledge. You can control neither your birth nor your death. It is a fact.

However, you can control a lot of what happens in between. Your unintended birth has given you a rare opportunity to experience life in all its hues and colors and learn from it whatever wisdom it can teach. It is why creation exists in the first place. If you believe in God and scriptures, you should believe in the value of your life also.

After a long and arduous climbing, on the top of a mountain you may see the grand spectacle of a vast landscape. You can make that experience even more memorable by remembering how you managed to reach there, how you prepared for it, dreamed of it, and overcame obstacles and self-doubts, before you took that last step and stood on the summit.

At the end of every journey in life, it is the totality of all that you had gone through, which makes it memorable and monumental. The monks, who renounce worldly pleasures, and do not keep any worldly possessions, exemplify this ideal. They live simple lives, but enrich their existence by focusing on the present, straightening their thinking, and living mindfully. They pay close attention to their minds and bodies constantly to understand how the process of living can cause so much pain and misery to people and how they can become free from it.

Happiness comes not only from having, but also from being and doing. The very state of existence, the condition of being alive with the ability to be and to become is in itself a great blessing which is worth more than any achievement or enjoyment. You may agree with me that some of the most memorable experiences in your life are the journeys that you made in your childhood and how you enjoyed them, not just what happened after you went somewhere. When your mind is filled with curiosity, you enjoy your life better.

Your present is what you can control, experience, enjoy, enrich, and remember. Your present moment is all that you can have at any given time. And your life becomes according to how you spend each of those moments for better or the worse.

There is nothing much you can do about your past or your future, other than learning to cope with them. What happens cannot be changed, and what is going to happen is uncertain.

Therefore cherish the moments that make your life's journey. Float on the waves of life when you can, and swim when you need to. If you live with this spirit, you will not suffer from disappointments and personal failures, even if you do not manage to reach your goals after all the effort. You will find solace in the memory of that journey, in the lessons you learned and the experiences you gained. You will remember your sorrows and you joys with certain nostalgia.

How to Motivate Yourself and Keep Your Morale High.

Some people begin tasks which they rarely finish. Some people begin new tasks with a lot of enthusiasm, but after sometime lose interest and limp along. You will also find some, who are so mentally deflated that they do not see any justification to plan their lives or achieve success. These situations arise when people lack interest or enough motivation. Our behavior is mostly motivated by desires. Motivation fuels our success. It is the desire for success, approval, recognition or fulfillment, garnished with purpose and inspiration, which propels you to achieve something or aim for something as part of your vision, purpose and self-preservation.

Self-motivation is your road to independence

Your motivation may arise from various external and internal factors. Of them, the internal ones are more compelling. There is nothing like self-motivation. It sets you free from your dependence upon others and your need for their approval, which most people are habitually conditioned to follow. Those who are not self-motivated, will not show initiative in their actions, unless they are asked, compelled, coerced, or instructed. The urge to do something or achieve some goal must come from within. If your desire is stronger, your commitment will be greater. In work place, you may be motivated by your organizational culture, your peers and superiors, or your career goals. But in real life, especially in personal matters and goals, you have to motivate yourself and keep your mind and body well conditioned.

It is necessary that you take personal responsibility for your motivation and the direction of your life. Your heart and mind must be properly aligned to your dreams and aspirations. If your motivation comes from within, your chances of sticking to the course you have chosen and reaching your goals will remain high. If you constantly depend upon others and look to them for support, encouragement and approval, the chances are you will drop the baton before you hit the finish line.

People are by nature selfish and self-centered. It takes a huge effort on their part to become selfless and help others without a motive or an agenda. This has been my experience. Unless they have a stake in your success, they do not care whether you succeed or not. In fact, most of them secretly want you to fail and humiliate yourself.

Their hidden animosity increases greatly if they are in a direct competition with you. Hence, you must be ready and well prepared to fight your own battles and keep your courage intact in the face of adversity, failures and setbacks.

Unfortunately, our motivation does not always stay strong. From time to time we relapse into our usual insecure selves. We lose interest or become distracted from our goals and aspirations due to various reasons. When it happens, we may wallow in self-pity and misery, and may even look for excuses and scapegoats to avoid hurting ourselves.

Repeated failures, disappointments, lack of encouraging environment, envious friends and family members, undue criticism, these and many other factors may discourage you from pursuing your goals and realizing your dreams.

In such circumstances, you have to gather your strength and courage, and move on with renewed enthusiasm. Perseverance comes with constant self-motivation. You should find ways and means to encourage yourself, keep your morale and enthusiasm up, and work relentlessly towards your cherished goals.

If you have chosen the right purpose and if you are engaged in activities and pursuits that you like most, if your goals are aimed to make the best use of your natural talents and abilities and if they are in harmony without your deepest hopes and aspirations, it would be easier for you to remain motivated and stay in the zone of peak performance.

Yet, even in such cases, you may have to constantly boost your motivation and keep your spirits high, because just as your body is prone to fatigue due to overexertion, your mind is also prone to distractions and mental fatigue, when you overstretch yourself and deprive it of its usual rest and sleep.

Self-motivation techniques

The following some suggestions are useful to overcome inertia and lethargy and remain motivated and enthusiastic in difficult circumstances.

1. Frequently Remember your goals and keep returning to them repeatedly.
2. Remember your mission or your ultimate purpose, what you want to do, and why you want to achieve success.

3. Remember your past successes, what made you seek success, and how you began the journey and dealt with problems in the past.
4. Practice positive affirmations to boost your morale and stay motivated. They will keep you in good spirits and protect you from the disapproval, negativity, discouragement, and jealousy that you face from others.
5. Avoid the company of negative people and energy vampires who discourage you, criticize you or find fault with you to keep your spirits down. There will be many people in your life who do not want you to succeed because of envy, hatred and personal reasons. Avoid them by all means.
6. Mingle with friends and family members who want you to succeed, who are genuinely interested in your progress, and upon whom you can rely in difficult times for advise or encouragement.
7. Have a few mentors who can give you advice on specific issues. If you can afford, you may also engage a professional counselor.
8. Read self-help books to remain motivated or keep your spirits high. You can return to them whenever you need inspiration or fresh guidance. You may also visit websites on Self-help for the same purpose.
9. Organize your work. Keep a daily to-do-list and a weekly or monthly planner. If you do not like the practice, at least keep a mental list of major tasks you need to accomplish for the day or week to reach your goals.
10. Remember your enemies and those who want you to fail. Success is the sweetest revenge, and the best way to deal with them is by achieving success beyond their imagination.
11. Visualize the end you want to achieve and the sweet rewards of success. With the end in your mind, you will remain committed to your goals and plans.
12. Join a professional club or association to keep yourself informed of the latest development in the field of your specialization, and meet like-minded professionals to know their plans and programs.
13. Have a few role models. Follow the lives of successful people, how they thought and dealt with their problems and how they achieved success. Imagine what they would do or think under similar circumstances.
14. Dispute your fears and negativity. Even if you successfully practice positive thinking and remain focused on the positive aspects of life, you may still be assailed by doubts, negativity

and irrational beliefs and fears. Learn to dispute them using reason and facts, before they consume your mind.
15. Have a mental trigger or a catch phrase to fire up your motivation instantly. You can do it by creating short and specific statements that remind you of your goals, abilities or determination. You can use them like mantras. For example, you can use phrases like "I am unstoppable," "I can," "I will," "Shake off your negativity."
16. Take a break from your work occasionally or go on vacation to charge yourself mentally and physically. While you are at work, pause and take a few deep breaths from time to time to invigorate yourself.
17. Keep good health. Bad health is one of the major sources of negativity, depression, and low motivation. Eating healthy food, doing exercise, keeping yourself physically active, counting your calories, watching your weight are a few important means by which you can remain in good health and remain motivated.

Self-motivation is the best way to remain committed to your ideals and goals. It is the best way to keep your life and destiny detached from the whims and negativity of others. Hence, change your life with self-motivation, and keep working for your success.

Are you Bored With Your Life

Do you remember what did happen yesterday or day before or two days before? If you are one of those who have gotten into a rut and been living the same routine in the same manner day after day, most likely you will not remember much of what happens to you every day. Many people eventually fall into a routine life, and lose track of the moments that make up their lives.

Routine is necessary, to some extent, because you cannot wake up every day and begin to worry what to do next. Routine normalizes your life and saves you from the stress of dealing with your everyday problems and familiar tasks. However, a routine life has its own disadvantages. It makes your life less adventurous, less exciting and less interesting.

Most people grow up, find a job, get married, have children and settle down. Then somehow, somewhere, almost imperceptibly, they fall into a dull and monotonous routine that make their lives increasingly uninteresting and even depressing. It is important to recognize the problem of monotony early, which is inherent in the modern life, before it becomes a problem. If you are one of them who suffers from frequent bouts of boredom and loneliness, you have to find ways and means to deal with it and live an active and fun-filled life.

What does routine do to you? On the positive side, it makes your life easier and somewhat predictable. On the negative side, it brings monotony, makes your life dull and miserable, and reduces your zest for life. It also affects your relationships, thinking and outlook, besides limiting your chances of improving your knowledge and skills, and achieving success. Many people suffer from depression after they retire from active life due to the monotony that sets in, and as they feel neglected, ignored, humiliated or helpless. Because of loneliness, alienation, and depression, some even fall sick or die.

Monotony reduces life into a long series of dreary and dull moments. When people feel that they are stuck in a rut, it drives them to desperation, while those who feel that their choices to break through that monotony are limited feel even more depressed.

How can you break the monotony of life?

If you are suffering from monotony and leading a dull and boring life, what are you going to do? It is important to remember that you choose monotony as a safe alternative to the risks that are inherent in stepping out of your comfort zone and dealing with the unknown and the unfamiliar. Here are a few inexpensive, simple and practical suggestions to deal with this problem. They do not require major adjustments to your current plans and priorities, career goals or general Wellbeing.

1. Change your daily routine.
2. Think from different perspectives.
3. Cultivate some new skills.
4. Find new friends.
5. Go on vacation.
6. Reward yourself with a sumptuous dinner or a good movie.
7. Spend time with your loved ones who care for you.
8. Find a purpose that is greater than you.
9. Find any passion or activity that gives you an opportunity to express your talents and skills.
10. If you are leading a sedentary life, join a gym or begin to exercise and walk.
11. If you are fit and healthy, participate in community events such as a marathon walk, cycling, or hiking.
12. Read motivational and inspirational books.
13. Revisit old places where you lived before.
14. Throw a party and invite a few friends.
15. Join a local club or a professional organization.
16. Have new goals and work for them.
17. Look for opportunities to improve yourself or enjoy your life.
18. Try to remain busy and active.
19. If your current job has become a dead routine, apply for a new one where you can feel more involved and creative.
20. Write a letter or send an email to someone you have not spoken for long.

These are general suggestions. Some of them may not suit you. Pick the ones that appeal to you, or use your imagination and creativity to find your own specific solutions. Find opportunities to live differently and break the routine that has made you unhappy and a prisoner of your own habits and behavior. As someone noted, the real joy in life comes from taking small steps into the inner freedom and towards enjoying small pleasures that life offers to you. It is moments that are filled with awareness and active participation, which create your life and keep you moving forward. If you take care of them, most likely you will experience fulfillment.

Therefore, do not ignore the problem if you are feeling bored and listless. You know that you can change it, with a few adjustments to your life, without feeling self-pity or blaming others, as if your life is someone else's responsibility. You may seek the friendship of others and spend happy moments with them, but do not expect them to cure your boredom, or make you happy. By doing so, you will not only push them away but also become even lonelier. Mental dependence upon others for happiness or excitement is counterproductive because it does not set you free, but binds your happiness to the moods and emotions of others. You do not want to fall into that trap and further complicate your life.

Freedom is happiness, and you can have freedom by increasing your wiggle space within the constraints of life that apply to you. Find every opportunity to break free from the chains that keep you bound to your fears, worries and anxieties. Life is unique, and too short. It does not always happen according to your desires and expectations. The moments that make up your life will not repeat in exactly the same fashion, except in your thoughts and memory. Once you leave this world or go out of sight, no one will be there to tell others the story of your life and the moments you savored. Even if they do, it is always their version, not what you might have actually experienced.

Your life is a precious gift given to you without your asking. It gives you a great opportunity to realize your dreams and become whatever you want you to be. Give it a personal touch with enthusiasm and confidence and see how far you can travel on the path to peace, joy, success, and happiness. You do not have to feel helpless and lost in the monotony of life, unless you want to wallow in self-pity and misery and find every excuse to avoid taking control of your life. Resolve the problem here and now, by making a strong self-commitment to take charge of your life and break free from the habitual patterns of your mind.

The Success Mindset

Mindset is an interesting concept. Mindset in a very general sense means how your mind is set or poised. Is it poised to remain fixated upon certain notions and concepts, or is it flexible enough to adapt itself to the challenges of life and willing to grow and mold with time and circumstances? Carol Dweck, a professor in Psychology from Stanford University and a noted psychologist who did research in this area, suggested that people had either a fixed mindset or a growth mindset and one could anticipate their behavior and responses once their mindset was determined. In her studies, Carl Dweck did not acknowledge any intermediary types, that is, people having aspects of both mindsets, a fixed mindset in certain areas of life and a flexible mindset in other areas. Her research focused mainly upon two mindsets. In real life it is difficult to find such a clear-cut demarcation of behavior and personality types. Human behavior is very complex and I therefore believe that there is more to human behavior than two clearly demarcated mindsets. The following discussion is about success mindset, and how one may cultivate it.

What is success mindset?

There is a mindset, which says, "I am like this, I will never change, I do not want to change and this is what I am." What this person tells you is that she is hopelessly caught in a time warp, with little hope or expectation.

Then there is the other mindset, which says, "I am like this, but I do not have to be like this. I can learn. I can improve myself. I can change. I can take responsibility for my life. I can learn, improve my knowledge and skills, to deal with my weaknesses, and keep adapting to the demands of life to achieve whatever I want to achieve and humanly possible."

You are probably familiar with both, and you may have either of the two. If you are serious about your life and accomplishments, your priority must be to cultivate the right mindset. With the right mindset you can reach whatever goals you decide to reach, even if you are born with certain with social or economic disabilities.

The key to a successful life is having the right mindset or the success mindset. Mindset means having a set of attitudes and beliefs that influences your thinking and actions.

Right mindset means having the right attitude, right temperament, flexibility, adaptability, realistic thinking, right resolve, belief in oneself, ability to deal with failure and willingness to grow, change and improve oneself.

Success mindset means having all these, plus the willingness to achieve your goals by taking direct responsibility for your personal growth, thinking and actions.

Growth mindset and fixed mindset

Carol Dweck identified the success mindset with growth mindset. In her book, "Mindset: The New Psychology of Success," she suggests that basically there are two types of mindset, a fixed mindset and a growth mindset.

The fixed mindset does not offer much scope for a person to change or improve. It makes him believe that his abilities and talents are more or less fixed and he cannot do much about it. Such thinking makes people rigid, resigned, passive, and follow the path of least resistance to resign to fate.

The growth mindset makes you think the exact opposite. It gives you greater flexibility and encouragement to change and improve your thinking and behavior according to the demands of the situation and accomplish your goals and dreams. It empowers you to succeed in life by making necessary improvements and adjustments to your thinking and actions.

Dweck suggested that it is possible for people to cultivate the growth mindset to realize their goals and achieve success and happiness. To be able to change or improve one must be able to see possibilities and opportunities. The growth mindset facilitates that process and helps an individual to move forward in life with right convictions.

To know whether you have the success mindset, or fixed mindset, you have to introspect and find answers to a few questions such as the following.

- Are you willing to learn?
- Are you willing to improve?
- Are you willing to adapt?
- Are you positive about change and growth?
- Do you believe a person can improve mentally and intellectually, and talent and intelligence are not fixed?

If you answer them affirmatively, it indicates that you have the right mindset, and you are poised for success.

To achieve success in life, more than wealth and resources, you need the right mind set, which empowers you to regard yourself as the master of your life and destiny. It gives you a valid reason to look at your life with hope, determination, and courage.

With right thinking and attitude, you can take control of your life, and develop the ability to adapt yourself, according to the goals you set, the challenges you face and the life you want to lead. You learn to forge ahead, without being stuck in the routine of your life. You keep yourself motivated and enthusiastic, as you learn new skills, acquire new knowledge, expand your sphere of influence and find ways and means to resolve your problems, overcome obstacles and stay ahead of others in competition.

How to cultivate the success mindset?

To cultivate the right mindset that leads to your personal growth and professional success, you should focus upon the following.

1. Positive beliefs in your abilities to change and adapt.
2. Knowing that you can always learn new skills and improve your knowledge and intelligence.
3. Knowing that each day is different and brings new challenges and opportunities.
4. Knowing that your success and failure depend upon you and your actions.
5. Knowing that with right effort you can overcome your limitations and weaknesses.
6. Willingness to learn and improve your knowledge and skills.
7. Flexibility and adaptability to adjust and respond to the demands of life.
8. Clarity of purpose.
9. Dedication and determination.
10. Perseverance.
11. Clear, specific, and measurable goals.
12. Focus.
13. Vision.
14. Hard work.

The following suggestions are also useful in this regard.

1. Have a few goals that are worth achieving, and remember them until they become your second nature. Build your life around them. Stay on course until you realize them.
2. Decide to be different and exceptional, even if it means facing disapproval from others.

3. Learn to take calculated risks, and step out of your comfort zone to be yourself or to reach your goals.
4. Aim for excellence, in whatever you do.
5. Be willing to make mistakes and learn from them.
6. Learn to accept failures and rejections.
7. Review your progress regularly.
8. Be honest with yourself in reviewing your actions.
9. Sharpen your skills and keep learning.
10. Learn to trust your instincts in making decisions, without ignoring the feedback from people you trust.

No one ever traveled on the highway to success, without ever making a wrong turn. Having a purpose, willingness to change and grow, determination, focus, commitment, self-study, self-motivation, faith, perseverance, hope and compassion, are a few important components of the success mindset, with which you can realize your dreams and reach your goals. Age is not a bar. But if you begin this journey early, it will help you in the long run.

A Brief Study of Intuition

What is Intuition?

Intuition is the ability to know directly and instantaneously without the aid of thought, reason, observation, inference or deliberation. The dictionary meaning of intuition is quick and ready insight, immediate apprehension or cognition. Intuition is an automatic mental process that defies logical thinking, but occasionally plays an important role in perception and problem solving. Hence, Karl Jung described it as an irrational function.

Intuition is part of our survival instinct. It is an ability that is not confined to human beings alone. Some animals seem to perceive threats in their environment intuitively. They have an uncanny ability to identify an enemy and stay away from danger.

Intuition is a rapid response mechanism of the brain that does not operate according to a set procedure or adhere to predictable conditions. Much of the intuitive process is hidden, beyond our grasp. We know it only when it happens in the form of a feeling, physical sensation, thought or a gut feeling. It appears that in intuition the mind is able to recognize hidden patterns instantaneously without the aid of any conscious cognitive process. From this perspective, we may say that intuition is an accelerated cognitive process in which many parts of the human brain participate.

In philosophical terms, intuition is viewed as a kind of subjective belief rather than a rational thought. It is also considered a mental state or a disposition that makes you believe in certain possibilities, expectations and outcomes.

Karl Jung suggested that extroverts and introverts differed in their ability to use their intuition. However, it is not clear whether intuition is universally related to personality types and orientation. Although it is unpredictable, intuition is a right brain activity, which plays an important role in problem solving, creative thinking, innovation and decision making.

While psychologists stayed away from intuition for long, presently cognitive scientists believe that intuition is an unconscious cognitive pattern recognizing process, which is difficult to explain but nonetheless an experiential fact. According to Gary Klein, the author of the book, "Seeing What Other Don't," insight leads to the recognition of new patterns when people see connections, coincidences, curiosities and contradictions in the observable world, whereas in intuition people use existing patterns which they have already learned or discovered to identify solutions, possibilities, and opportunities. He also stated that about 90 percent of our critical decisions are based on intuition, and far from being a sixth sense, intuition is an essential skill which can be learned like any other skill.

Intuition as a spiritual faculty

Intuition is a faculty of the higher intelligence or the spiritual mind. It also goes by the popular name, the sixth sense or the inner voice. Spiritual people have a better intuitive ability because they are well connected with their inner consciousness and they are free from the usual distractions and disturbances of the mind. They develop extra sensitivity through pure observation, which also make them extra intuitive.

Spiritually speaking, a calm and stable mind, which is free from afflictions, desires, attachments and expectations, is better equipped to receive intuitive thoughts and sublime messages because of fewer distractions and less mental noise. From a spiritual perspective, it is believed that your intuition may arise from within yourself or from an external source such as a divine entity or the Universal Mind when you are in harmony with it.

You may also consider intuition a type of higher mental awareness in which the usual inner chatter is absent and the mind is free from the burden of fears and anxiety and the influence of the negative self-talk. If you are not careful, you may mistake your self-talk for intuition. If you have a clear and stable mind, you will have a greater ability to process the incoming information and provide insight and intuition into the nature of things.

What makes you intuitive?

In his book "Blink : the power of thinking without thinking," Malcolm Gladwell explained how some people possessed the ability to filter a lot information in an instant and made choices in an instant or in the blink of an eye. Some people were good at it because of the way they processed information and weighed the various options and variables.

While intuition is a mysterious process, certain factors tend to increase our intuitive ability such as knowledge, experience, mindfulness or heightened observation, pattern recognition, sensitivity, empathy, feelings, effective listening, open mindedness, non-judgmental awareness, visualization and creativity. People with years of experience in a particular field or profession develop an intuitive way of understanding things and make on the spot of judgments about people and problems. Probably knowledge, experience, and habit, coupled with confidence, give them a unique ability and a clear perspective to "think in a blink." People who are sensitive, introverted, spiritually inclined and those who practice yoga, meditation, visualization and similar practices regularly also show greater receptivity to intuitive and subliminal messages.

Myths and facts about intuition

The following are certain important myths and facts about intuition.

1. **Myth**: Intuition is a mental faculty, or the ability whose functioning is difficult to determine.
2. **Myth**: You can always rely upon your intuition because it is divine.
3. **Fact**: Intuition is not a magical ability but a mental ability, and very human.
4. **Fact**: People differ in their intuitive abilities and the method and the manner in which their intuition works. It is because they differ in their thinking, perception, knowledge and interests.
5. **Fact**: There is no such thing as an intuitive person. Intuition is a latent faculty, which almost everyone occasionally uses as part of his or her survival mechanism to think and recognize threats and opportunities.
6. **Fact**: With effort and practice we can become more intuitive. As you pay close attention to the world around you and to the thoughts and feelings in you, you become increasingly intuitive.
7. **Fact**: Intuition has no correlation with birth, intelligence or education. Everyone has it and can use it to solve problems and overcome threats.
8. **Fact**: There is no guarantee that your intuition will always be correct or right. It is not under your conscious control. You cannot make your intuition happen when you want it. Hence, it is not always reliable.
9. **Fact**: Since it mostly happens by chance, you cannot expect to use your intuition as your only problem solving strategy. You have to use it along with other methods to resolve your problems and make intelligent, and balanced decisions.
10. **Fact**: Intuition may arise in various ways and you cannot easily predict how it may happen. It may be triggered by unusual insight, perceptions, connections, inconsistencies,

coincidences, associations, patterns, or it may happen internally during sleep or dreaming.
11. **Fact**: Intuition is not a magical ability. It cannot be enhanced through magical formulas or mantras.
12. **Fact**: Knowledge and awareness can contribute to intuition. For example, in long-term relationships, people tend to become more intuitive towards their partners.
13. **Fact**: Intuition seems to develop with repeated use and testing.

How to Develop Intuition?

The following factors are conducive to intuition.
1. A calm and composed mind.
2. Believing in yourself.
3. Attentiveness.
4. Curiosity and interest.
5. Freedom from judgment.
6. Freedom from attachments, prejudice and expectations.
7. Freedom from fear and anxiety.
8. Concentration.
9. Meditation.
10. Steady breathing.
11. Positive relationships.
12. Receptivity.
13. Humility.
14. Gratitude.
15. Self-knowledge.
16. Trust.

Your intuition arises from accumulated knowledge, wisdom and experience. Its source is what scholars call in eastern traditions higher intelligence or discriminating intelligence (buddhi), which gives humans beings the power of discernment or the ability to see patterns and connections, and know one thing from another. Ordinarily human intelligence is adulterated with many impurities such as desire, greed, fear, anxiety, instability and other afflictions and modifications of the mind. Therefore, it is believed that self-purification and inner transformation can greatly enhance the intuitive faculty of our minds. A calm mind, a healthy body, virtue, character and integrity are very conducive to intuition. The intuitive ability that is present in human consciousness points to the evolutionary possibilities of the human mind and in which direction humanity may eventually evolve as a species.

Improving Intuition

The following is a brief discussion of developing intuition. Some of the ideas presented in this section are already discussed in the previous essay. Intuition is the ability to know or feel automatically or instinctually what is going to happen or what may be necessary or appropriate or the right solution in a given situation. It is a kind of premonition, a gut feeling or a hunch, which lets you know exactly how things are shaping out or in what direction you are progressing.

In intuition you do not deliberately use reason and analysis. They happen in the background without your active involvement. What you get from your intuition in the end is the understanding, conclusion, or awareness about something or some situation. However, how do you know that your intuition is going to work as expected and it is not mere guesswork? There is no real answer to this. Only time will tell whether your intuition was right or wrong. An important truth about intuition is that you cannot force it to happen. It happens mostly on its own, without your active participation. Another important truth is that at times your intuitive choices can be wrong.

If you have a strong ego and rigid mind, very likely you may not be able to think intuitively. With hard work and intelligent effort, you may force yourself to think intelligently and strategically, but you cannot do it in case of intuition. You can, however, train your mind to develop gut feeling and solve your problems in an instant. You can do it by cultivating a passive and mindful observation, nonjudgmental awareness, detachment and by not filtering your thoughts and perceptions with set beliefs and rigid attitude.

If you are flexible, with an ability to see patterns and connections, you will be more intuitive. By developing sensitivity and inner tranquility, you can allow your intuitive mind to recognize those patterns and connections and gain insight. The following factors improve or enhance your intuition and help you become intuitively aware of the people and the world around you.

1. Be sensitive to your thoughts, feelings, and surroundings. Learn to label them clearly. Do not suppress them because you are feeling uncomfortable.
2. Pay attention to the world around you to notice any patterns, connections or coincidences. At the same time, be mindful of

the happenings in your mind and body because intuition may arise as bodily sensations, gut feelings, or vague thoughts.
3. Practice mental stability. Let your mind remain calm and composed and free from disturbances. If you are anxious, disturbed, or agitated, you will lose the touch with your intuitive mind and remain distracted.
4. Stay in the present and keep yourself fully awake and alert. A keen sense of observation is essential to intuitive thought process or to recognize unusual or hidden patterns.
5. Listen attentively. When you actively listen to people, you will allow your mind to draw its own conclusions about the verbal and nonverbal clues coming from them and think intuitively.
6. Feel empathy and compassion for others. You are sensitive and intuitive to the extent you empathize with others and feel for them.
7. Practice detachment. If you are detached, you will let your intuitive mind speak through your wakeful mind, as you will not interfere with its movements with your desires, expectations, and preferences.
8. Keep your mind empty. When you empty your mind by interrupting your thoughts and feelings and create a center of calm in you, you allow other people's thoughts to reach you and your own intuition to respond to you.
9. Be honest. Intuition is a higher faculty. Its source is the higher intelligence, which functions well when you are pure and when you are honest and truthful to yourself and others.
10. Feel oneness with the Universal Self. You are an integral part of God's universal body. You may think that you are a separate entity, but you are an inseparable part of the universe and the Universal Mind. When you identify with it and feel connected to it, your intuition gathers strength and flourishes.
11. Practice yoga and meditation. They purify your mind and body and let you to experience peace and stability, which are necessary to experience intuition.
12. Suspend your judgment, since it interferes with your ability to think freely. You become more intuitive when you are free from judgment, prejudice, and preconceived notions. Therefore, stop being critical and judgmental about what disturbs you or irritates you.
13. Minimize your expectations. Expectations prevent your mind from recognizing unusual patterns, hidden trends or contradictions and inconsistencies. Hence, you have to free

your mind from anticipation, expectation, and preconceived notions.
14. Express gratitude. Whenever you receive help from your intuition, say thank you. You do not have to react negatively, or express anger and frustration, if your intuition has failed you. It is not necessary that your intuition will always be right or deliver the right message. It can be contaminated by your own thoughts and expectations.
15. Avoid the urge to control your intuition, situations, or other people. Free your mind from any anxiety you may feel about your future, or the urge to control your life and destiny. Do what you can and leave the results to themselves, with the understanding that you can control your actions, but not their outcome.
16. Let go of your fears. If you are afraid, nervous or depressed, your intuition will remain suppressed.
17. Slow down. In our fast paced world, we miss noticing many things that are important and have a value and relevance to our lives. Therefore slow down, whenever possible, and take a calmer and deeper look at things and the world around you.
18. If you think it is necessary, keep a journal to record and analyze your intuitive experiences. It will eventually help you to know the conditions and circumstances in which your intuition works better for you.

How to Create Happiness in Your Life

Happiness is a positive state of mind and having positive feelings. We experience happiness frequently almost every day. However, since we do not pay enough attention, we do not mostly remember the occasions when we were happy. It is also true that in most cases our happiness do not last for long.

There are two aspects to happiness, the experience of happiness and the state of happiness. The former is about the happy moments we experience in our daily lives, and the latter points to our general state of mind, attitude and propensity.

From experience we learn that usually we are happy under certain circumstances such as the following.

1. When we do what we love most.
2. When we have a definite purpose in life.
3. When we are in harmony with ourselves and others.
4. When our dreams and desires are fulfilled.
5. When we learn to adapt ourselves to the demands of life.
6. When we help others.
7. When we are recognized, rewarded and appreciated.
8. When we are loved and cared for.
9. When we have security and stability.
10. When we are in control of a situation.
11. When we are in the company of people we love most.

From the above, it becomes clear that we can make ourselves happy by creating situations and conditions that are conducive to our happiness. While some amount of frustration and dissatisfaction may still remain deep within our minds and hearts, and certain unpleasant facts about our lives and circumstances may still bother us, even within such limitations we can find opportunities to create, sustain, or increase our happiness.

The general assumption is that if you have more luxuries and amenities you will become happier. However, if you happen to visit poor countries, you will notice that people living there also find occasions and opportunities to smile and be happy. It gives credence to the conclusion that if you are determined, and if you use your intelligence and creativity, you can be happy and make yourself happy. Your thinking, beliefs and attitude play an important role in creating and sustaining your happiness. Sometimes, happiness means being at peace and in harmony with yourself. In this regard, the following suggestions are relevant. They help you become or remain a happy and cheerful person.

1. Smile even if there is no specific reason to smile, if necessary by forcing yourself. A forced smile is a good antidote to feeling of depression. If it does not cheer you up, at least it will cheer up those around you.
2. Do what you love most. If you cannot leave your current profession, use your free time to pursue your hobbies and dreams.
3. Have a higher purpose in your life, which gives you a sense of direction and the ability to bear suffering, with hope and resolve.
4. Spend time with the people who are happy and who love you and respect you. People who love you boost your self-esteem and make you feel good about yourself.
5. Avoid the company of critical people and those with whom you cannot get along. At times, it is better to avoid the company of negative people and motivation busters rather than trying to impress them and win over them.
6. Find time to help others. Invite your friends and family for lunch or dinner, participate in some voluntary activity or mentor children who need help and who lack a proper home environment. Such activities can greatly enhance your happiness.
7. Whether at work or at home, make yourself useful, helpful and friendly in whatever you can.
8. Live within your means and invest your savings wisely even if it is not much. A good bank balance can keep you free from financial worries and anxieties.
9. Avoid taking undue risks whose consequences you cannot resolve.
10. Give health a top priority and make sure that you keep yourself mentally and physically healthy.
11. Focus on your strengths and achievements and learn to forgive and accept yourself unconditionally.
12. Avoid hurting and harming others for personal gains or to make yourself feel good. You have to recognize other people's right to happiness just as you acknowledge your own.
13. Have a pet, preferably a dog. There is no better solution to feeling needed and loved than having a pet by your side that loves you unconditionally.

Remember that you have but a limited time to live upon earth. On a cosmic scale, a hundred years is too small a time to experience anything deeply, or understand the immeasurable and infinite purpose of human life. After we are born, and as we grow, we lose sight of the very nature of human life and become caught up in many activities that do not really matter in the end. Occasionally, it is necessary to withdraw from frivolous actions and refocus your mind upon the critical and important aspects of your life that lead to your happiness, mental stability, peace and harmony. Therefore, wisely spend your time, focusing upon the positives, thoughtfully choosing your priorities, and finding occasions and opportunities to make yourself happy, contended, cheerful, purposeful, energetic, inspired, and determined.

Cultivating Wisdom and Intelligence

There are some people in the world, who may know their names, the names of their friends and relations, the streets and the places where they live or go, but do not know much about anything else. There are some, even among the educated ones, who do not show much interest in what happens around them. Ask them who Da Vinci was, and they may ask you with a puzzled look whether it is the name of an Italian recipe or a restaurant! In a world that has been increasingly becoming complex by day, it is important that we live with certain awareness, knowledge and wisdom.

Considering their level of interest, knowledge and awareness, we can classify people broadly into four categories.

1. **People who live like plants**: They do not go much beyond where they were born or know what exists beyond their noses. They remain rooted to their past, and to their rusted, obsolete mindset, refusing to move with the times.
2. **People who live like animals**: They spend their time and energy in satisfying their desires and live very much like pets, cattle, or zoo animals.
3. **People who live like humans**: They possess humanity, awareness, and show understanding and compassion. They use their knowledge and intelligence to solve their problems, and adapt to the world in which they live. They also possess sensitivity to respond to events and situations that arise in their lives, even if they are not directly affected by them.
4. **People who live like higher beings**: They are comparable to gods or angels, with an enlarged vision, who see life from a wider perspective and think of it as a gift, blessing or a great opportunity to transcend their human limitations and find unity and harmony with the universe.

We have these four classes of people in our present day world. We meet with them, interact with them, and at times deal with them. They were present before, and they will be present in future also. In fact, they were always present in the history of the mankind. In the Vedas, they were recognized as the four classes or castes of human beings. It is a different matter that such distinctions have been used in the past and now for wrong purposes.

If you examine carefully, you will realize that the four classes of human beings exist universally, in every nation, region, community and society. You may recognize them under different names and in different forms, but they do represent the above mentioned four distinct divisions of the humanity.

The four classes do not enjoy equal status. The first category of people suffer from many social and economical disabilities due to their lack of knowledge and wisdom. However, mentally, the worst sufferers are those who belong to the fourth category. They are comparable to gods or angels, but to due to their heightened awareness, they suffer from moral conflicts and dilemmas. Their suffering increases exponentially if they have to deal with the plant or animal kind, interact with them regularly or depend upon them for their survival.

Our purpose upon earth is nobler than what most people believe or care to think about. It is to discover our humanity, make full use of our rationality, if possible rise above our limitations, and develop a wider vision and higher intelligence, not just for ourselves but for the entire existence. The successes we achieve and the abilities we cultivate will help our future generations and make their lives even better. For that, we do not have to make elaborate plans. We have to live our lives responsibly and try to manifest the best and the noblest of the human nature in us. We also need to make a sincere, spiritual effort to cultivate an intense aspiration to transcend our weaknesses and show our humanity. Most importantly, we need to rise above our pettiness. Then, with such perfections and refinements, and with our hearts and minds set upon that singular purpose, we can use commonsense approaches to improve our knowledge and intelligence.

With the help of the following four simple techniques, you can expand your awareness and grow mentally, intellectually and spiritually into a higher being. You can consider them the four feet of wisdom or the four candles with which you can illuminate your mind, and elevate your thinking, vision and worldview into a higher plane. Opposing these four positive approaches are the four negative ones, which you may call the four feet of delusion. They are indolence, negligence, falsehood, and perversion. These four negative qualities lead one down the path of self-destruction and moral degradation.

Read

Reading and knowing give you the status of the twice born. Many people think that reading is for children only, or for those who are engaged in academic or scholarly pursuits. In this information age, it is important to cultivate good reading skills and habits, and keep yourself well informed. It is not good for your intellect to confine your reading to film magazines, gossip columns, and sports journals. It may fill your hours, but would put you in the animal realm, just above the plant category. Instead, read interesting and useful books and magazines, which will help you personally, professionally and spiritually to progress in life and change the way you think and perceive the world around you. If you have a local library, visit it frequently and get into the habit of reading books and magazines.

Nowadays, one can download a lot of information from the Internet into a computer, phone or an electronic device. You can use it to enhance your knowledge, memory and thinking skills. However, when you do it, you have to ensure that the information is relevant, useful and good for your mental and spiritual development.

Do not let a day pass by, without reading something and absorbing useful information. Read wherever and whenever possible to keep your mind well nourished. Reading is to your mind what eating is to your body. If you want to go for an extra mile in this effort, try to develop fast reading skills so that you can gather more information in a shorter time.

Observe

Although we remain awake for at least 15 hours to 16 hours a day, we hardly pay serious attention to anything, unless we are engaged in performing critical tasks or when we perceive threats to our security and wellbeing. This is natural, because our minds are made to conserve our energies and keep us distracted from anything that is not important to our existence or survival. Therefore, we perceive a fraction of what happens to us or around us. As a result, we live the same lives every day, develop rigid habits and routines, indulge in rituals, and play games to avoid intimacy and inconvenience or to stay in our comfort zones. Thereby, we miss noticing many things and live rather unmindfully. When we meet people we do not register their faces or names, and when we pass through the streets we do not notice much.

The truth is, for the most part of our lives, we remain on an autopilot. While it may not be a good idea to always remain awake and attentive since it will be exhausting and distracting, it is necessary that you become a good observer and become insightfully aware of the word in which you live. You should observe the people you meet, the situations you face, the things you seek, the way you act and react and the way other people deal with you and respond to you. Good observation skills, which lead to mindfulness or attentiveness, will help you see things clearly, and discern problems and opportunities, and friends and foes. It helps you to identify problems well in advance even before they happen and remain proactive.

Listen

Effective listening is a skill. Effective listening means the ability to listen with full attention and absorb most of what you hear, without any distractions or mental chatter. Most of us are not good listeners. For one reason or the other when we meet people routinely, we shut down our minds and take them for granted. As a result, we may displease them, make them feel uncomfortable, or miss many opportunities to forge good relationships with people who might help us in future.

To be a good listener, you have to set aside your opinionated and judgmental mind, and open your heart and mind. You have to cultivate sensitivity and empathy, and show readiness to invest time and energy in building relationships with others, resisting the temptation to dominate them or defend yourself in front of them.

Effective and empathetic listening is the best and the least stressful way to gain knowledge and wisdom. You may experience stress from reading because you have to focus your mind and assimilate the information. In listening also you need concentration and effort. However, if you are genuinely interested in people, you will not feel stressed at all. You can become a good listener by removing the barriers to good listening, such as egoism, judgment, impatience, preconceived notions, negative emotions such as fear, envy, and anger, and selfishness.

Reflect

To reflect means to make an intelligent analysis of what has been going on in your life. As events happen, you have to think and draw rational conclusions about the people you meet, the situations you experience, and the life that happens to you. You have to think about solutions and strategies to deal with your problems and achieve your goals. If you do not reflect upon your experiences, you will not learn from them. If you do not learn from them, you will commit the same mistakes repeatedly and make your life difficult. You can learn from your failures and successes only when you reflect upon your plans, decisions, actions and interactions. The other three qualities or approaches which we have discussed before are useless unless you cultivate this important quality.

Reflection means thinking and reviewing what has been read, heard or experienced. It is an important quality, which sets you apart, and gives you a distinct personality and character of your own. It also puts you on par with the most intelligent beings upon earth, besides helping you to become analytical, observant and insightful, which in many ways adds depth and character to your learning.

Most people live without reflecting upon their perceptions and experiences. They become mentally lazy and mechanical as they harden their senses and stop feeling and responding. While it may temporarily shield them from the harsh realities of life, it stifles their mental and intellectual growth. Those who do not reflect upon their experiences seldom develop their individuality. They live other people's lives and try to fit into the roles society thrusts upon them.

You should put your rationality to regular use because you are not a plant or an animal, but a thinking, feeling and living person. You are endowed with many talents, skills, and abilities to make decisions for yourself and to experience and express your life in your own unique ways. Since you have curiosity and adaptability, you should use them to your advantage. People respect you more, if you have individuality, if you follow your own principles and live by your own convictions, if you have a certain way of looking at things and understanding them, and if you help them with your unique perspectives when they need them. It is possible only when you reflect upon your life and glean wisdom from it.

You can practice reflection, by becoming a keen observer, asking questions, and drawing conclusions. You can also develop it by keeping a journal, practicing meditation and contemplation, validating your beliefs and perceptions in the light of your own experience. A reflective person refuses to be charmed and deluded by the superficial aspects of life. He goes deeper into his own experience in examining things to understand his life and himself.

Thus, through the four channels of reading, observing, listening, and reflecting, you can increase your knowledge and wisdom, and your understanding of the world and yourself. Make them the four windows or the gateways of knowledge through which you can interact with the world in you and around you, and become a better and wiser human being.

Focus on the Positive Aspects of Life

Positive thinking is greatly helpful to control your negative emotions, deal with your problems, and progress in your life and profession. However, it may not always be useful or appropriate. Sometimes you have to adapt to circumstances and use defensive pessimism or negative thinking to ground your mind in reality, deal with tough situations, anticipate problems, and act proactively.

Defensive pessimism, or having doubts and concerns about the outcome of certain situations over which you do not have full control, becomes the norm when you are required to be realistic about problems and people, and act according to the situation rather than your preconceived notions, beliefs, and conditioned responses. It is definitely the right approach to deal with the problems that need an immediate and timely resolution. However, in routine and normal situations, you should stay positive and keep your negative emotions under control, rather letting them overwhelm you. Overall, positive thinking helps you live your life with courage and conviction and remain in control. Besides, when you are free from anxiety and self-doubt, you will see better options, solutions, and opportunities to solve your problems, which you may otherwise overlook.

Optimism is a learned response. We are not conditioned to always remain positive or appreciate life when we have problems and difficulties. We are naturally conditioned to remain on the defensive and safeguard ourselves against the threats that are present in our environment. You may try to be positive, but for that you have to go against your natural thinking and fight your instincts. Since no one can predict future correctly or find ready-made solutions to problems, it is difficult for anyone to live without fear and anxiety or focus only on positive outcomes. Thus, optimism, like courage, has to be cultivated and maintained with effort in the face of grave problems. Unless we toughen our minds and focus on the brighter aspects of life, we cannot readily enter the positive state of mind.

Many times in your life you will have a choice either to let negativity rule and ruin your life or to take control of it and allow positive thoughts to guide your actions. Such opportunities arise many times in your life as you perform actions, make decisions, choose your relationships, deal with your problems, work on your goals or adapt to your environment. When you make right choices by using your discretion, you will learn to trust your instincts, take responsibility for your actions and decisions, develop faith in your methods, and feel good about your achievements.

In any given situation there are always some positives and negatives, opportunities and threats, where you can use your knowledge, skills, abilities and judgment to bring out the best in you and manifest the best you can. When the outcomes are not predictable or disappointing, you may use them as learning opportunities. If you cultivate a growth oriented mindset, and see possibilities and opportunities for self-growth, you will have better chances of feeling positive about your actions and their outcomes.

In this world, no one is perfect. We make mistakes, stumble and fall, hurt and disappoint others. At times, we lose our balance, or let lose our emotions that may lead to lasting consequences. You, as everyone else, will always have such weaknesses, and like everyone else you may not always win, or be right or righteous. Yet, you cannot allow those concerns and limitations to hamper your motivation or weaken your resolve to overcome obstacles.

An important lesson which is not generally taught in schools is how to cultivate positive thinking and make it an integral part of your consciousness and behavior. As you grow and mature, you have to learn it on your own to address your fears and force your mind to think positively until it becomes a habit. The following suggestions are useful in this regard. They help you cultivate the habit of positive thinking and ingrain it deeply in your thinking beliefs.

1. Develop the habit of thinking both positively and negatively about people, problems and situations in your life. This will give you an all round knowledge, and free you from errors in your thinking and judgment.
2. Question the assumptions in your decisions and how far your expectations are based upon facts and reason.
3. Avoid mind-reading and jumping to negative conclusions about other people without proof. Give them the benefit of doubt until you have the right information.
4. Choose the positive in a gives situation unless there are compelling reasons to ignore it. To the extent possible, and unless you have a reason not to, focus upon opportunities, solutions, strengths, positive outcomes, gains, benefits to sustain your effort and progress.
5. Dispute you negative thoughts and feelings to understand from where they are coming, whether the causes are justified and how you can deal with them.

6. Be realistic in your thinking and approach. If at all you have to be negative, do so as part of a deliberate strategy to achieve certain positive ends.

Life is a mixture of opposites. You can neither avoid unhappiness nor choose only happiness. Most of the time in your life you have to settle for what life offers to you or what you can make out of your circumstances. Within those limitations and between the dualities of suffering and elation that define your life, you can learn to choose wisely and create conditions for your inner Wellbeing.

A monk learns to remain equal to all. He reacts alike to both happiness and unhappiness as he conquers his desires and passions. Of all the solutions, it is still the best one. However, it not possible for people who cannot transcend their desire for material things. For them the best course is to stay positive, choose their goals wisely, and learn to make the most out of their abilities and opportunities.

Understanding and Accepting Your Emotions

You have heard many times that when you are angry you should count the numbers one to ten. The underlying idea is that when you take your mind off the cause or the source of it, your anger will disappear. Did you ever try it and see whether it works? Most of the time, in critical situations, people just do not remember to do it. When they become angry or frustrated, they forget everything and let out their anger. Do you know why it happens?

You may have also heard about the ways in which you can control your anger, such as disputing your negative thoughts, practicing breath control, taking adequate rest, doing meditation and cultivating mindfulness. No doubt, these techniques may occasionally help you and others to achieve mental stability and emotional control. However, do you know whether they always help you to control your negative emotions? The answer is clearly no.

Emotions are difficult to control. If you are one of those millions of ordinary people who are habitually prone to emotions, you might have learnt from your experience that emotions cannot be easily controlled. You may try hard, but there will be times when you cannot simply get rid of certain powerful emotions. As they invade your mind, you cannot help being angry, irritated, frustrated, afraid or anxious.

The problem with emotions is that you cannot simply take them out of your system. They are an essential and inseparable part of your consciousness and personality. They are part of your survival mechanism built in you by Nature, which allows you to cope with the ups and downs of your life both physically and mentally.

For example, fear may not be good for your self-esteem, but fear is necessary for your survival. Anger may not be good for your health and relationships, but anger may help you defend yourself against possible threats. These emotions let you know how you are doing in your life and what opportunities and problems may be present in your environment.

Emotions act like indicators in the systems that control and regulate your life. They prepare you and cushion you like shock absorbers against the bumps and shocks you face. By becoming aware of them you can protect yourself from breaking down when things go wrong.

Without emotions you will not be able to live your life normally or humanly. If you suppress them or turn them off, you will not be able to establish normal relationships or experience positive emotions such as pride, love, the sense of achievement, fulfillment or belongingness.

The social cost of trading with your emotions

Your emotions are meant to help you to relate to the world, know it, communicate with it and deal with it. Unfortunately, society forces you to hide the unpleasant aspects of your behavior behind a mask of acceptable behavior, social rituals and conditioned responses. By hiding them or manipulating them, you may gain social approval, recognition and acceptance, but if you believe in certain values you may feel conflicted. For example, if you believe that you are not true to yourself, the same strategy may very likely make you feel guilty and uncomfortable. From experience you may know that those who are good at manipulating others with their emotions under control are deceptively more pleasant and popular than those who are honest in their opinions and actions, but cannot control their emotions.

A question which is relevant in this context is to what extent you are willing to trade your genuine emotions for the love and appreciation of others. When you hide your emotions and true feelings, you stop being genuine, spontaneous and authentic in your relationships. You may pretend intimacy, but in unguarded moments you will betray it. When we put on cultivated and polished faces and hide our true feelings for the satisfaction of others, we stop being true to ourselves and others. While socially it may satisfy our need for approval and belongingness, morally it raises serious doubts in our minds about our character, faith and trust.

Although humans are more advanced and intelligent, many animals are more genuine and authentic in their behavior and responses than humans. The more educated and socially polished people are, the less transparent and reliable they become. Hence, in civilized societies, it is really a challenge to find genuine friendships and people who are willing to speak their minds without fear. People in such societies are drawn to pets because pets do not lie.

Understanding your emotions

Understanding how emotions arise and what purpose they serve in your survival is necessary to accept them and use them for your wellbeing. Here are few important facts about emotions which will help you to understand them and cope with them.

1. Accept your emotions rather than suppressing them: One of the first steps in dealing with emotions such as anger or fear is to acknowledge them as normal and human. There is nothing sinful or immoral about being emotional, unless your emotions make you inhuman, insensitive and cruel to others. Feelings of guilt associated with emotions are more devastating and damaging than the experience of emotion itself. So when you deal with the problem of emotions, you should learn not only how to control them but also how to accept them and manage the guilt and remorse arising from them.

2. Emotions make us human: People may love to see a tobacco chewing film star who would not bat an eyelid when the guns are blazing at him or when someone tries to provoke him with an insulting word. But let us admit, in real life you may not feel very comfortable with that person because you cannot tell how that person is responding or what is happening inside his mind. When it comes to friendship and relationships, we prefer emotionally vibrant people to the cold and calculated types, whose minds and hearts are difficult to fathom.

3. Emotions are useful: There is a reason why emotions are so difficult to control. There is also a reason why probably we may never be able to completely control them. Our brains are made up of two components, one primitive and one modern. The primitive part constitutes the core. It is what we have in common with the rest of Nature. The recent or the modern one is the most human and rational part. It constitutes the outer core. It is where our exclusive human faculties are located. Our senses are wired primarily to the primitive mind and through the primitive mind to the more recent one. Nature intended this design for our survival and continuity. However, in the process it also created some problems and consequences.

4. Emotions are part of a complex decision-making process: Although we are different from animals and mostly rely upon reason and thinking, the primitive core of our personality still plays a vital role in our survival and wellbeing. It is where the external stimuli and perceptions are first received and processed before they are transmitted to the outer core for further processing, analysis and control.

The outer core works approximately like a regulator or a controller. It decides what to do with the information that is coming from the primitive core, and whether to modify the incoming, primitive, and instinctual responses from it or let them go unchecked and unchanged.

To the extent we develop our outer core and polish our thinking and reasoning skills, we can control our primitive and habitual behavior and bring out the more civilized and thoughtful responses. It is why education and overall awareness are such important factors in the development of human personality and in controlling one's behavior.

5. We can control our emotions only partially: Most of the time, the rational mind controls the information coming from the primitive core and makes its own decisions about what to do and how to respond. This is the norm. It is what happens when you are talking to strangers, riding a rollercoaster, or watching an emotionally intense drama. You remain in control and let the emotions slide through you harmlessly and almost unnoticeably.

However during critical situations, especially when a threat is perceived, the outer core loses control and fails to regulate the impulses and instinctual responses coming from the primitive brain. As a result, you let disturbing thoughts and emotions arise in your consciousness and succumb to your primitive behavior. At times, the rational Mind goes into a faulty mode of thinking and aggravates the primitive responses instead of countering them rationally and realistically. Irrational thinking is therefore a key factor in our failure to manage our emotions.

6. You can learn from your emotions: Since emotions arise primarily in the primitive parts of your consciousness, and since the senses are primarily wired to them, it logically follows that if you can control your primitive mind, you can control your emotions. Unfortunately, it cannot be done so easily.

The primitive mind is wild, basically in an auto mode, and mostly uncontrollable. It is self-regulated, autonomous and spontaneous. You can only control it and endure it through the rational, analytical and human part of your brain.

Emotions are natural to human behavior. There is nothing sinful or immoral about them. They are a natural and inseparable part of your consciousness, which play an important role in ensuring your survival and enriching your consciousness. When you experience them, you should learn to decode the message they want to convey, rather than feeling sorry about them.

The two minds that are hidden in your consciousness, are like day and night. They are the inseparable twins, often symbolized in the mythology as good and bad. One is primitive and independent and the other rational and analytical. Together they make you who you are, human, a mixture of opposites and a subject of duality. Your behavior depends largely upon which part of your mind is active and how much control your rational mind exercises over your primitive mind.

Learn to live with your emotions. In times of emotional turmoil, remember that emotions arise because your senses are wired to the primitive part of your mind and your rational mind cannot always deal with it effectively. The messages that your emotions deliver are part of your survival and existential mechanism, and should not be stifled simply because emotions are unhealthy and betray your weaknesses. When strong emotions arise, instead of stifling them, pay attention to them and try to understand what they are trying to say. This way you make use of your emotions without losing your balance and inner stability.

Listen to the Messages Life Delivers

If you are a hardcore realist, who only believes in the perceptual reality, you may ignore the following discussion and move to the next. Here we talk about cultivating deeper awareness that arises from pure observation, in which your mind becomes an observer rather than an active processor of perceptual reality.

We look to friends, family members, specialists, institutions, books and spiritual masters for guidance, inspiration and help. Sometimes, they help you and sometimes they do not. Sometimes, you may also need to spend time and money or make an extra effort to receive their help.

While you may continue to use these options to guide your actions or solve your problems, you may also consider another option, which is freely available to you and for which you do not have to depend upon others but use your own discretion, intuition and intelligence. The method has been used and tested by people since ancient times. It does not require any technology. You too can practice it anywhere and anytime.

You can do it by paying attention to what is going on around you and inside you, and by looking for the hidden messages the universe constantly keeps sending you. To practice it you have to be awake, aware and attentive, the 3 A's, which can connect you to the universe and provide you with solutions that your reason may not be able to find.

We rarely look within ourselves and search for answers or pay attention to the messages that keep coming to us in various forms. Thereby we miss many subliminal messages, the signs and omens that keep coming to us from various sources.

You may be surprised to know that you have an invisible connection with the world and the universe. You are part of them and you are forever connected to them both physically and mentally. Since you are inside them, you are an integral part of them, just as the blood cells in your body are a part of you.

You are also immersed in an ocean of intelligence. You may never see it, but know that you are a representative of it. The universe speaks to itself through you. You do its work in the microcosm. You are its probe. Your mind is part of that intelligence only.

Just as you depend upon it for your survival and just as you acquire from it your power to think and conceptualize, Nature or the Universe looks upon you as a work in progress and uses your knowledge, experience, talents and abilities to constantly update and improve its own designs and programs and unfold the further course of evolution.

You can harness the same power of observation, learning and assimilation in which Nature as a silent observer excels. With some effort and training, you can open your mind to its intelligence and establish a two way communication, whereby you not only enrich the intelligence of the universe with your unique experiences and learning, but also benefit from the intelligence that wants to guide you and help you.

Every day, you receive subliminal messages as advice, warnings, and solutions. Unless you are well prepared and receptive, you will miss them as most people do. In fact, many people do not notice them because they are preoccupied with other matters and concerns.

How to receive guidance from such messages?

You may ask, "How can anyone recognize such messages? How to tell that it is not your imagination or your desire speaking for itself?" It is true that desires, prejudice, and expectations can interfere with your thinking and mislead you. It means you need some preparation and self-purification to keep your mind stable, peaceful, detached and non-judgmental.

Ideally, the messages should come from sources that are beyond your will and control. They must surface in your consciousness on their own, without your interference. If you are expecting them, probably it may be an illusion of your mind, and untrue. You must cultivate discretion to distinguish the thoughts and ideas you create from those that happen on their own. When you have that discernment, you can easily open to the messages that are coming from the universe.

Look for events that happen on their own, fortuitously, passively, unexpectedly or coincidentally. Actions and events that happen due to the will and actions of others or due to the acts of God happen for a reason. You have to find out what they mean to you, what message they deliver, and how you are connected to them.

How to decode the messages

Here is a simple suggestion to receive guidance from the invisible forces of the universe or your inner world. Analyze any experience that manifests in your mind or perception by itself and catches your attention. It may be a dream, an unexpected event, an object, a chance meeting, an unusual or uneasy feeling or foreboding, a conversation, or any event that bothers you or disturbs your peace and happiness. Ask yourself, what message could be hidden in it and what it was trying to convey to you.

In every experience, there is some visible content and some hidden content. The visible content is what is immediately perceptible in that experience. It may be totally deceptive and misleading, because the messages are rarely straightforward. They are delivered mostly in a cryptic or symbolic language. The hidden message may be connected to your past or your future. It may be connected to your past lives or a future birth. It may be about something you wanted to do but forgot, or it may be a mistake or imperfection you are letting to continue.

Hence, you have to look for the hidden content in the message, which can surface only when your mind is clear and free from desires, expectations, fears, judgment, preconceived notions and prejudice. Many people fail to decode the messages because they have not risen to that level of purity and objectivity.

One way to find the hidden message is to observe the visible content with an open mind and ask yourself questions such as the following

What is it trying to teach me?

Why did it happen to me?

What thoughts are arising in me spontaneously in response to it?

Are there any lessons I can learn from this experience?

Does it have any relevance to my past or present?

Can I label the feeling and connect it to my past?

Why is this happening?

If you ask such questions in your daily life when any event or situation catches your attention, you will learn to perceive the hidden messages that life throws at you. You can use them to improve yourself, solve your problems and safeguard yourself from unforeseen situations.

Factors that can help your intuition long-term

As stated before, you cannot read the messages that are coming from outside unless you are mentally prepared and balanced. You should be passively attentive, without becoming too involved with what you observe. To enhance your intuitive abilities, you have to cultivate the following qualities.

1. **Detachment**: If you are detached from external things, you will have greater clarity in receiving the messages.
2. **Expectations**: Keep your mind free from desires and expectations. It helps you maintain objectivity.
3. **Freedom from fear and anxiety**: Fear and anxiety may either block the messages or distort them. Hence, develop a calm mind.
4. **Beliefs**: You must believe in your ability to receive message. If there is no faith, you may not be receptive to the messages.
5. **Nonjudgmental attitude**: You must let the messages come to you freely without evaluation, criticism and judgment.
6. **Confidentiality**: It is better to keep the messages you receive to yourself. If you want to help others, you may do so, but you should do it without telling them. If you disclose them to others, they may confuse you with their own interpretation or mislead you.

Your learning never stops. Most of your learning in life comes from pure observation. Education is a modern concept. In the ancient world people learned purely from their observation. Nature does not have formal education, but it always learns. So is the case with all animals. They learn and adapt. Learning is thus part of our survival.

Education definitely helps you to improve your observation and draw better conclusions from your perceptions and experiences. If you have a degree or formal education, it does not mean your learning has stopped. In fact, you may have to do some unlearning to improve your intuition and observation and continue your learning from them. Humility, openness, detachment, non-judgmental awareness, faith, courage, sameness, discernment, keenness, and wakefulness are a few qualities that can greatly enhance and strengthen your ability to connect to the universe and find answers to your problems. If you persist in the practice and cultivate appropriate attitude and mindset, you will be able to benefit largely from the hidden messages the universe constantly keeps sending you.

Before we conclude this discussion let us not forget the importance of gratitude. Whether the messages serve you any purpose or not, make sure that you express your gratitude to everyone who facilitates your survival and continuity.

How to Use Defensive Pessimism

"Positive thinking" is one of the most commonly discussed subjects in self-help writings. You might have read about it several times In books, articles, quotations, training programs, and message forums. It is often presented as the panacea for all your problems in life. Almost every book on self-help speaks about it and the importance of cultivating it. While we do not know how many people genuinely practice it and find it useful, there is clearly a perceptible bias in society towards positive thinking.

It is not easy to remain positive and keep up your good spirits in today's world and look in another direction, when you have to deal with difficult problems and witness unpleasant events. People are also attracted to unusually negative news. Read any newspaper or journal, and you will know the power of negative thinking. Human beings are instantly drawn to negative news: wars, conflicts, murders, crimes, shootings, rapes, corruption, pollution, drugs and death, while the actions of good people are rarely noticed unless they make negative comments or indulge in inappropriate behavior. Besides, as part of their survival, people are conditioned to remain pessimistic and fearful of the world in which they live. Therefore for all practical purposes, you can consider negative thinking the natural condition of the human mind whereas positive thinking is a temporary and cultivated fabrication, which most people forget when they are overwhelmed with negative emotions.

Although it is difficult to stay positive, we cannot minimize the importance of positive thinking in overcoming problems, reaching goals, and dealing with tough situations. Despite the arguments against it, positive mental attitude is still important to feel good about yourself, your life and future, and the outcome of your actions. You can use it strengthen your motivation and complete your tasks with resolve when circumstances are unfavorable.

It is also true that since the world is a combination of dualities and opposites, you cannot always remain positive, or use positive thinking only to guide your actions. Just as you cannot choose only happiness or unhappiness, or good or bad, you cannot choose only positive thinking as the guiding principle of your life. In challenging situations, when reality stares at you, you have to keep all your options open and think of all possibilities and threats. Since you are not in full control of the world in which you live, you cannot escape from the feelings of self-doubt and vacillation. When it happens, you have to know how to use your negative thinking to your advantage and remain in balance and control.

Life is all about balance

Life is a mixture of opposites. Days and nights, good and evil, heat and cold, and many such dualities create the sum of your life. They also produce in you conflicting thoughts and desires. They create uncertainty, but at the same time give you an opportunity to choose what is good for you. Problems arise when you cling to the extremes of life to find happiness or avoid unhappiness. Preferences and expectations reduce your choices and opportunities to deal with your problems.

Many times, true happiness lies in accepting life for what it is. You do not have to change everything about your life. Sometimes, it is better to go with the flow and embrace what life offers to you, even if it gives some discomfort. The extreme positions in any situation are difficult and even troublesome. A better course is to stay in the middle and keep moving forward. In spiritual life, you are advised to rise above the dualities and remain equal to all situations. Sameness and having a balanced attitude towards all aspects of life are positive virtues, which come when you practice detachment and inner stability. It is difficult to achieve, but if you succeed, you will enjoy immense freedom from the usual anxieties and concerns to which people are subject.

Defensive pessimism

Negative thinking is useful in certain situations and has its own value. We cannot undermine its importance to deal with adverse and unpleasant situations that cannot be fully avoided or ignored. It is a good defensive strategy in your self-preservation to remain on guard. This approach is better known as defensive pessimism, which involves thinking the worst case scenarios to take care of the negative outcomes of the actions and decisions you may take.

Its purpose is essentially self-protection and prevention as in case of defensive driving. As you know, even if you have good driving skills, it is better to drive carefully and save yourself from the mistakes other drivers can make. You cannot control their behavior or know what they are going to do. Hence, it is better to anticipate the common mistakes people make while driving and remain on the defensive.

It is the same with your life. You can only control your side of any relationship, or your side of the bargain. You can control only certain aspects of your thinking and behavior. The rest depends upon others, chance or acts of God. Hence, there is a strong need to use defensive pessimism in certain aspects of your life.

Put to use the power of negative thinking

Positive thinking is helpful to focus upon your goals and dreams and sustain your actions and motivation. However, while you remain positive, you must use negative thinking to deal with the contingencies. Whether you like it or not, sometimes you have to deal with negative situations and negative people to safeguard yourself and your interests from their negative influence. You have to balance your positive thinking with defensive pessimism and develop backup plans to deal with the problems and the unforeseen consequences of not only your actions and decisions but also of others. You have to be careful about people and situations that are not entirely under your control. It is especially important if your work involves other people or depends upon their contribution.

This is not to suggest that you have to be suspicious, distrustful or paranoid, but careful, diligent and watchful, just as you are when you perform complex and critical tasks such as climbing a ladder, sawing a tree, or giving an important presentation on which your career depends. It is what defensive pessimism is about. It keeps you prepared without being too pessimistic or fearful. Since life is uncertain, and people are unpredictable, you have to remain defensive to avoid getting hurt, despite your enthusiasm and positive outlook. Even when things are going on smoothly, you have to keep evaluating situations to notice any warning signs and problems that may take you by surprise.

Negative thinking in health and relationships

One of the areas where defensive pessimism is effectively useful is healthcare. People generally tend to overestimate their health conditions and health choices. Many people do not usually follow the good advice given by doctors and healthcare professionals regarding exercise, dieting, and healthy lifestyles, under the assumption that their situation is not that serious and somehow they are not going to be effected by their unhealthy actions. Defensive pessimism can help them see the negative consequences of their actions and habits and protect themselves from their own irrational beliefs.

Another important area where you can use this principle is relationships. Since human beings are complex, most relationships need a lot of maintenance. By nature most people are sensitive and need to feel assured and reassured in their relationships and dealings before they can develop trust and accept people as they are. Sometimes innocent remarks and small incidents can break relationships. Hence, it is necessary to deal with your relationships with a certain degree of pessimism, at least in the beginning stages until the relationship is cemented and stabilized. It is better to take certain precautions, and remain discreet about your behavior and expectations, to make other comfortable and allow your relationships to grow.

Suggestions to practice defensive pessimism

You should use defensive pessimism a part of a wider strategy to combine the power of both positive thinking and negative thinking to solve your problems, and reach your goals. You can use both approaches to assess situations that arise in your life to identify threats and opportunities and work on them. Use it as a preventive measure to temper your expectations, reevaluate your decisions and judgments, and prepare for difficult times. You can also use it to remain balanced and realistic. In this regard the following suggestions are worth remembering.

1. Have an open mind.
2. Stay positive but be realistic.
3. Do not take people or situations for granted.
4. Develop contingency plans.
5. Be ready for any eventuality.
6. Trust in your abilities but know that everything is not under your control.
7. Do what you can, hope for the best but have a backup plan for every situation.
8. When things go wrong, take responsibility and focus on the solutions.
9. Learn from your failure and keep moving on.
10. Enjoy your life, knowing well that it will not last forever.

Knowing the value of pessimism in accomplishing your goals is critical to remain levelheaded. You should also know the value of pessimism in your relationships as well. Those who understand it rationally react to negative comments and criticism of others, accepting it as a feedback to review their actions and learn From it. If you believe in the value of defensive pessimism, you will value the relationship of those who speak their minds, who are transparent and do not mislead you with polished diplomacy. It is better to have such friends rather than those who want to tell you what you want to listen, but may say its opposite behind your back.

Dealing with Emotions

There can be a thousand reasons why we experience emotions and why we are frequently overwhelmed by them. Emotions are indicators, which help you label your experiences and interactions with the external world. The most common emotions such as anger, fear, guilt, resentment, happiness, joy, and anxiety are common to all of us, although it is not clear whether we all feel them exactly in the same manner. We constantly experience them, in response to the events and problems we face. The truth is emotions color our perceptions and make us human. They define our lives, character and personalities, shape our relationships, and color our experiences. It is a matter of choice whether you let your emotions rule you or you make use of them intelligently to enrich your life and live it fully.

We are so frequently assailed by emotions that we do not remember most of our emotional experiences at all, unless they affect us intensely and leave an emotional scar. Since emotions are so common and frequent, we experience them rather habitually and do not pay them much attention. We remember some, such as the emotions related to falling in love, getting the first job, witnessing a tragedy, or being laughed at by friends or colleagues in a party, but eventually we forget most of them as we move on with times. Generally speaking, we do not remember positive emotions as much as we remember the negative ones where we experience pain, trauma, unhappiness, depression, neglect, abuse, anger, humiliation or insult.

Emotions affect us both physically and mentally. They have a physical and mental component. Hence, we physically experience them as sensations in the body, and mentally as feelings and mental states. The physical expression of emotions makes it harder for us to hide them from others, unless we learn to mask them well and stay in control of difficult situations.

It is rightly said that emotions are meant to protect us from ourselves and the world in which we live. They are part of our survival mechanism. Through them we come to know about ourselves, our environment, our relationships and what is going on with our lives and choices. Emotions are the windows to the world and your own heart. If you are sensitive and intelligent, you will learn from them and make progress in your personal and professional life with the knowledge you gain. You will learn more about yourself and the world by observing them as you deal with people and problems.

It is necessary to pay attention to your emotions and become familiar with them and the message they want to convey. You have to train yourself to control your emotions as well as to understand them, so that you can minimize the damage they do and maximize your chances of experiencing positive and healthy emotions.

The first step in this regard is the realization that emotions are healthy, necessary, unavoidable and largely responsible for your actions, thoughts, relationships, attitudes, intelligence, peace, success and happiness. If you do not pay them attention and learn from them, the problems associated with your negative emotions may remain unanswered and harm you. Moreover, if you neglect them, they may persist in your consciousness as latent memories long after the events that triggered them were forgotten.

They may also impair your health, as negative emotions leave a residue of harmful toxins in your body, which may lead to other complications. It is similar to what happens if you ignore the warning signs coming from the panels of any system or machine. Eventually it will fail, causing you some inconvenience. The same happens to your body if you ignore your emotions or suppress them habitually. Suppressed and repressed emotions may harm your health and cause mental abnormalities.

How would you deal with your emotions, especially the negative ones? This is an important question that you have to keep asking yourself until you find an answer. You cannot escape from your emotions. It is certain. Even if you escape into a remote cave, your emotions will stay with you. They are so deeply embedded in your consciousness that you experience them even in sleep.

Life teaches us many lessons. In our lives, as we grow and mature, and as we gather experience, knowledge and wisdom, we learn many skills, some good and some not so good, to deal with our emotions in our own unique ways. We also gain insight into how they work and what leads to them. The following are a few such insights associated with emotions, which you can use to gain a better understanding of them.

1. Beliefs and emotions: Your beliefs play an important role in creating your emotions. Such beliefs may be either rational or irrational. Irrational beliefs are more troublesome than the rational ones. They are also difficult to identify since they influence the way you look at things and make sense of them. One better way to deal with your emotions is to understand the underlying beliefs and assumptions associated with them. You can do it by repeatedly looking for them whenever you experience them, especially those that overwhelm you negatively and refuse to subside. Irrational beliefs are difficult to resolve, if their causes are deep. For that you need introspection, objectivity and sometimes professional help.

2. Perceptions and emotions: It is wrong to attribute your emotions to extrinsic factors or blame others for what happens to you at the emotional level. Sometimes, you may feel cheated, betrayed, hurt or angered by others. While their actions or words may trigger those emotions, in reality it cannot happen unless you allow it to happen. Your response to such events is a choice you make and certainly it is not the only choice you have. You could have reacted in other ways too, but you decided to act in that particular way because you felt it was the right choice. Whenever you are driven by emotions, you should remember this.

You are making yourself angry, fearful, depressed or unhappy by your thoughts and decisions. You are labeling your experiences with particular emotions because you are conditioned by your habitual thoughts and responses to do It External events are not primarily responsible for your emotions, but your perceptions and interpretations are. In other words, it is the way you look at things and interpret your experiences and interactions, which influence your thinking, perceptions and emotions. Since those reactions stem from internal causes, people vary greatly in the manner in which they respond to situations and express their emotions. The same situation may invoke in them different feelings and reactions, and prompt them act differently.

3. Emotions and control: You must have heard several times or read in several self-help books that having control over your emotions is crucial to your relationships, success and wellbeing. People always admire cool characters in the movies, especially the cowboy movie types who keeps firing away with guns blazing in their hands as they hide behind a rock or some vantage point, smoking a cigar. They remain cool, and show no sign of fear, even when a hundred enemies have surrounded them from all sides and constantly firing at them.

Unfortunately, in real life it is very difficult to find such characters. Most people experience fear and anxiety in the face of danger. It is not easy to always control your emotions even with the help of the best therapists in the world. Emotions happen despite your best efforts. No ivy school education will help you to stop them at will because humans are primarily emotional beings. They are born with a brain that is partly primitive, and largely ruled by emotions and instincts.

Therefore, in any given situation, people begin to think and reason only after they experience emotions. The human brain first filters the information with the help of emotions to identify the nature and intensity of threat, before passing it on to its rational part where logical thinking and executive functions happen. Thus, you may think before you act, but it is highly doubtful whether anyone can think rationally in the face of threat without first experiencing emotions. In any problem situation, you experience emotions before you take control of them and think about solutions. This is the natural order of things. You can use this natural process wisely to your advantage by letting your emotions rise to the surface and experience them without feeling guilty or uncomfortable. You can then sense their underlying message and act upon it.

4. Environment and emotions: Environmental factors such as education, cultural values, upbringing, social and family background can play an important role in shaping your emotional behavior. For example, in certain cultures children are expected to be afraid and obedient to their parents and elders, but ferocious and courageous when dealing with an enemy or opponent. Both positive and negative emotions are universally associated with certain events across all cultures, such as birth, death, marriage, love and betrayal.

Genetic factors also play an important role in shaping people's emotional behavior. For example, predisposition to depression, anger, and fear may arise partly due to hereditary reasons, while their actual expression may depend upon other factors. However, most emotional responses shown by people are learned by them from their parents and peers, or from others as part of their value system and survival strategy. If parents are emotional, most likely their children will also turn out to be emotional. The good thing about this is we can use this knowledge to our advantage by learning to change our emotional behavior, controlling our responses, changing our thinking, and interpreting our perceptions differently.

5. Expression and suppression: You can deal with your emotions positively by expressing them and negatively by withholding them. Both approaches are useful and practical in their own ways. Positively, you can allow your emotions to run their course by experiencing them consciously and trying to understand their underlying causes. You may also even express your emotions before those who understand you, whom you trust and with whom you choose to be transparent and trustworthy. This way, you can gain insight into your emotional behavior and learn to accept and release your emotions safely without aftereffects. However, this solution may not always be appropriate, especially in social situations, when you have to deal with people who may not appreciate emotional behavior and may interpret your emotions as a sign of weakness, instability and lack of control. In such cases you have to control your emotions and keep them to yourself.

6. Emotions and self-awareness: The key to deal with your emotions is to become familiar with them and in the process with yourself. You have to know and understand why you act in certain ways and experience different emotions. The more you gain insight into your own thoughts, beliefs, habitual reactions and actions, the greater will be your ability to cope with your emotions and release them. For this you have to study yourself with keen interest and understand how your emotions are triggered in different situations, what beliefs and thinking patterns sustain them and feed them.

7. Emotions and yoga: The practice of yoga is also a great help in knowing your emotions and dealing with them. Yoga is primarily meant to curb the mind and its modifications. Its ultimate aim is to stabilize the mind so that with a calm and composed mind one can experience equanimity and sameness and see life as it happens without the usual filters we apply to our perceptions. For this the classical yoga suggests various practices, such as self-control, postures, controlled breathing, concentration, meditation and self-absorption. All these practices have been proven to be very effective in controlling one's emotions and establishing peace and tranquility. Yoga has by far been the best and the most proven method in the history of the world to establish control over the human mind and body. It is a holistic program, which tries to deal with the instability of the mind from every possible angle, so that in the end, it has nowhere to go but surrender to its master.

There are many other ways in which you can deal with your emotions, such as talking to someone you trust, learning to appreciate yourself unconditionally, helping others, seeking professional help, exercising the mind and body, practicing relaxation, going on vacations, labeling your emotions, going to a new place, cultivating a purpose, having healthy and achievable goals, avoiding negative people, making yourself busy and so on.

Whatever may be the technique or approach you would prefer following, taking responsibility for your life, your thoughts, actions and emotions, and for the choices you make is crucial to deal with your emotions and minimize their negative impact. With all the practice and effort, you may not achieve complete success with your emotions, but you will succeed greatly in enriching your emotional life and bringing vitality and energy into your thoughts and actions.

Core Values For a Principle Centered Life

When we look back and review our experiences, certain principles about our lives become apparent. The following are few such ones. It is not that they are the only ones you may ever think of. However, they are the commonest ones to which many people arrive based upon their experiences and perceptions.

The Core Principles

1. **Life is filled with suffering**: Whether you are big or small, young or old, rich or poor, you cannot escape from suffering. Our imperfections and vulnerabilities make our suffering even more difficult to resolve.
2. **You are not in full control**: You cannot control every aspect of your life because you have limited information about almost everything that you deal with. It includes the knowledge that you have about you and others. Therefore, you have but a limited control over what happens in you and around you.
3. **You do not know everything**: You cannot fully comprehend the truths of life because you lack intelligence, and the all-round vision that is necessary to comprehend truth from all sides. Besides, we are prone to emotions, logical fallacies and prejudices. Our vision goes only up to a certain point, beyond which everything is hazy and dark.
4. **You create your life**: You are largely responsible for your life and actions. While you may be subject to certain random events and natural processes that are beyond your control, in retrospect your life is largely shaped by your thoughts, actions and choices. Ironically, while you shape your future, you cannot always predict it accurately.
5. **You are caught between opposites of life**: You are never free from duality and pairs of opposites such as pain and pleasure, and heat and cold. You are also a mixture of opposites in a world of opposites. Due to attraction and aversion, you are drawn to them or repelled by them, and in the process become attached to them positively or negatively.
6. **Our morals are relative**: We do not know whether morality is always the right choice. In a world ridden with temptations, distractions, and competition, it is difficult at times to justify

the virtue of virtuous living. It appears that largely the world favors those who break rules and conventions and disregard virtue and honesty to achieve their individual goals.
7. **You cannot always follow the example of Nature**: We live in a very violent world where the values the humanity cherish seem to be either silent or absent most of the time. Nature has its own sense of justice and right and wrong. There is no place in Nature for such human values as virtue and compassion. It promotes and favors brute force, control and competitiveness. Hence, those who succeed in controlling others and securing the resources enjoy better chances of survival and more opportunities to prevail over others.

Core Values

Living in such an unpredictable environment, what are we supposed to do? It is not easy to answer this question because it depends upon many factors and variables. What type of life you may choose and how you may want to express it through your thoughts and actions depend upon your experiences, perceptions, beliefs and a number of other factors including your awareness, social conditioning and mental attitude. However, whatever lifestyle you may choose, you cannot secure peace and happiness without honoring the following values of our lives.

1. **Good health**: Health comes before everything else. Whatever profession or occupation you may choose, you have to ensure that you remain in good health.
2. **Wealth and comforts**: We live upon earth for a limited time, and in that limited time we must have at least few comforts to make our living a positive experience. Some people may argue that wealth and comforts are evil. Hoarding excess money or earning it through dishonest means is certainly not good for your spiritual welfare. However, to achieve peace and balance in your life, you must aim for financial security.
3. **Security and stability**: Life is uncertain. We cannot entirely remove the uncertainty surrounding our lives. However, we must address our concerns and anxieties and try to stabilize our lives by building necessary safeguards, cultivating good habits and not taking undue risks.
4. **Peace and happiness**: If God suddenly appears before you and asks you to seek just one boon, what would you choose? An Indian spiritual master once said that one should choose peace and happiness above everything else, because if you have peace and happiness, it means you have everything in

your life and you are completely satisfied and at peace with yourself.
5. **Fulfilling relationships**: You should have healthy and harmonious relationships with people who care for you and whom you care, people who respect you and whom you respect, and people who do not try to regulate your life or want to be controlled in turn. Such relationships are not bound by expectations and demands, but thrive upon trust, freedom, compassion, understanding and genuine love.
6. **Opportunities to grow and prosper**: Growth oriented people are seldom happy with their progress or achievement and always look for opportunities to grow and prosper. Although, they may not always succeed, they would not let an opportunity go by, since they know that it can change their lives and contribute to their growth and prosperity.

These are the ideals or conditions which you should actively pursue to experience peace and happiness. In countries and places where people do not have enough opportunities to realize them, you will find that the general level of discontent among people remains very high. Such societies also remain relatively unstable and suffer from many problems including violence and crime.

Presently, the world is so structured that it favors a few at the expense of many. The rich and the powerful sections of society corner most resources and enjoy the best comforts. The excess wealth may also result in wastage and frivolous spending.

Someone recently purchased an old comic book for three million dollars, which is probably double or triple the amount any ordinary middle-class person can ever dream of making in a lifetime. When you hear such stories, you may feel that the world is unfairly balanced and favors a few individuals.

The inequalities of our world have the potential to create bitter acrimony between communities and nations. You can expect them to grow further in future as people will have to compete for dwindling natural resources and remain content with a narrowing window of opportunities.

While we have made rapid progress in the field of science and technology, spiritually we seem to be marching backward as people are increasingly turning to materialism for creature comforts and renouncing their spiritual beliefs and values.

Core virtues

Apart from principles and values, certain virtues are also important to bring balance into your thinking and actions. The following are a few important virtues that can lead to peace and balance.

1. Deeper awareness about life, its purpose and value.
2. Right thinking in your decisions, actions, choices, and problem solving.
3. Right conduct in your behavior and relationships.
4. Love and compassion towards yourself and others.
5. Understanding and tolerance in your dealings with others.
6. Respect for life in all forms.
7. Forgiveness towards yourself and others.

You can make your life according to your dreams and desires within in the limitations to which you are subject. Whether you believe in multiple births or a single birth, you cannot deny that your actions and decisions will have consequences for you and others and you can build your life and future largely on the principle of reciprocity.

Knowing and Being Who You are

Unfortunately, most people do not live their lives and do not like to be themselves or express themselves freely. As they live their lives according to the expectations and desires of others, they allow others to pull their strings or make important decisions for them. This trend is more pronounced in countries that are ruled and regulated by totalitarian regimes, rigid religious laws and social values. It is also considerably felt by people who live in traditional communities where parents and elders have a greater say in the lives of their children and where social pressures are acute.

From an early age, we are brainwashed to live in a certain way and believe in certain things. When we are grown up, we are constantly flooded with propaganda and subliminal messages to buy certain products, support certain belief systems and ideologies and pursue interests and goals that are not entirely conducive to our personal wellbeing or our economic welfare.

We know that we cannot have everything going our way, and we cannot always push our personal agendas at the expense of others. However, we must have enough opportunities to express ourselves or use our unique talents and skills. Otherwise, we may become disenchanted and frustrated about the world, and mechanical in our thoughts and actions. We must have opportunities to express ourselves and grow individually and responsibly.

There are many powers and factors in the world which limit our freedom and choices. Even in countries, which boast of democracy and individual liberty, people are not truly free. Their lives and minds are chained to ideologies, group think, racial and gender biases, conditioned ignorance, and religious pressures.

Sadly such conditioning and invisible influences greatly affect our lives. It not only limits our freedom but also prevents us from being genuine to ourselves. Most importantly, it limits our ability to use our greatest asset in life, which is our own uniqueness.

Every human being in this world comes with a valuable asset, which is his or her unique and distinct individuality. It is shaped by many factors. Unfortunately, we have to sacrifice this uniqueness in return for acceptance, belongingness, approval and appreciation from others. In our eagerness to blend in and be part of the world, we compromise our values and beliefs. As we submit to the norms of society, we forget who we truly are and rely upon others at the cost of our own individualities to make our decisions.

It is very difficult to be yourself in this world. In this regard, we are our own worst enemies. We are conditioned to deal with the known and the familiar, and with people who are predictable. People do not usually trust those who are assertive or want to be themselves. The same goes with organizations. They speak about leadership but prefer the sheep to perform routine jobs. In the recruitment process, they want to see how much you will confirm to the norms of the organization and fit in rather than stand out.

You can tell from your experience that people are generally apprehensive of those who want to be different and independent. They mistake your individuality and independence for impudence or arrogance. You may be called rude if without discretion you speak your mind or reveal your true feelings to others. The odds of success will be stacked against you if you want to follow your own path and stand your own ground. It does not mean that one should be a social rebel or question the authority of established institutions. You may live your own life and do whatever you want, but you cannot hurt others or ignore the damage you may cause to them.

We should respect society, established traditions, laws, and institutions because they are products of humanity's collective wisdom and meant to ensure the order and regularity of various processes that are vital to our survival. Further, to live in peace and harmony with others, we have to respect our relationships with them and our obligations towards them. At the same time, we should remember who we are, what we can do as individuals, and how we can express ourselves creatively and freely without being corrupted by fear and dependence mentality.

If you can harmonize these two approaches by following the middle path, knowing when to follow others and when to be yourself, you will have better chances of accomplishing more than just being a cog in the wheel of society. The following suggestions are useful in this regard

1. Accept yourself unconditionally, whatever may be your weaknesses and shortcomings.
2. Be honest with yourself, with your thoughts and feelings. Accept them without rationalizing them or manipulating others.
3. Learn to be self-forgiving. It is important to avoid feeling guilty or ashamed to uphold your individuality and break free from the conditioning that society enforces on you.

4. Avoid judging yourself and beating yourself with negative self-talk and self-criticism. Many people sabotage their own lives and success, as they fail to appreciate their individuality and uniqueness.
5. Acknowledge your strengths and weaknesses. Build your life around your strengths and work out suitable alternatives to deal with your weaknesses.
6. Pay attention to your deepest thoughts and feelings and your gut feelings. The core of your being is filled with your essence, your personal history and hidden potentials. Tap into it through silent awareness, meditation, and intuition.
7. Rely upon your own experience rather than the authority of others.
8. Learn to trust your thinking and decisions. Sometimes you have to take risks and learn to trust yourself.
9. Learn to say No. It is the first step to being assertive, stand up to bullies in your life and stay in control of your life and destiny.
10. Learn to be assertive without being aggressive. It means you should not only assert your rights, but you must also be responsible enough to acknowledge the rights of others.

How to Reduce Anxiety By Changing Your Thoughts

Anxiety may arise from both physical and psychological causes. Here, we will discuss mainly the psychological factors or the mental conditions that lead to anxiety. Anxiety is produced by the way people think about themselves and their future, and how they interpret their experiences. Simply put, anxious thoughts arising from both internal and external causes produce anxiety.

Understanding such causes is important, because they may be real or imagined, and distinguishing them poses some problems. It is the imagined ones, and the irrational ones, which make anxiety even more difficult to resolve. In normal situations, anxious thoughts arise from real causes. For example, if you know that a certain difficult situation is about to happen and you cannot deal with it or prevent it, you are bound to experience anxiety. When real threats are present, it is human to be afraid. However, problems arise if the threat is imagined or exaggerated by your irrational and thoughts and unrealistic expectations.

Those who are emotionally unstable and sensitive may experience anxiety because of not only their irrational thoughts and imaginary threats but also their negative interpretation of what happens to them. Normal people quickly recover from shocks and setbacks and move on. They deal with unpleasant situations, and take failures and disappointments in their stride as part of their living. When adversity strikes, they may initially experience pain and suffering, but eventually they move on. Anxious people not only overreact in such situations but also take them personally as if they were responsible for them. Hence, they fail to get rid of their negative feelings even long after their happening. It is this tendency, which is troublesome and needs our attention.

When normal situations, which could have been easily ignored, begin to bother you, it is an indication that you have a problem and it requires your attention. Anxiety becomes a problem, when people are unable to overcome the thoughts that produce anxiety, and when they cannot reason with themselves to face the problem and deal with it. It is not what happens in such situations, but how they regard what happens, and how they interpret such experiences and imagine their consequences, which makes them anxious and incapacitates them to think and act normally.

Thinking styles that produce anxiety

People who frequently suffer from anxiety have to cope with their own personal demons that aggravate it. They have to realize how their negative perceptions, attitude, beliefs, and interpretations are responsible for it. Studies in cognitive therapy show that certain habitual thought patterns, beliefs and assumptions, increase anxiety in people and render them incapable of managing their fears, and living normally.

Hence, the best way to remedy anxiety is by identifying associated thoughts and behavior, and address them. Those who are prone to anxiety should examine their thinking and know how their anxiety is caused by their unverified and irrational thoughts and beliefs so that they can counter such thoughts, and respond to them rationally and realistically. Following are some of the thinking styles which create fear and anxiety and make people worrisome.

Exaggerating the probable outcome: It is also called overestimating the probable outcome. Anxious people over react to situations, thinking that what they fear or expect to happen is bound to happen, whether in reality it is going to happen or not. It is true that in real life, most outcomes that people fear will happen do not happen. However, they cannot help feeling afraid, as they expect negative outcomes that may never happen. In case of anxious people, the problem is even worse. Due to their negativity, irrational thinking, and lack of confidence, they imagine the worst even though the chances of it happening are very minimum.

Examples: "I may be ridiculed or insulted if I speak out." "I may lose my job if I do not resolve this problem on time."

Mind reading: Anxious people suffer from persecution complex. They are constantly assailed by the near certain belief that other people are thinking about them negatively and critically, even if they may not be doing it or may not be paying them any attention. This nagging feeling makes them uncomfortable in the presence of others. It is true that when we meet people, they may make judgments about us or form their own opinions about how we look or what we say. However, unless we know clearly, we should not jump to any conclusions about what they may be thinking.

Examples: "She must be thinking I am stupid." "Everyone in this group must be thinking that I am an odd person here because I am not well dressed for the occasion."

Taking things personally: Anxious people take personal responsibility for the negative situations in their lives, even if they have not caused them or contributed to them. They also take responsibility for other people's behavior, even if they are not directly responsible for them. For example, they may attribute other people's fear, anger, sorrow, frustration or disappointment to themselves, thinking that they might have somehow caused it, whereas in reality the real reasons may be entirely different.

Examples: "I made my boss angry with a stupid remark." "We lost because I failed to score a goal."

Unreasonable expectations: Anxious people hold unreasonable, realistic, and perfectionist expectations about how things ought to be or how they and others should behave in a given situation. Since it is difficult, if not impossible, to meet such expectations, it makes them stressed and disturbed. This behavior is manifested in their frequent use of words like, "should," "never," "always," and "must."

Examples: "I have to break the annual sales record in half the time." "That guy never finishes his work in time. It is making me sick."

Catastrophic thinking: This is to believe that the outcome of a negative event or situation is going to be catastrophic, even if it is a minor incident with little or no chance of it ever happening. As people imagine the worst in their extreme pessimism, even if there is no such possibility, they experience fear, anxiety, depression, and even guilt. For example, an anxious person may truly believe that that she is certain to be robbed or raped if her car breaks down in the night while she is returning from office. It will make her nervous, even before she even starts driving from her office. A fashion show model may become nervous if she believes that the long dress she is wearing might fall off on the ramp and cause her embarrassment.

Examples: "I am late. My boss is going to fire me today." "She did not greet me well. Looks like she is plotting to fire me."

All or nothing thinking: Anxious people have trouble dealing with ambiguity and uncertainty. Since they expect the best or the worst, their conclusions also reflect their extreme thinking. They judge people as good or bad, like or dislike something, or view people as friendly or hostile. This all or nothing thinking, which arises from their inability to see the middle ground or the grey area, subjects them to feelings of anxiety, fear of failure and guilt. It also makes them overreact to their failures and setbacks, instead of learning from them and moving on.

Examples: "I am done talking to her because she said I should switch off the phone in the classroom." "I made three mistakes during the presentation. It was a complete disaster." "This project is a total failure because we got delayed by a few days."

Selective thinking or cognitive bias: Anxious people tend to pay undue attention to specific aspects of their experiences or specific types of information, according to their beliefs and anxieties, which tend to aggravate their anxiety further. Thus, they may focus on certain parts of their experiences or remember only certain aspects of their interactions with others or certain negative memories. Such behavior reinforces their anxiety producing thoughts and beliefs and keeps them restless. Even if overall they had positive interactions and experiences with others, they remember only the negative ones that are consistent with their beliefs and ignore the rest. It makes them critical in their thinking and attitude towards others and resolving their anxiety even more difficult.

Examples: Remembering a few negative conversations one might have had with one's spouse in the past and ignoring the pleasant moments they both might have spent together. Focusing on those who are too critical and ignoring those who are largely appreciative.

Core beliefs: These are the assumptions and beliefs that become deeply integrated into one's consciousness and become part of one's worldview. They play a vital role in creating and sustaining one's feelings of anxiety. They also include long standing negative assumptions one develops about one's self-image and self-esteem and about others and the world in general. Further, they determine how individuals cope with their problems and difficulties and how they regard themselves in personal relationships and difficult situations.

Examples: "You cannot trust people." "People find me rather aloof." "If you get too closely to people, you might get hurt."

Coping with anxious thoughts

We have seen that anxiety is created by our own beliefs, assumptions, exaggerated and imaginary fears, irrational thoughts and habitual thought patterns. The solution to anxiety, therefore, lies in paying attention to our own thinking and knowing what thoughts, beliefs and assumptions create our anxiety so that we can devise effective strategies to change them effectively. In this regard, the following suggestions are useful.

1. **Be realistic**: Validate your beliefs that produce anxiety with facts and reason and subject them to reality check by looking for evidence, using your own experience and observation as the basis.

2. **Challenge your thinking styles**: This is necessary to counter the all or nothing thinking, catastrophic thinking, mind reading and selective thinking.
3. **Use your strengths**: Focus upon your strengths and compensate for your weaknesses. At the same time be willing to acknowledge your limitations in perfecting yourself, achieving excellence, performing actions, resolving problems and reaching your goals.
4. **Accept yourself**: Learn to accept who you are, no matter what your personal deficiencies are. Acknowledge your imperfections, weaknesses as part of your growing and learning. Know that you have limitations in your skills and abilities.
5. **See as others do**: Learn to observe yourself objectively as others do to balance your thinking and overcome your self-deprecating thoughts, which you may experience in social situations.
6. **Stay positive**: Refuse to accept your habitual negative thoughts and reactions and dispute them constantly when they arise with logic, facts, evidence, counter arguments and empowering thoughts.
7. **Acknowledge your imperfections**: Know that you cannot be perfect in every situation and impress everyone. Besides, you may have to occasionally deal with unpleasant situations, face failures and experience frustrations and disappointments. Acknowledging those possibilities and accepting your limitations will help you cope with failure and rejection without feeling devastated.
8. **Face your fears**: You will develop confidence when you do what you fear, and when you take calculated and manageable risks to test them. Alternatively, you can visualize new responses to the situations that produce fear and anxiety.
9. **Step out of your comfort zone**: Learn how to distract yourself with pleasant thoughts and emotions by doing something different, seeking newer experiences and learning to make the most out of your life within the limitations and constraints to which you are subject.
10. **Practice visualization**: Imagine situations that produce anxiety and deal with them mentally through visualization. By facing your fears in your mind through visualization, you can learn to respond differently to anxiety producing events and situations.

The Power of Positive Thinking in Daily Life

Positive thinking is a powerful and potent force in manifesting your reality and accomplishing tasks successfully. It is a habit of your mind, which is formed by these two important resources of your inner world.

1. The attitude with which you approach your life and view the world in general.
2. Having basic trust in yourself, your abilities and in the higher power which you accept as your mentor, giver and guide. Even if you have reservations about theistic beliefs, having a belief in yourself would be a very powerful source of positive thinking.

How to practice positive thinking

The habit of positive thinking can be cultivated carefully by following some of the suggestions given below. These suggestions are effective if you frequently refer to them until they are deeply integrated into your subconscious mind. It is still better, if you not only remember them but also practice them so that you gain a direct insight into the value of positive thinking and how it can make a difference in your life.

1. Focus on what you want to be, what you want to achieve and how you would like to see yourself in future. In a hundred words or so, using the most positive expressions write down how you would like to see yourself and your achievements in a year, in two years and five years from now.
2. Use positive beliefs, expressions, and expectations to guide and direct your subconscious mind. To begin with, have a positive and empowering belief in the power of positive thinking itself. Truly and strongly believe in what you want to accomplish and what you wish to happen so that your mind is saturated with it and will manifest the desired end. Belief is a powerful force that can manifest your destiny and change your reality. For that to happen, you must believe in the power of the belief Itself. To make your subconscious mind do its work effectively, you must have a child like faith in its ability and the possibility, and constantly affirm to yourself what you believe in.

3. Fully appreciate and enjoy what you already have, expressing gratitude for what has been already given to you. The mental state of contentment and gratitude prepare you to be ready for the things yet to come. It will also help you focus upon the positive aspects of your life.
4. Act as if you already have what you want and seek, expressing gratitude as if your wishes have been granted and the reality you wish to see is being manifested by the power of your thoughts, actions and feelings.
5. Improve your chances of success by combining your positive thoughts with positive beliefs and positive action. Focus your mind on what you want to manifest and bring in the synergetic power of positive thoughts, positive beliefs and positive actions.
6. Allow your higher mind to take over and give shape to your thoughts and beliefs. Stay focused but relaxed, and allow the higher mind to do its magic.
7. Stay in the present. It may require a lot of practice to keep your mind in the present, but it is worth the attempt because it sustains your positive thinking and helps you stay focused on the tasks you need to perform to reach your goals. If you are in the present and mindful, you remain attentive and responsive to events and situations spontaneously giving little opportunity to your worries and anxieties to shape your thoughts and actions.
8. Through meditation, positive affirmations and other mental exercises, cultivate positive emotions and states of mind such as elation, spontaneous joy, unconditional love, compassion, magnanimity, contentment, detachment, dispassion and so on.
9. Read books and articles on positive thinking until your mind is saturated with inspiring and powerful thoughts.
10. Accept yourself unconditionally. To be yourself and let go of your faults and blemishes is not easy. It would require years of effort and insight into your own thinking and behavior. However, the effort is worth taking.
11. Meet like-minded people who can reinforce your thoughts. In India religious and spiritual people organize the gathering of like-minded people in their homes and public places. The practice is popularly known as satsang, which means friendship with the truthful or the pure hearted. Such meetings are held because of the belief that when good people come together and pray together, their positive energies become intensified and their minds become purified

by their collective thoughts and vibrations. We can extend this concept into our relationships and associations. Try to cultivate the friendship of positive minded people, who uplift your mind and soul and encourage you to be happy and successful. The Yogasutras, which is a 2500 years old scripture on Yoga, says that you should cultivate the friendship of happy people and show consideration and compassion towards those who are unhappy. Likewise, you should work for companies that have sound business policies and practice positive leadership styles.

12. Chose your words carefully when you speak or write. Use positive words and expressions in both verbal and oral communications, especially in your daily conversations and personal memos. There is always a way to speak positively whatever be the situation or circumstance. It may take years of practice to sound consistently positive, but in the end it will bring rich rewards as positive relationships and success.

13. Stop criticizing anyone or anything, unless it is extremely necessary. The same scripture, Yogasutras, says that you should praise those who are virtuous, but resist the temptation of judging those who are not. You can avoid criticizing many things, which have no bearing upon your life. For example, people criticize movies, celebrities, sports teams, film stars, politicians, political parties and certain trends and events they observe in daily life. It makes sense only if you are personally involved with social reform or community related issues. Otherwise, there is no point in filling your mind with negativity, when your criticism is not going to reach the people or the organizations against which it is intended.

14. Embrace the dualities in an uncertain world since you cannot always choose what you want. Accept the negativity, failures and suffering that you may occasionally experience as learning opportunities for self-growth and progress in the journey of life. By positively embracing the problems, challenges, and negative situations that life throws at you, you create opportunities to learn and grow, find peace and harmony within yourself, and appreciate the blessings of life even more.

Taking Responsibility for Your Life

It is easy to dodge our responsibilities, but we cannot dodge the consequences of dodging our responsibilities. Josiah Charles Stamp.

You must take personal responsibility. You cannot change the circumstances, the seasons, or the wind, but you can change yourself. That is something you have charge of. Jim Rohn.

For the truth is, we control our life. We control how lucky we are. We create our fortune with our effort. We alone have the power. Rick Pitino, Basketball Coach.

A politician thinks that it is his duty and responsibility to blame others, while not acknowledging his own. Jayaram V

In a general sense, responsibility means honoring the obligations and accountability in performing certain tasks and accepting any consequences that may arise from them. It is taking ownership of your actions, decisions and their consequences, without trying to put the onus on others, or making excuses. Taking responsibility means any of the following.

1. Being answerable to the task.
2. Accepting the obligation to accept the conditions and produce expected results.
3. Keeping your promises.
4. Accepting the consequences arising from your actions and obligations, whether they are positive or negative, and rewarding or unrewarding.
5. Honoring your commitments.
6. Taking initiative.
7. Showing leadership.
8. Owning the task and taking it to the finish line.
9. Defending and protecting the people and resources for which you are responsible.
10. Controlling, delegating, monitoring and managing tasks and their performance and progress until the obligation is met.
11. Knowing the limits of your duties and responsibilities.
12. Following the rules, discipline, and procedures that apply to the performance of such duties.

Duty is synonymous with responsibility because both are obligatory. A person's responsibilities can be categorized as personal, social, moral, legal, political, financial, religious, spiritual or professional. They may arise from birth, a position of authority, social background, family status, economic and geographic conditions, financial obligations, profession, relationships, religion, agreements, laws, self-will, coercion or physical threat.

For example a person who lives in a desert has certain additional responsibilities compared to a person who lives in the mountains, or in plains. The same applies to all conditions and circumstances. In each case, people have to perform their duties and responsibilities according to their lifestyles, aims, environment, social status, and individual needs.

A person's duties and responsibilities may also change with age, time, gender roles, circumstances and similar factors. While some responsibilities are optional, some cannot be avoided. People also have some duties and obligations towards society, country and the government, which cannot be ignored. There are also some gender specific obligations that are expected from everyone and they need to be honored.

Duties and obligations also arise from our moral sense and religious beliefs. For example, in almost all religions it is the duty and responsibility of every individual to honor scriptures, practice virtue, fulfill family obligations, help others, respect traditions, and work for one's salvation.

In carrying out their responsibilities and meeting their obligations, people are expected to make sacrifices and, if necessary, undergo difficulties, pain and suffering. Parents have a responsibility towards their children and have to make necessary sacrifices to bring them up. In the process, they may even suffer from the displeasure of their children who may not appreciate the decisions they make either to enforce discipline or teach them right values.

Many problems arise in life when people do not recognize their responsibilities or take them sincerely. When people do not perform their duties and responsibilities, chaos and disorder follow. The worst sufferers are those who are directly affected by their negligence and irresponsibility, such as their children, and forced to live with the consequences.

The very process of living implies certain duties and obligations, which cannot be ignored. When you are part of society and a family, you have to do your part to keep things in order and ensure your welfare and that of others. Your self-image, the respect you command from others, your sphere of influence, relationship with others, status in family and society, financial and physical wellbeing, self-esteem, peace and happiness, future, and several other factors depend upon how effective you are in performing your expected duties and carrying out your basic responsibilities. Those who neglect them are not well respected in society.

Therefore, for your own welfare and that of your loved ones, it is necessary to recognize the importance of living a responsible life, performing the tasks and meeting the obligations that are expected from you. In this regard the following are worth remembering.

1. Prepare a complete list of the various roles you are expected to perform in your personal and professional life and the duties and obligations that associated with each of them. Prioritize them and resolve any conflicts that you may experience in undertaking them.
2. Teach your children to acknowledge their responsibilities towards themselves and others and honor their obligations. Make them accountable for their actions and accept the reward and punishment that come with it.
3. Examine whether you are neglecting any personal or professional responsibilities and how you may overcome your mental blocks and change your thinking and attitude towards them.
4. Accept accountability for your actions. When things go wrong, instead of blaming others and finding scapegoats, have the courage to own the failure and admit your mistakes.
5. Examine whether you harbor any deep seated resentment against your parents, teachers and others for your personal failures. See whether you blame them because you believe that they were responsible for your life and happiness.

In life we do often hold others responsible for our failures and successes. Generally, it is human to take credit for one's success and hold someone else responsible for the failures. This is the norm. While it may temporarily help you to escape from feelings of guilt, it does not solve the problem of failure or help you in your progress.

If you are responsible for your success, you are equally responsible for your failures. Extraneous factors may play a role, but overall, your life is your responsibility. You should not expect others to take care of you or your life, unless you are a small child, or unless you have health issues that do not allow you to live by yourself. When you hold someone responsible for your life, you lose your inner freedom and develop a dependence mentality, which will practically limit your chances of achieving success and happiness.

There is no shortage of people in the world who envy the success of others and hold them responsible for their personal failures and negligence of duty. Politicians make their living by creating divisions within society to secure their base. They may tell you that your suffering is caused by the greed of others and you have a rightful share in the wealth of others. Some people may be bad and selfish, and earn their wealth at the expense of others, but it is not a cause enough to ignore your basic responsibilities.

If you believe in karma, you know that your life and salvation are your sole responsibility. Your thoughts, decisions and actions shape your life. The Bhagavadgita states that you should perform your obligatory duties, and if you neglect them you will incur sin, because by not meeting your obligations you contribute to chaos and disorder and thereby cause your own downfall and the downfall of your family and society. Even God performs His duties and obligations, although He has no desires and no interest whatsoever in the existence or nonexistence of the world.

Broadly speaking your responsibilities can be categorized as shown below.

1. **Responsibilities towards yourself**: They are meant for your physical mental and spiritual wellbeing.
2. **Responsibilities towards your family**: They include your responsibilities towards your parents, spouse, children, elders and other dependent members.
3. **Responsibilities towards the world**: They include your obligations towards fellow human beings in promoting peace, harmony, happiness, cooperation and coexistence. As a responsible member of society, you have to abide by the prevailing social norms, values and traditions, and avoid disrupting and destroying the order and regularity of life upon earth.
4. **Responsibilities towards other living beings**: The earth does not belong to humans only. Except for self-defense or to protect yourself from possible harm, you are not expected to indiscriminately destroy life upon earth. All beings that live upon earth have an inalienable right to exist and live within their spheres. You are not only obliged to protect them but also as a self-aware intelligent person help them in their survival.
5. **Responsibilities towards your ancestors**: You are responsible for your family reputation and that of your ancestors. You have an obligation to ensure that you do not undermine the name or the reputation of your family and you ancestors by your actions. You also have an obligation to teach your children to follow the same and continue the tradition.

6. **Responsibilities towards God**: There is something more to life than what you can see or reason. You have a deeper awareness, which you can bring into play to meet your spiritual obligations towards your deeper Self, other human beings and living beings. You have an obligation towards life itself, which means you cannot throw away your life or the opportunity that has been given to you to experience it. You have to show gratitude to God, Nature and all the invisible powers, forces, and circumstances that made your birth and existence possible. It is called gratitude, and you cannot live without it. Whether you know it or not, countless people shape your life and influence its course. Whether you believe in God or not, you should know that you played no obvious role in your birth, and you cannot live all by yourself, without Nature and the Universe doing their part. Therefore, you have to honor your hidden connection with the rest of the existence, acknowledge its role in your life and actions, and repay your debt by doing your duty towards others, society, and the world.

The Self-confidence Gospel

Many people do not finish what they begin. Along the way, they lose heart, become distracted and give up their cherished dreams that might have changed their lives. Often we come up with great ideas or set difficult goals to improve our skills, knowledge or our chances of success, but do not find the courage to give them shape. People entertain wishes, hopes and dreams, but underperform in reaching them, because they lack initiative, courage and conviction, believing that they do not have the resources or the ability. They deny themselves success because in some mysterious ways they hold back and deny themselves opportunities to achieve success and make a mark for themselves. In short, they lack confidence in themselves, in what they think, believe and aim to achieve.

What is self-confidence?

Confidence means having the belief or the assurance that you are dependable, and you will succeed and can succeed in what you aim to achieve. Confidence comes from having the trust in yourself and in your abilities, and having commitment to achieve goals and perform tasks. Without it one may find it difficult to make progress. Thus, your confidence stems mainly from your belief or faith in yourself and your abilities. As Norman Vincent Peale said, "What the mind can conceive and believe, and the heart desire, you can achieve." The most difficult part is holding that trust and belief as your inherent nature without self-doubt, fear and anxiety.

Self-confidence gives you the strength and hope to use opportunities that you either create or find in your life to achieve success, peace and happiness. Unfortunately, many people lack it either totally or in specific areas, which prevents them from being effective and successful in their lives and careers.

Recognizing the problem of low self-confidence

You may not be able to explain what confidence is, but you know from experience when you had confidence in your life and when you suffered from the lack of it. It is not difficult to perceive self-confidence in yourself or in others. Self-confidence speaks for itself in your thinking and actions. A self-confident person has the following distinguishing marks.

1. Believes in his skills, abilities, plans, and actions.
2. Is willing to take risks.

3. Has positive self-image.
4. Acknowledges his failures and mistakes and learns from them.
5. Does not indulge in blaming others, or finding excuses and scapegoats.
6. Takes responsibility for his actions and their consequences.
7. Remains committed to his goals and dreams.
8. Listens to the advice given by others, but keeps his own counsel.
9. Is open to suggestions and ideas even if he does not agree with them.
10. Accepts compliments and criticism graciously.
11. Has the heart to appreciate the virtues and achievements of others.
12. Does not engage in self-destructive actions or denial.

A self-confident person does not indulge in the following negativity.

1. Making decisions or performing actions to seek other people's approval.
2. Avoiding taking risks or stepping out of his comfort zone.
3. Avoiding responsibility for his life and actions.
4. Undermining his own abilities or underselling himself.
5. Putting other people down to feel good.

It is a myth that anyone can remain confident forever and in all situations. Under certain conditions even the most confident people lose their nerve. When provoked beyond tolerance, a person who is otherwise timid and nervous may show extraordinary courage. Self-confidence stems from many natural factors, such as your appearance, education, knowledge, social and family background, past experiences, geographic and cultural factors, physical and mental health, and social skills.

A person who is lacking in self-confidence suffers from nagging self-doubts about himself, which shows up as fear of failure and rejection, and anxiety about the outcome of his actions. He usually remains silent in a social conversation, readily agrees with the opinions of others, hesitates to speak his mind, does things to gain attention and approval of others, and waits for others to lead and give directions. He rarely takes risks or steps out of his comfort zone or ventures out to experience new and unfamiliar situations. Since he is afraid to stand for himself, he is not effective at negotiations. He keeps low expectations about himself and mostly underperforms and undersells himself.

How to build self-confidence?

You cannot build self-confidence by focusing on your confidence alone. Your self-confidence is part of your mindset and attitude. Therefore to build self-confidence, you must address basic issues which prevent you from not only being your normal and confident self but also using your potentials to your best advantage. You have to uncover the blockages that prevent you from being your natural self. It means you have to look deeper into yourself to find the root causes of your fears and self-doubts, rather than dealing with the problem superficially. To build self-confidence, you have to understand the factors which contribute to it and build them. It means you have to spend time knowing yourself and increase your self-awareness.

Here are a few areas where you can build your self-esteem, and thereby your self-confidence to bring out the best in you.

1. **Self-esteem**: Your confidence directly stems from your self-esteem. If your self-esteem is strong, your confidence will be strong, and vice versa. Self-esteem means how you stand in your own estimation and how you regard yourself in relation to others. It is directly related to the self-image you hold in your mind and your feelings of self-worth. Your self-esteem practically depends upon the same factors as your self-confidence. Therefore, if you want to build self-confidence, you must first address your self-esteem issues. With positive self-esteem, you will naturally feel confident.
2. **Self-talk**: How you talk to yourself is important to your confidence. Your self-esteem is also related to it. We all have an inner critic, who keeps constantly evaluating and judging our actions and keeps telling us how we are doing in our lives and in specific situations. We are conditioned to listen to this inner critic who can be toxic and destructive at times. To build self-confidence, it is necessary to counter the inner critic with reason, facts, positive thinking and affirmations.
3. **Knowledge and competence**: Knowledge, competence and confidence go together. If you have more knowledge and competence about something, you will be more confident in making use of it, performing your tasks, and reaching your goals. It is especially true if the knowledge is related to your career or profession. Knowledge empowers you to make decisions, express your opinions, and solve your problems on your own. Therefore try to improve your knowledge and skills in whatever you do.

4. **Strengths**: You are endowed with many natural abilities, strengths and weaknesses. You must identify them, analyze them, and explore opportunities to use them to reach your goals and achieve success. If you rely upon your strengths and take care of your weaknesses, you will have greater chances of achieving success and feeling confident. Therefore, identify your strong points and accordingly plan your life.
5. **Weaknesses**: No one is perfect in this world. We have our own weaknesses and imperfections. With effort and training we may manage some of them, while we may never be able to overcome some. It is not even necessary to remove all your weaknesses, considering the costs and time involved. You must be intelligent enough to know what you can overcome, what you cannot, and how you can circumvent those that cannot be overcome. For example, if you lack knowledge or expertise in a particular field, you can always hire professionals or experts who can help you in that field.
6. **Thinking and attitude**: Positive thinking is vital to feel good and having confidence. We have already examined how negative self-talk can lower your confidence. Therefore, using reason, visualization techniques, and positive affirmations, you must dispute your irrational fears and negative thinking to improve your perceptions and understanding. You must also focus upon your strengths, achievements and successes to overcome your doubts and fears.
7. **Experience**: Your self-confidence is directly related to the successes you achieve in your life. If you are more successful in your life, you will have more confidence in facing problems and challenges, or dealing with people. Conversely, if you fail frequently, your confidence weakens. One way to build self-confidence is by setting small goals in the beginning and achieving them so that with each success you will feel more confident.
8. **Expectations**: Examine your own expectations. Generally, people with low self-confidence have low expectations. Are your expectations realistic? Are they in harmony with your hopes and aspirations, and your strengths and abilities? Are your expectations influenced by your own thinking or the demands and expectations of others? By attuning and adjusting your expectations according to your abilities and keeping them realistic, you can increase your confidence and feel good about your chances of achieving success.

9. **Emotions**: Negative emotions such as fear and anxiety have a direct bearing upon your self-confidence. By resolving them you can increase your self-confidence.
10. **Grooming and appearance**: Your appearance is part of your self-image. Therefore, it is important to improve your physical fitness, grooming, and appearance to feel good about your appearance and self-image. You can do it by leading an active life, doing exercise, eating healthy food, improving your speech and behavior, wearing clean clothes, smiling and being happy in the presence of others.
11. **Helping and Appreciating**: Appreciate those who genuinely and generously deserve it and learn from them. Help those who lack it, need it or seek it. When you appreciate others, they will appreciate you in return. It will not only strengthen your relationship with them, but also reinforce your belief in your skills and abilities. It also increases positive feelings in both. The same happens when you help others. Their appreciation and gratitude will reinforce your positive self-image and increase your self-confidence.

How to Deal with the Monotony of Life

I am not easily bored. It was true even when I was a child. I grew up under the care of my grandfather who was an ex-police officer and a stickler for rules. He put a number of restriction on me to make sure that I would not waste my time playing with friends outside the house, which he sincerely believed would interfere with my health, education and discipline. He was concerned that if I was allowed to go out freely and mix with my friends I would climb trees or swim in the local ponds and canals and endanger my life.

He also felt that since my parents put me under his care, I was his personal responsibility and he should justify the confidence and trust my parents put in him. Therefore, he kept a close watch on me and did not let me frequently go out and spend time with my friends. I was allowed to go outside only during particular hours and return by the appointed time. Any failure on my part to comply with his instructions invariably resulted in punishment and more restrictions.

I resented the controls, but they helped me to put my creativity to great use. I learned to deal with the problem by tapping into my inner freedom. Whenever I stayed at home, I invented my own mind games and kept myself busy. I also used the spare time to memorize whole lessons so that I did not have to study in the night.

In the night, my grandfather insisted that I should loudly read the textbooks for at least two hours before I went to sleep, and answer any questions me might ask during the reading. I sincerely recited the lessons I memorized before at the top of my voice to make him believe that I was following his instructions, while I was doing something else and taking my little revenge. My grandfather listened to my loud reading from the other room as he smoked a cigar, and was happy that I was sincerely following his instructions and making progress.

Fortunately, at a very early age I learned to respond constructively to the problem of enforced routine without being oppressed by it. The trick to boredom is to be creative and keep yourself busy. I learned it very early in my life, thanks to my grandfather. Many children do it in their own creative ways to deal with loneliness, lack of freedom, sadness, or boredom, because they are inventive and possess a fertile imagination.

There is no connection between boredom and laziness. Laziness does not necessarily lead to boredom and boredom is not necessarily caused by laziness alone. A number of factors are responsible for the monotony or boredom experienced by people. Everyone occasionally experiences it, when they have nothing to do, when they are lonely, or when they are forced to do some work against their will.

However, in some cases the feelings may persist for long and require special attention. People who suffer from Attention Deficit Disorder experience boredom frequently as they quickly lose interest in what they do. Some are easily bored by routine and seek variety and novelty in their daily lives. They may also complain about boredom and lack of activity.

The following are a few suggestions to deal with the monotony experienced by people in normal circumstances. Those who recurrently and persistently experience boredom may have to look for hidden causes, and seek help.

1. **Find a purpose**: You can keep boredom away by finding a purpose that is larger than your life and extends beyond your personal interests and individual needs. It will keep you remain motivated and busy to do something that will make you happy and fulfilled, or make others happy.
2. **Keep yourself busy**: It is the best cure for boredom. Find something creative and new to do. Expand the scope of your actions or duties. Bring novelty and variety into your household duties or office responsibilities. If you are employed, find ways and means to take up additional work.
3. **Do things differently**: There are many ways in which you can perform your daily tasks. Try experimenting with ordinary household tasks such as cooking, watching television, shopping, learning, reading, walking, or dressing.
4. **Work on your relationships**: Find opportunities to interact with your friends and family, without overdoing it and reducing it into a predictable routine. Find new friends who are happy and positive.
5. **Have goals**: Create and work for a few personal or professional goals which will not only keep you busy but also lead you on the path to success, excellence, and achievement. If you have specific goals, it will help you remain busy and focused, and keep yourself engaged.
6. **Do regular exercise**: Exercise makes you active and energetic. If you are physically in good shape, your mind will be in good shape.
7. **Help others**: Help your children in their homework, in having fun time, visiting a local museum or a historic site, or

learning new skills. You may also help friends, family, or join a voluntary organization to help those who need help.
8. **Become a good observer**: Pay attention to the world around you. Even though you may visit the same places, meet with the same people, or find yourself in the same situations, your experiences are never the same. There will always be something new in what you see, feel and experience. If you pay attention, you will certainly notice them. A friend of mine died a few months ago. Another friend of mine did not know about it for over six months because he never bothered to notice his absence. Each time you meet people, or visit places, you can notice subtle changes by paying attention and having some curiosity. When you are mindful and pay attention to the world around you, you will not experience boredom.

Life as a human being is a precious opportunity to be aware, alive, and experience the simple pleasures of life. Consider the odds of any person taking birth upon earth as a human being. What are your chances of ever coming back to this planet in the same form and with the same set of friends, family and circumstances?

Sadly, many people do not recognize the value and uniqueness of human life. Having the opportunity to live as a human and experience the world through the mind and the five senses is in itself a great blessing. The world will never be the same. It is always in a flux. Impermanence is inherent in our lives. Everything within us and around us keeps constantly changing.

Therefore, there is no reason for us to experience boredom. In a way, feeling boredom is disrespecting life and wasting away an opportunity to experience it. We suffer from boredom because we do not respect life and the precious opportunity we have got. We experience it when we freeze our minds mentally and refuse to acknowledge the life that happens to us. Being mindful, staying in the present, and paying attention to the constant flow of life are the best remedies for dealing with boredom. If you have the right attitude and open your mind to the experience of life, you will not find excuses for boredom and loneliness. Therefore, if you feel bored constantly, you should examine your thinking and free your mind from the usual filters to experience here and now the wonder called life.

Finding Happiness in the Simple Pleasures of Life

What will happen if you are too preoccupied with your daily chores and do not find time to enjoy the little pleasures of life, or if you do not relax and enjoy quiet moments? As it happens in case of several people who are too busy to relax, your life will become increasingly stressful as you experience unhappiness and dissatisfaction. On the path of life, you cannot run forever. There are limitations to what you can and cannot do. Rest and recuperation are vital to your wellbeing. Those who do not respect the limitations run into trouble as their bodies wear out and as they suffer from physical and mental fatigue. You must know when to run, when to pause and take a fresh breath. Balance is the basis of a stable and secure life. For your health and happiness, you should remain balanced in your thinking, habits or actions, and avoid extremes.

In spirituality we call it moderation or staying on the middle path. The essence of moderation is that you respect the laws of Nature and the limitations to which you are subject and prefer living within those confines to the best of your ability. You can always try to transcend your conditions and circumstances, but it should not be done with a tortuous mentality, risking your own life and survival. In simple terms, you should avoid treading on the edges of ambition, and instead choose stable paths that are grounded in reality.

Happiness does not last forever. However you may try, you are bound to suffer from the impermanence of life. Impermanence is woven into our existence. You cannot escape from it. You may win a few battles against it here and there, but in the end impermanence wins. It is certain that whatever you build here on earth is but a castle in the sands of time. It will collapse when death walks over it. What you think is yours today will not stay that way forever. You should always remember this simple truth. You do not have many options against the imminent destructibility of life. You can make peace with it, ignore it, or fight with it. If you remember it frequently you will become wiser in your thinking and actions.

By understanding peace and impermanence, you can learn to adapt to the conditions they create and make the best out of the little moments of happiness that life offers to you, or you create on your own. If you choose happiness as your priority, you will improve your chances of experiencing happiness. If you frequently remember that you are entitled to peace and happiness, you will find happiness in unexpected places. The following affirmations are meant to help you in this regard. Remember them occasionally, until they are firmly etched in your memory and become part of your consciousness.

1. I deserve peace and happiness: I know a well-educated lady who spent her whole life trying to impress her husband and win his approval. She somehow felt she was born to sacrifice her comforts for his. Although she was well qualified, she chose to remain a housewife. Her orthodox parents ingrained in her mind that her job was to make her husband happy. Eventually, he divorced her, since she could not bear children, and married a younger woman.

Her life is a lesson for others. You should not condemn yourself to drudgery because you have to prove to others how good you are, or allow yourself to be humiliated by your own negative self-talk, which wants to tell you that you are never good enough. You are not here to impress others, earn their approval, or win their acceptance. You are not here to fit into the clothes that society wants you to wear.

You are here to be yourself, and express your uniqueness, even if it means earning some social disapproval. You should not also let your inner critic ruin your life. Your uniqueness is your gift to the world. What else can you give to the world, other than the individuality that you have? Therefore, know that you are the master of your life and you deserve peace and happiness. When you feel oppressed by excess work or the burdens of life, affirm to yourself, "I deserve peace and happiness."

2. I can choose to be happy: Do you really choose to be happy? Think about it. Have you ever made happiness a priority in your life? Have you ever tried to make yourself happy consciously? Many people think about being happy, but do not choose to be happy.

Happiness is a choice. Your happiness depends upon how you interpret your daily experiences and what choices you make to keep yourself peaceful and happy. If you choose to be happy, you will guide your thinking and actions accordingly. You will try to look for opportunities to make yourself happy. You will cultivate a positive mindset to shield yourself from the difficulties of life.

If you have chosen to be happy, it should reflect in your thinking and actions. Your choices should increase your chances of happiness, rather than decreasing it. If you have chosen to be happy not now and not here, but somewhere after another twenty years, and after marrying off your youngest child, you have not chosen well. You must seek happiness here and now, in whatever circumstances you may find yourself, and it must be reflected in your actions.

3. I can aim for happiness in the simple pleasures of life: Do not look for happiness at the end of the road. You should look for it in the simple things of your life. Every day, you can have countless opportunities to experience peace and happiness. For example, you can pause during a hectic schedule, take a deep breath and relax for a moment. You can drink tea or coffee and refresh yourself. You can look around or look out of the window near your desk and enjoy the view outside. If it is the right time, you can open your lunch box and eat your food with gratitude and love for the person who prepared it.

There are many ways in which you can find happiness in the simple pleasures of your life. You can talk to a friend, meditate, go for a walk or go on a drive when the time permits. If you are sincere, you will find many such opportunities to enjoy life and lighten up. It is the little moments that make up most of your life and it is where you can find many opportunities to choose happiness instead of depression, anxiety, and gloom.

4. I can make others happy: Too much of selfishness is not good. Selfish people experience a great vacuum in their lives. It is not proper to think just about your own happiness or try to be happy at the expense of others. You might have seen enough ignorant people who make fun of others with sadistic pleasure to keep themselves laughing. Those who crack jokes against others in a demeaning way do so because of a deep sense of inferiority.

If you want to experience true happiness, you should think of others' happiness too. You can make happy the people in your life with whom you interact, by being pleasant and courteous, paying attention, listening, appreciating, helping, letting them be themselves, and sharing with them your positive feelings.

Happiness is the greatest gift that you can give to others. It does not cost you any money. You do not have to throw an expensive party to make them happy. You do not have to take them to dinners, or shower them with costly gifts. You can do it if you can afford the money and the lifestyle. However, you can make them happy by just being human, kind, considerate, polite, and humble. If you do it, you will have no shortage of friends and well-wishers, and through them, you experience still more happiness, love, and belongingness.

5. I can share other's happiness: Happiness is contagious. Unless you are envious or have issues with your self-esteem, you will feel happy when you see others happy. By meeting happy people, you can become happy. One of my friends has few close relations, who live in the same town where he lives. In fact, they live within a few minutes distance from his house. During normal times, they never care to talk to him, call him or visit him. They also ignore his invitations to attend parties in his house. However, whenever he is hospitalized because of the chronic health problem from which he suffers, they invariably visit the hospital to see him. My friend even wonders whether they come because they enjoy visiting hospitals or watching him being sick and helpless.

It is important that you should share other's happiness whenever you find an opportunity. You can console people who are going through adversity, but you should also remember to talk to them when they want to share their happiness with others. Find time to congratulate people when they achieve success or cross a milestone. Show them that you are happy for them and you care for them.

Happiness is a choice. It depends upon your thinking, beliefs and interpretations, not necessarily upon the conditions and circumstances of your life. You can choose to be happy by accepting the conditions life offers to you and making the best out of them. Happiness is also a gift that you can give to yourself and others by just being good to yourself and to them. It does not cost you any money to be happy. You can find happiness in the simple pleasure of life by choosing happiness as your priority and opening your mind and heart to the innumerable opportunities life offers to you to experience it.

How to be Assertive and Tolerant

You might have seen a few people in your life who want to have their say in everything as if it is their right, but become angry and restless if anyone opposes them or disagrees with them. People who are accustomed to certain social, economic or political privileges for long tend to do it. It is proper to live your life according to your choices, values and beliefs and use your resources and judgment to achieve your goals.

However, problems arise if you do not recognize other people's right to do the same. In some cultures its value and importance in social life and personal relationships are not recognized. Children in such communities grow up being either aggressive or submissive. They are driven by either anger or fear, but seldom by reason. Aggressive people want to silence their opposition. They do not want to listen or appreciate any viewpoint which they oppose or dispute.

People with such attitudes thrive in feudal and totalitarian systems, but will have problems when they live in places where the rule of law prevails and everyone enjoys equal rights and opportunities. Human aggression shows up in many ways. Sometimes people channel it as national pride, racial superiority or religious bigotry. The same people, who are aggressive, tend to become timid and fearful when they feel helpless or perceive threat to their own safety.

If you notice the current social trends, you will see a growing number of people holding such values. Today we live in a very divided society. If you have a doubt, please visit the Internet and check the messages posted there. There is a lot of intolerance among people from all ages and all sections of society. Most of them possess a tunnel vision and do not care what you think or feel or how their words are going to hurt others. They communicate aggressively or thoughtlessly as if they want you to either put up or shut up.

People are not an assembly of pixels on a web page. They have hearts and minds just like you and deserve to be themselves. Before you post any message on the Internet, think whether it will be appreciated if you say it directly to anyone in person. If you think it is going to hurt, you should avoid posting it or rephrase your words. To grow mentally and intellectually you have to keep an open mind and recognize other people's right to have their own opinion. It is not that important whether you agree with them or not because you are not the measure of universal truths. You will have an open mind and respect for others when you practice the following.

1. You must value yourself and others equally.
2. Recognize and respect other people's right to express their opinions.
3. Do not depend upon the opinions and approval of others to feel good.
4. Do not patronize them, or let them patronize you.
5. Act according to the situation not according to your fixed beliefs and notions.
6. Pay attention to others rather than being lost in your own thoughts.
7. Be willing to negotiate and compromise when necessary rather than posturing and threatening.
8. Avoid talking down, aggression, impatience or hostility in your behavior and communication.
9. Learn to say no, but let others know why you did it.
10. Be assertive, rather than aggressive, in your dealings with others.

You may often come across people who are intolerant of what others say or write. What is even more striking is that many people do it in the name of religion and spirituality, which are meant to make us humble and tolerant. You can genuinely feel concerned about the events and conditions that you see in today's world and respond to it. You can even criticize those who disrupt peace and social harmony. However, you have to remember that you are part of the vast humanity and others have the same rights as you to live their lives and pursue their goals.

You should be assertive rather than aggressive. Just as you have the right to stand for yourself, protect your integrity and interests, and live according to your best judgment, others have the same rights. Unless the idea is deeply ingrained in you, you cannot easily practice it. The true test of whether you have it or not is to see how you deal with people who are less privileged than you and who do not enjoy as much power, wealth or position as you.

Thinking Outside The Box

What is thinking outside the box means?

You might have heard of the phrase thinking outside the box. You might have also done some exercises and puzzles in school or college which require a fresh thinking and creativity to find unusual solutions. Many problems and puzzles require you to think creatively outside your normal and routine thinking and find solutions in a flash of illumination. It is as if you have to jump into another dimension and awaken a new awareness in you to see thing differently.

In a metaphorical sense the box is the world you create in your mind. It is a world that is made up of your beliefs, assumptions, irrational thoughts, mental habits, perceptions, desires, expectations, emotions, attachments, and memories. It is the Meta Program which constitutes your beingness or individuality, and which guides your thinking and actions. The box is really a cage in which you hold yourself as a prisoner because you find in it comfort and security. It serves you the same purpose as a dog-crate serves a dog. When you are afraid or uncomfortable, you jump into it and sit there. It also serves as your filtering mechanism by which you perceive the world according to your needs, desires, expectations and conditioning. You rarely notice it because you are inside it most of the time, and like a fish that does not know that it is inside the water you do not know that you are inside the cage.

It is also described more technically as paradigm shift or paradigm change. In psychology it is termed as creative illumination, and in spirituality as self-realization or liberation. Out of the box thinking unleashes your creative and innovative thinking and helps you to generate new ideas and thoughts, or see the world differently from different perspectives. To make it possible, you have to do the following.

- Change your perspective.
- Step out of your comfort zone.
- Embrace the opposites that you dislike.
- Think in different ways.
- Jump out of your routine thinking.
- Refuse to accept the surface thoughts and solutions.
- Stop acting as if you alone are right.
- Stop arguing with people that they are wrong.

- Believe in the possibility that we cannot know the truths of life but only shades of truth.
- Acknowledge the theory of perspectives known in Jainism, according to which truth is relative to the perspective from which it is seen.

Why it is important

You may think you know everything and you are a free individual, but the truth is you are not truly free. You are chained to your own habitual ways of seeing and thinking. You are practically like a prisoner who takes prides in his chains and wears them like those who wear gold necklaces and bangles to flaunt them in functions and festivities.

When you are limited by the filtering mechanism of your mind, your ability to see things clearly and know them correctly also becomes limited. If the filtering mechanism is too opaque, you may not see the truth at all or see it only through a narrow window. When it happens to you, you take a partial truth for complete truth.

Fanaticism, narrow-mindedness, intolerance, and authoritarian attitude are a few extreme examples of the inside box thinking. People who entertain them not only live as prisoners inside the box, but have a limited view of the outside world, as if they are shut inside a dungeon.

What you think the world is may not be the world in the real sense because it is what you have allowed yourself to believe or see, or what your feelings and beliefs have allowed you to know. For example, you may see a beautiful sunset on a beach and feel totally uplifted by it. Another person sitting by your side may think that the dust and the sand flying in the air are annoying and he needs to go home and relax. That person may not have even paid attention to the setting sun, but may have kept thinking about an argument she had with someone few hours before.

What happened in that situation was that your perceptions were colored by your emotions and attitude. It does not mean that you were right and your friend was wrong. It only means that you both were experiencing the world differently even though you were at the same place and time, because your mind was relatively free, while your friend's mind was overwhelmed with negative emotions.

It also proves that what you both felt about the sunset has nothing to do with the sunset. The same sun at the same time must have made a million other people to think differently and react differently. Some people may carry that sun for years, if they had gone through a very bad experience at that time. That sun had nothing to do with any of these experiences, yet people would carry that sun along with the pain, as if there is a connection between the two. Some may even develop an aversion to it.

Experiences and observations such as these prove clearly that what we think real or believe to be real need not be real because we put ourselves between the reality outside and our perceptions. It shows that we should not rely totally upon our feelings beliefs and assumptions and consider the truths we know are the only truths. It also means that you are not really free because you see the world through the opaque walls of the box you create mentally.

What are its implications in real life?

As you become too comfortable with seeing and thinking from inside the box, you lose opportunities to see the world really. As you become too attached to your thoughts and opinions, you lose your freedom and flexibility to know and learn. It is the spiritual blindness, which the Upanishads remind people not to cultivate. They firmly declare that those who see only the spiritual side of the truth and those who see only the material side of the truth, both enter the world of darkness (ignorance) because they do not see the truth. Only those who see the truth from both perspectives enter the sunlit domains of the heavenly world.

The moral of this is that you should not live here attached to your thoughts and opinions as if they only are true. The tolerance of Hinduism comes from this simple but great truth. You cannot say, "It is my way or highway," or indulge in "all or nothing," thinking. You cannot put up an argument that only a particular prophet or a guru can take you to heaven and the rest are idiots. The Bhagavadgita says that the paths to God are many, and one can reach Him by any of the ways. It is an example of outside box thinking. Imagine if there was only one way to reach New York! That road would be jammed with traffic and nothing will really move on that. Here are a few more truths for your contemplation.

- Truth sets you free. If it has not set you free, you should know that it is you who have not set yourself free.
- Truth does not depend upon you for its validation. You do that validation for your own satisfaction or to reinforce your belief system.
- You will not know the truth if you think and act as if you already know it.
- Your seeing is adulterated by your memory of the objects you see. Therefore when you see, you may not really see the

objects of the outside world but the objects that exist in your mind as impressions or stereotypes.
- You cannot achieve true liberation if you remain bound to your ideas and beliefs and condemn everything else.
- Bondage to life means you are stuck in your life and not making any progress, because you are lost in routine and habitual thinking.
- You do not have to impart too big a meaning to liberation. Becoming free from the oppression of your own opinions and judgments is in itself true liberation.
- If you are not free physically and mentally, how can you be free at all in the highest sense?

How can you come out of the box?

You can cultivate a free mind and liberate yourself from your inner conditioning by cultivating an all inclusive vision. It is what we call, seeing yourself in all and all in yourself, which is considered the highest state in the Upanishads. You can do it by the following.

1. By not excessively relying upon your learning and convictions as if they are the sole truths.
2. By paying more attentions to your motives, assumptions and beliefs when you make judgments, draw conclusions, or make decisions.
3. By keeping an open mind and not becoming attached to things.
4. Learning to see the world without the usual mental noise and without the values, which you habitually use to measure it.
5. By knowing that you create your own illusions, and your great dramas to justify your thinking and behavior and to cling to your fear, anger, hatred and negativity so that you can protect yourself from your memories or gain the sympathy of others.

How to see things as they are

Ignorance means seeing the world in duality, as divisions, categories and opposites without the underlying unity. True realization means seeing it all as one indivisible truth like a wheel having different spokes that are connected to a central connecting hub. It is the wheel of Truth and Existence. It is also the highest goal of yoga. If your mind is fluctuating or unstable, you cannot see truth, or discern things clearly. Therefore, you should look inward and remove the distortions to stabilize your mind and see the world as it is. Seeing things as they are means breaking out of the box inside you and learn to be really free from the burden of your conditioning and habitual thought patterns.

That burden is also caused by your past actions (karma), which provides you with a lot of material to build the box. Your karma restricts your ability to see things or live your life holistically. If you are hurt in the past, you develop defensive reactions. If you suffered pain, you do your best to avoid it. If you enjoyed pleasure repeatedly, you tend to cling to everything that promotes it or creates it. It is karma in action. It is your past dictating your present. You can free yourself from it in the following ways.

- By giving it up, and forgiving yourself and all those who might have hurt you or harmed you in the past.
- By becoming unstuck in your life, pulling yourself out of it mentally.

You can move forward in your life and feel free, when you are not held in chains by your past. Here are few more suggestions that may help you to set yourself free from the mental habits and inner conditioning that arises from your karma.

1. Dispute your own opinions and assumptions.
2. Examine the assumptions underlying your decisions and conclusions.
3. Listen to others with an open mind.
4. Acknowledge the diversity of opinion.
5. Avoid coercing others to submit to your opinion.
6. Tolerate the things that you cannot accept.
7. Know that there is always more than one way to know, act, decide or understand.
8. Avoid becoming a fanatic.
9. Keep an open mind.
10. Avoid being judgmental and critical.

How Should We Deal With Our Bad Memories?

You cannot remember only the good and forget the bad. Memory is a function of the mind. It is better to leave your memory management to the natural functions of your mind, rather than to your judgment since you do not have complete control over it. The best approach to it is to take advantage of the strengths of your mind, and find solutions to deal with its weaknesses that interfere with your memory. It is also technically possible to suppress bad memories using hypnosis or self-hypnosis, but it is doubtful whether it will solve your problems.

Studies show that most of the painful memories of your past become part of your subconscious mind, and from there may indirectly and imperceptibly influence your thinking and behavior. Psychologists call them repressed memories. They influence your thinking and behavior and create defensive mechanisms, which you may use to manipulate your reality and protect yourself from perceived threats. In some rare cases they may even lead to mental abnormalities and unusual behavior.

Therefore, suppressing your memories is not the right solution. Besides, why do you want to do it? If you do it you would be silencing a part of yourself, and hide it from yourself. It is a form of denial and self-violence. What enters your mind becomes a part of you. If you frequently keep remembering it, it becomes part of your active memory and wakeful consciousness. Over time, it even becomes part of your identity and individuality.

Therefore, you should not try to consciously suppress your memories. Your memories are all that you will be left with. They constitute your history, the record of your life, or what you carry in your mind as your past. They also represent your past actions (karma). Good or bad, you should let them stay with you. You may leave behind all your relationships and give away all your wealth. However, you cannot do it with your memories. They will stay with you and remain part of you as long as you do not lose your identity, sanity, and individuality.

The question that arises then is what you can do about troubling or unpleasant memories. Some of them may be very painful and trouble you even when you are busy with your routine life like thorns stuck in your mind. You may attribute various reasons for your suffering and may even hold other responsible for it. Whatever may be the cause, you must take responsible for your life and for your past. If you take responsibility, you have better chances of dealing with it. You suffering might have been caused by others in the past, but it is not an excuse to keep suffering. If you are still suffering from your past pains, it means you are repeatedly reenacting your past and keeping it alive. Your present life is your immediate responsibility. While you cannot change your past, you can certainly take control of your present life and deal with any consequences that may arise from your past. In this regard the following truths are worth remembering.

1. The external world has nothing to do with your present suffering. It is a choice you make.
2. You cannot change situations after they happen. You can only manage them.
3. You can change your thinking, actions and responses. It is where you can hope to find solutions to any problem.

With this understanding, let us look at the following solutions to deal with the problem of unpleasant memories.

1. Know that you are the source: Your memories have nothing to do with your suffering. You are the one who uses them to continue your suffering and unhappiness. You may do it because it has become a habit with you, or you have developed an attachment to your suffering. It may also be because you want to justify the notion that you are a victim to rationalize your helplessness or to hide your fears and vulnerabilities. Whatever may be the reason, the truth is you cause your suffering, using your memories to fuel the fire, while you always have the option to respond to it in better ways.

2. Accept who you are: Your pain and suffering, and all your deficiencies and weaknesses are part of your identity. To be at peace with yourself, must accept them and embrace them, even when you try to resolve them. You may hide the unpleasant aspects of your body behind expensive clothes, but what can you do with the memories and thoughts that live inside you? Unless you totally and unconditionally accept who you are, you will not be at peace with yourself. You must find acceptance from yourself first. More than anyone, you deserve your love, compassion, tolerance and acceptance. You will have peace and harmony when you accept yourself unconditionally, and unapologetically, even if you have many faults and cracks in your personality. You do not have to hide them from yourself, or feel remorse. You do not have to escape from the reality of who you are or pretend to be someone else. Accept who you are, and learn to be the unique person that you are.

3. Change your response: You have probably developed certain habitual ways of responding to the world around you and inside you. You may be doing it to perpetuate your resentment and anger, or to cling to your past so that you do not have to deal with the reality of your present moment. You are probably stuck in your past and do not want to take charge of your life, or you may be looking for someone to come and rescue you. You should examine why you tend to react in certain habitual ways and what is that you collect in return. Once you understand the reasons, you can learn to change your responses.

4. Focus on the positive: You cannot remove memories from your mind. However, it is possible to rewrite them and create an alternate reality so that you can believe that certain events in your life did not happen or happened differently. It seems some people tend to do it to deal with their uncomfortable past. They exaggerate or falsify their past memories to feel good or to lie to themselves. Although it has some advantages it is not the right solution because no one knows its long-term consequences.

For example, in one movie, the protagonist in the story suffers from an identity crisis after he becomes so engrossed in his acting that outside the studio he does not know whether he is living his life or sill acting in it. If you create false memories, you may suffer from a similar fate. It may impair your self-image and cause you an identity crisis. Instead, it is better to focus upon your good memories and positive aspects of your life. Balance is the hallmark of existence. Rather than trying to suppress your negative memories, you should balance the negative in you with the positive, and strengthen your empowering memories to remain positive. It is the natural way to deal with the negativity in your mind without the harmful consequences.

5. Develop detachment: We cling to many things in the world. Everything we touch repeatedly becomes a burden. This clinging is largely responsible for our fears and insecurities. The world in which we live is unstable, impermanent and subject to decay and destruction. Everything will disappear from your life at some point. If not, in the end, Death will take you away. Therefore, it does not make sense to live like a prisoner of your own attachments. If freedom is your goal, you must learn to take things lightly and let go of the chains that hold you back.

The world is made up of pairs of opposites. Everything in life comes in pairs. You buy one and you will get the other for free. When you seek happiness, know that behind that happiness sorrow lurks. Since you do not have all the information about life and full control over it, you cannot always be sure what consequences may arise from your actions and expectations. "I want this, I do not want that," thoughts like these are responsible for much of our suffering.

Idealists think that they can shape the world and people in certain ways. The truth is the world is made of dualities. You cannot just eliminate one side of it, so that you can live on the bright and beautiful side. Like the world, you are also a mixture of dualities. Both good and bad live in you. You cannot say that you never lied, never desired anything that is socially unacceptable, or never thought of hurting and harming anyone. Even if you try hard, you cannot fully kill the darkness in you or wish it away. You have to find a way to manage the unpleasant aspects of life and live with them, without being limited by them. Life is more complex than making positive choices and avoiding the negatives. Once you understand it, you will know what to do with the negativity in your life.

Being Alone and Feeling Lonely

Note: These suggestions are not solutions but pointers. The solutions must come from within yourself. You have to choose and then customize the suggestions according to your requirements and circumstances.

Being alone and feeling lonely are not the same. Being alone refers to any physical situation when no one is around you and you are on your own. Feeling lonely refers to a state of mind when you feel as if you are missing something or someone, left out, disliked or rejected by others. It is mostly about how you feel about others and yourself. It is a condition, in which a person feels uncomfortable when he is with others or when he is alone. It is not because he is troubled by others, but because he is troubled by himself.

The causes of loneliness are mostly internal. You can be alone and still not feel lonely, and you can be in the middle of a big crowd watching a game and still feel lonely. Thus, loneliness refers to a morbid state of mind in which a person may experience depression, fear, unhappiness, fear, or withdrawal. Loneliness is a common problem. It is a social malady, as more and more people feel alienated, discriminated, rejected and unwanted.

Psychologists suggest that feelings of loneliness may arise because of low self-esteem when people do not like themselves or feel good about themselves. Such people are habitually too judgmental about themselves and others. As they project the same attitude upon others, they avoid their company and prefer to stay alone. However, since they cannot escape from themselves and their negative self-talk, they do not find any comfort in being alone.

When people are alone, they tend to become introspective and think about themselves. If they think that others are better than them and their proximity makes them happier, they feel even more uncomfortable in their absence. When people do not like themselves, they elevate others in their esteem and give them more credit than they deserve. If you like the company of other people but do not like to be alone, most likely you do not like being yourself. This is the key to overcome loneliness, you must accept yourself and feel comfortable with yourself, even if you have several flaws. Then, whether you are with others or alone, you will not feel loneliness inside you. Here are a few suggestions to deal with the problem.

1. **Accept yourself**: You are the person with whom you spend most of your life and time. If you want to be happy and peaceful, you must learn to accept yourself unconditionally. It

means you have to tolerate your shortcomings and failures, and treat yourself with compassion.
2. **Be yourself**: You do not have to measure yourself against other people's opinions. There is no need to impress others or win their approval, just to feel good. You may do it when you have to secure support or win them over, but you do not have to do as if it is your life's mission. You have to live your life for your happiness, to express yourself and your potentials, and to reach your goals, but not to solely impress others. You may accept their opinions and criticism for your self-growth, without taking it personally.
3. **Know yourself**: If you increase your self-awareness, you will understand better your motives and behavior, and control your thoughts and emotions effectively. Whether you are alone or in the company of others, pay attention to your own thoughts and how you feel about yourself, rather than worrying about what others may think about you. The best way to do it is to spend time in meditation and contemplation.
4. **Spend your free time wisely**: When you are alone, use your time wisely. It is the best opportunity to spend quiet moments with yourself and review what is going on your life, and how you are managing your circumstances. If there is nothing else to do, just do nothing. Stay with the moment and enjoy being alone.
5. **Get busy**: The best cure to loneliness is to get busy with some activity. Busy people do not feel lonely, unless they get busy to escape from themselves. You can use your spare time to learn new skills and hobbies, do housekeeping, volunteer, invite a friend, write a blog, help others, network, join a club, etc.
6. **Learn to appreciate**: Loneliness arises from self-deprecating attitude, which often manifests as too critical behavior. People who are prone to loneliness push people away with their negativity. You can improve a lot of relationships with positive attitude and sincere appreciation, rather than with arguments and showmanship. Learn to appreciate things and people, even forcefully if necessary, and you will notice the difference. Learn to forgive them mentally, so that you do not have to think about them and feel angry and resentful.

Being alone is a blessing, a rare opportunity to introspect and be yourself. You should find opportunities to spend quiet moments with yourself. If you are having feelings of loneliness and missing other people in your life, examine the underlying cause. See whether you can deal with it by learning to like yourself and be yourself. If you like yourself, you will never feel lonely and you will not suffer from a dependence mentality. You will feel not feel as if you cannot live without some people around you.

How to Manage Worldly Success?

What do you do when you reach a goal or cross a milestone? You probably celebrate the occasion and move on. That one success, may not radically alter your life, but adds some weight to your self-esteem. It also does not guarantee that you will be successful next time. It may even put more pressure on you as you expect more from your and others also. Success is thus a double edged sword. It not only brings rewards, name and recognition, but also complicates your life and increases your responsibilities.

Your life is a series of happenings. Some make you happy, some bring you down and some do not leave any mark. Some happen because of you, some happen in spite of you, and some without even your knowledge or intervention. Amidst all this, what matters is your attitude. Ideally, in both success and failure you should manage to keep your balance and restrain your reactions. You should not be carried away by success or lose your confidence and morale because of failure. However, in life we see that both success and failure change the way people think and act.

Success does not necessarily mean making it big in life. If it is the only definition, only a small percentage of people in the world can be considered successful. A truly successful life is one which is made up of many great moments, which need not have to arise only from achieving success, or having an abundance of wealth. It can arise from any event in which you experience elation and fulfillment.

You experience success when you fulfill your desires, reach your goals, achieve your desired ends, or meet with your expectations. When you succeed in these, you experience happiness and fulfillment, and feel good about yourself. Your desires and expectations need not be about wealth. They can be about anything, which you consider important in each situation.

Having desires and fulfilling them is one of the many ways in which you can enjoy life and experience fulfillment. It is the worldly approach, in which you tie your happiness to having things and enjoying them. Our scriptures tell you that it is not a good strategy because it can potentially make you unhappy, whenever you fail to fulfill your desires or meet with your expectations.

Experience teaches that we cannot always expect to fulfill all our desires because we are subject to many limitations and cannot control every process and power that shape our lives. It may not be even a sane idea to entertain such a notion. The limitations put a heavy burden on all of us. They make even the most successful and wealthiest people in the worldly unhappy, uncertain and anxious, because although they are very successful, they are equally, if not more, vulnerable to failures and disappointments in future.

What this means is that if peace is your aim, you should have both worldly goals and spiritual goals. The latter ones prepare you for setbacks and failures and protect you from shocks and disappointments that you may face in pursuing your materialistic goals. They keep you sane and balanced in a competitive world, and also help you uphold your character and integrity in worldly matters.

The following spiritual goals will teach you to stay in control and persevere when the going gets tough.

1. To remain undisturbed by success or failure.
2. To give your best in every task and not take any failure personally.
3. To learn from your failures and move on.
4. To take responsibility for your actions.

You may consider them your principles rather than goals, and practice them to in your life. Strengthen your character with spiritual aims while you build your life with material goals and ambitious plans. To experience fulfillment and the sweet rewards of success, you should have both material and spiritual goals and work for them. It is the most balanced, intelligent and holistic approach to a lead a fuller and balanced life.

Recommended Reading

Achor, Shawn. The happiness advantage: the seven principles of positive psychology that fuel success and performance at work. 1st ed. New York, Crown Business, c2010.

____. Before happiness: the 5 hidden keys to achieving success, spreading happiness, and sustaining positive change. First edition. New York, Crown Business, 2013.

Acuff, Jonathan M. Start : punch fear in the face, escape average, do work that matters. Brentwood, Tenn., Lampo Press, c2013.

Antony, Martin M., and Richard P. Swinson. The shyness & social anxiety workbook : proven, step-by-step techniques for overcoming your fear.2nd ed. Oakland, CA, New Harbinger Publications, c2008.

Arthur, James Ray. The Science Of Success: how to attract prosperity and create harmonic wealth through proven principles, SunArk Press, 2006.

Bancroft, Lundy. Why does he do that? : inside the minds of angry and controlling men. Berkley trade pbk. ed. New York : Berkley Books, 2003.

Baum, Kenneth, with Bob Andelman. Mind over business : how to unleash your business and sales success by rewiring the mind/body connection. 1st ed. New York, Prentice Hall Press, 2012.

Beattie, Melody. Codependent no more : how to stop controlling others and start caring for yourself / Melody Beattie. 2nd ed. Center City, MN, Hazelden, 1992.

Becker, Gavin de. The Gift of Fear: survival signals that protect us from violence, Dell Publishing, 1998.

Bellisario, Gina., illustrated by Renée Kurilla. Keep calm! : my stress-busting tips. Minneapolis, Millbrook Press, 2014.

Besant, Annie W. (1847-1933). Thought power, its control and culture. Theosophical Pub. House , 1973.

Bourne, Edmund J. The anxiety & phobia workbook. 5th ed. Oakland, CA, New Harbinger Publications, c2010.

Bourne, Edmund J., Lorna Garano. Coping with anxiety : 10 simple ways to relieve anxiety, fear & worry. Oakland, CA, New Harbinger, c2003.

Bowen, Will. A complaint free world: how to stop complaining and start enjoying the life you always wanted. 1st ed. New York, Doubleday, c2007.

Brady, Teresa. Ignite your psychic intuition : an A to Z guide to developing your sixth sense. 1st ed. Woodbury, Minn., Llewellyn Publications, 2011.

Brantley, Jeffrey. Calming your angry mind : how mindfulness & compassion can free you from anger & bring peace to your life. Oakland, CA, New Harbinger Publications, Inc., 2014.

Brantley, Jeffrey., and Wendy Millstine. Five good minutes in the evening : 100 mindful practices to help you unwind from the day & make the most of your night.Oakland, CA : New Harbinger Publications, c2006.

Brassell, William R. edited by Tilley, Leslie. Belonging: a guide to overcoming loneliness, , New Harbinger, 1994.

Bristol, Claude M. (Claude Myron), 1891-1951. TNT : the power within you : how to release the forces inside you and get what you want. Bristol and Harold Sherman. Edition: First Fireside edition, New York : Simon & Schuster, 1992, c1954.

Brockman, John, Ed. Thinking : the new science of decision-making, problem-solving, and prediction. First edition. New York : Haper Perennial, 2013.

Brown, Brené. The gifts of imperfection : let go of who you think you're supposed to be and embrace who you are. Center City, Minn., Hazelden, c2010.

Browne, Mary T. The 5 rules of thought: how to use the power of your mind to get what you want. Atria Books, 2009.

Bourke, Joanna. Fear, Shoemaker Hoard: Distributed by Publishers Group West, 2006.

Buffett, Peter. Life is what you make it. 1st ed. New York, Harmony Books, c2010.

Burton, Valorie. Successful women think differently / Valorie Burton. Eugene, Or., Harvest House Publishers, c2012.

Canfield, Jack, and D.D. Watkins. Jack Canfield's key to living the law of attraction : a simple guide to creating the life of your dreams. Deerfield Beach, Fla., Health Communications, Inc., 2007.

Canfield, Jack, with Janet Switzer. The success principles : how to get from where you are to where you want to be. 1st ed. New York, HarperCollins Publishers, c2005.

Carnegie, Dale, 1888-1955. How to win friends and influence people. New York, Simon & Schuster, 2009.

Carper, Jean. Your miracle brain. 1st ed. New York, N.Y., HarperCollins, c2000.

Cacioppo, John T. and William Patrick. Loneliness: human nature and the need for social connection, W.W. Norton, 2008.

Chamorro-Premuzic, Tomas. Confidence : overcoming low self-esteem, insecurity, and self-doubt. New York, Hudson Street Press, 2013.

Chapman, Gary D. Anger : handling a powerful emotion in a healthy way / Gary Chapman. Chicgo, IL, Northfield Publishing, c2007.

Chast, Roz, author, illustrator. Can't we talk about something more pleasant? : a memoir. First U.S. edition. New York, Bloomsbury, 2014.

Chittister, Joan. Happiness. Grand Rapigs, MI, Wm. B. Eerdmans Publishing, 2011.

Chopra, Deepak. Reinventing the body, resurrecting the soul : how to create a new you. 1st ed. New York : Harmony Books, c2009.

___. The seven spiritual laws of success : a practical guide to the fulfillment of your dreams. San Rafael, Calif., Amber-Allen Pub. : New World Library, c1994.

Christensen, Clayton M., with James Allworth, and Karen Dillon. How will you measure your life? New York, NY, Harper Business, c2012.

Chua, Amy, and Jed Rubenfeld. The triple package : how three unlikely traits explain the rise and fall of cultural groups in America.New York, Penguin Press, 2014.

Clabough, Casey. Creative writing. New York, Alpha Books, 2014.

Coffey, Tabatha. Own it! : be the boss of your life--at home and in the workplace. First Edition. New York, itbooks, 2014.

Corley, Thomas C. Rich habits : the daily success habits of wealthy individuals : find out how the rich get so rich (the secrets to financial success revealed). Minneapolis, MN, Langdon Street Press, c2009.

Covey, Sean. The 6 most important decisions you'll ever make : a guide for teens. New York, Simon & Schuster, c2006.

Covey, Stephen R. The 7 habits of highly effective people : restoring the character ethic. [Rev. ed.]. New York, Free Press, 2004.

Covey, Stephen R., with Breck England. The 3rd alternative : solving life's most difficult problems. 1st Free Press hardcover ed. New York, Free Press, c2011.

Dalai Lama XIV Bstan-'dzin-rgya-mtsho, and Cutler, Howard. C. Art of Happiness: A Handbook for Living. New York, Riverhead Books, 1998.

David Susan A. David, Boniwell Ilona, Conley Ayers Amanda, eds. Oxford, UK, Oxford University Press, 2013.

Davies, Clair., and Amber Davies. The trigger point therapy workbook: your self-treatment guide for pain relief, foreword by David G. Simons, MD. Third edition. Oakland, CA, New Harbinger Publications, Inc., 2013.

Davis, Martha. Elizabeth Robbins Eshelman, and Matthew McKay. The relaxation & stress reduction workbook. 6th ed. Oakland, CA : New Harbinger Publications, c2008.

Dawson, Roger. Secrets of power problem solving. Pompton Plains, NJ, Career Press, c2011.

De Becker, Gavin. The gift of fear : survival signals that protect us from violence. New York, Dell, 1999, c1997.

Dennett, D. C. (Daniel Clement). Intuition pumps and other tools for thinking. 1st ed. New York, W. W. Norton & Company, 2013.

Diamandis, Peter H., and Steven Kotler. Abundance : the future is better than you think. 1st ed. New York, Free Press, 2012.

Diener, Ed , Diener, Robert B. Happiness: Maiden, MA, Unlocking the Mysteries of Psychological Wealth. Blackwell Publishing, 2008.

Dooley, Mike. Leveraging the universe : 7 steps to engaging life's magic. New York : Atria Books; Hillsboro, Or, Beyond Words, c2011.

Dumm, Thomas. Loneliness As A Way Of Life, Harvard University Press, 2008.

Dungy, Tony., with Nathan Whitaker The mentor leader. Carol Stream, Ill., Tyndale House Publishers, c2010.

Dutton, Kevin. The wisdom of psychopaths : what saints, spies, and serial killers can teach us about success / Kevin Dutton.1st ed. New York, Scientific American/Farrar, Straus and Giroux, 2012.

Dweck, Carol S. Mindset : the new psychology of success. Edition: 1st ed. New York : Random House, c2006.

Dyer, Wayne W. Change Your Thoughts-Change Your Life (Easyread Large Edition). ReadHowYouWant, 2009.

___. Pulling your own strings. New York, T.Y. Crowell Co., c1978.

Epstein, Mark. The trauma of everyday life. New York, The Penguin Press, 2013.

Evans, Richard Paul. The four doors : a guide to joy, freedom, and a meaningful life. First Simon & Schuster hardcover edition. New York, Simon & Schuster, 2013.

Ferriss, Timothy. The 4 – Hour Work Week: Escape 9-5, live anywhere, and join the new rich. Crown Publishers, 2007.

Ford, Debbie. Courage : igniting self-confidence. First HarperCollins paperback edition. New York, Harper One, an imprint of HarperCollins, 2014.

Frankel, Bethenny, with Eve Adamson. A place of yes : 10 rules for getting everything you want out of life. 1st Touchstone hardcover ed. New York, Simon & Schuster, 2011.

Frankel, Lois P. Nice girls don't get the corner office : unconscious mistakes women make that sabotage their careers. Revised and updaged, First revised edition. New York, Business Plus, 2014.

Funk, Mary M. Thoughts Matter: The Practice of the Spiritual Life. The Continuum International Publishing Group Inc, 2005.

Gawain, Shakti. Creative visualization : use the power of your imagination to create what you want in your life. 25th anniv. ed. San Rafael, Calif., New World Library, c2002.

Gelb, Michael.How to think like Leonardo Da Vinci : seven steps to genius every day. New York,Delacorte Press, 1998.

Gilbert, Daniel. Stumbling on Happiness. New York, Random House, Inc., 2007.

Givens, Charles J. SuperSelf : doubling your personal effectiveness. New York : Simon & Schuster, c1993.

Gladwell, Malcolm. The tipping point : how little things can make a big difference. 1st Back Bay paperback ed. Boston, Little, Brown and Co., 2002, c2000.

___. Blink : the power of thinking without thinking. 1st ed.New York, Little, Brown and Co., 2005.

Godin, Seth, illustrated by Hugh Macleod. The dip : a little book that teaches you when to quit (and when to stick).New York, Portfolio, 2007.

Goldstein, Noah J., and Robert B. Cialdini. Yes! : 50 scientifically proven ways to be persuasive. 1st Free Press hardcover ed. New York, Free Press, 2008.

Goleman, Daniel. Emotional intelligence. New York : Bantam Books, 2005.

Goulston, Mark; foreword by Ferrazzi, Keith. Just Listen: discover the secret to getting through to absolutely anyone, American Management Association, 2010.

Grant, Adam M. Give and take : a revolutionary approach to success. New York, Viking, c2013.

Haidt, Jonathan. The happiness hypothesis : finding modern truth in ancient wisdom. New York, Basic Books, 2006.

Hamblin, Thomas H. The Power of Though. U.S.A., Murine Press, 2007.

Hanson, Rick, with Richard Mendius. Buddha's brain : the practical neuroscience of happiness, love, & wisdom. Oakland, CA, New Harbinger, c2009.

Hanson, Rick. Hardwiring Happiness: The New Brain Science of Contentment, Calm, and Confidence. New York, Harmony Books, Crown Publishing Group, 2013.

Harris, Russ., foreword by Steven Hayes. The confidence gap: a guide to overcoming fear and self-doubt. Boston, Trumpeter, 2011.

Harvey, Steve, with Denene Millner. Act like a lady, think like a man : what men really think about love, relationships, intimacy, and commitment. 1st ed. New York, Amistad, c2009.

Harvey, Steve, with Jeffrey Johnson. Act like a success, think like a success : discovering your gift and the way to life's riches. Edition: First edition. New York : Amistad, 2014.

Hay, Louise L., and Mona Lisa Schulz, M.D., Ph. D. All is well : heal your body with medicine, affirmations. 1st edition. Carlsbad, California, Hay House, Inc., 2013.

Henderson, Jeff. If you can see it you can be it : 12 street-smart recipes for success. 1st edition. Hay House Inc 2013, New York, NY, SmileyBooks, 2013.

Hendricks, Gay. The Big Leap: Conquer Your Hidden Fear and Take Life to the Next Level, HarperOne, 2009.

Hill, Napoleon. The science of success: Napoleon Hill's proven program for prosperity and happiness. New York : Tarcher, 2014.

___. The Law of Success: in sixteen lessons: teaching, for the first time in the history of the world, the true philosophy upon which all personal success is built, BN Publishing, 2007.

___. Think and Grow Rich: The Original Classic. Chichester, West Sussex, UK, Capstone Publishing Ltd. (A Wiley Company), 2009.

___. Grow Rich! With Peace of Mind. New Yor, Plume, Penguin Group, 2007.

Hogshead, Sally. How the world sees you : discover your highest value through the science of fascination. First edition. New York, NY, Harper Business, an imprint of Harper Collins Publishers, 2014.

Huffington, Arianna Stassinopoulos. Thrive : the third metric to redefining success and creating a life of well-being, wisdom, and wonder. First edition. New York, Harmony, 2014.

Jackson, Phil, and Hugh Delehanty. Eleven rings : the soul of success. New York, Penguin Press, 2013.

Jakes, T. D. 64 lessons for a life without limits. 1st Atria Books hardcover ed. New York, Atria Books, 2011.

___. Instinct : the power to unleash your inborn drive. New York, FaithWords, 2014.

Jamison, Terry., and Linda Jamison. Psychic intelligence : tune in and discover the power of your intuition. 1st ed. New York, Grand Central Life & Style, 2011.

Jantz, Gregory L., ith Ann McMurray.Overcoming anxiety, worry, and fear : practical ways to find peace.Grand Rapids, Mich., Revell, c2011.

Johnson, Spencer. Who moved my cheese? : an amazing way to deal with change in your work and in your life. New York, Putnam, c1998.

Johnston, Joni E. Psychology. 5th edition. Indianapolis, Alpha, 2014.

Jordan, Bernard E. The laws of thinking: 20 secrets to using the divine power of your mind to manifest prosperity. Hay House, 2006.

Kahneman, Daniel. Thinking, fast and slow. 1st ed. New York, Farrar, Straus and Giroux, 2011.

Kaku, Michio. The future of the mind : the scientific quest to understand, enhance, and empower the mind. First edition. New York, Doubleday, 2014.

Kay, Katty., and Claire Shipman. The confidence code : the science and art of self-assurance-- what women should know. First ed. New

York, NY, HarperBusiness, an imprint of HarperCollinsPublishers, 2014.

Keller, Gary, with Jay Papasan. The one thing: the surprisingly simple truth behind extraordinary results. 1st ed. Austin, Tex., Bard Press, 2012.

Kerry Patterson, [et al.]. Change anything: the new science of personal success . 1st ed.New York, Business Plus, 2011.

Kiley, Dan. Living Together, Feeling Alone: healing your hidden loneliness, Prentice Hall Press, 1989.

Klein, Gary A. Intuition at work : why developing your gut instincts will make you better at what you do. 1st ed. New York, Currency/Doubleday, 2003.

___. Seeing what others don't : the remarkable ways we gain insights. First edition. New York, PublicAffairs, 2013.

Knaus, William J. The cognitive behavioral workbook for anxiety : a step-by-step program. Oakland, CA, New Harbinger Publications, c2008.

Knight, Bobby, with Bob Hammel. The power of negative thinking : an unconventional approach to achieving positive results. Boston, New Harvest, c2013.

Kratz, Dennis, & Kratz, Abby Robinson. Effective Listening Skills, McGraw-Hill, 1995.

Layard, Richard. Happiness: Lessons from a New Science. New York, Penguin Books, 2006.

Lebauer, Susan R. Learn to Listen, Listen to Learn 1: Academic Listening and Note-Taking, Pearson ESL, 2010.

Lee, Jennifer., foreword by Chris Guillebeau. The right-brain business plan : a creative, visual map for success. Novato, Calif., New World Library, c2011.

Lehrer, Jonah. Imagine : how creativity works. Boston, Houghton Mifflin Harcourt, c2012.

Lerner, Harriet Goldhor. The dance of anger : a woman's guide to changing the patterns of intimate relationships. 1st Perennial Currents ed. New York : Perennial Currents, 2005.

Leslie, Ian. Curious: the desire to know and why your future depends on it. New York, Basic Books, 2014.

Levine, Madeline. Teach your children well : parenting for authentic success. 1st ed. New York, Harper, c2012.

Longknife, Ann, and and K.D. Sullivan. Easy writing skills step-by-step : master high-frequency skills for writing proficiency---fast! New York, N.Y., McGraw-Hill, c2012.

Lucado, Max. Fearless: Imagine Your Life without Fear, Thomas Nelson, 2009.

Lynch, James J. A Cry Unheard: new insights into the medical consequences of loneliness, Bancroft Press, 2000.

Lynch, Margaret M., with Daylle Deanna Schwartz. Tapping into wealth : how emotional freedom techniques (EFT) can help you clear the path to making more money.New York, Tarcher/Penguin, c2013.

Madelyn, Burley-Allen. Listening: the forgotten skill: a self-teaching guide, John Wiley & Sons, 1995.

Mandino, Og. Mission : success! Toronto, New York, Bantam Books, 1986.

Marra, Thomas. Depressed & anxious : the dialectical behavior therapy workbook for overcoming depression & anxiety. Oakland, CA : New Harbinger, c2004.

Martin Shepard. Dying: a guide for helping and coping, G.K. Hall & Co., 2000.

Mason, Douglas J., and Spencer Xavier Smith. The memory doctor : fun, simple techniques to improve memory and boost your brain power. Oakland, CA, New Harbinger Publications, c2005.

Mason, Paul T., M.S. Stop walking on eggshells : taking your life back when someone you care about has borderline personality disorder / Paul T. Mason, Randi Kreger. Second edition. Oakland, CA, New Harbinger Publications, c2010.

Mathews Gordon, and Izquierdo Carolina, eds.Pursuits of Happiness: Well-being in Anthropological Perspective. New York, Berghahn Books, 2009.

McKay, Matthew., Patrick Fanning, and Patricia Zurita Ona. Mind and emotions: a universal treatment for emotional disorders. Oakland, CA, New Harbinger Publications, c2011.

Maurer, Robert. One small step can change your life : the kaizen way. New York, Workman, c2004.

Maxwell, John C. How successful people think : change your thinking, change your life. 1st ed. New York, Center Street, c2009.

___. Make today count : the secret of your success is determined by your daily agenda. 1st Center Street ed. New York, Center Street, 2008.

___. The 21 irrefutable laws of leadership : follow them and people will follow you. Rev. and updated. Nashville, Tenn., Thomas Nelson, c2007.

___. Success 101: what every leader needs to know, Nelson, 2008.

Maxwell, John C. The 5 levels of leadership : proven steps to maximize your potential. 1st ed. New York, Center Street, 2011.

McArdle, Megan. The up side of down: why failing well is the key to success. New York, Viking, 2014.

McGraw, Phillip C. Life code : the new rules for winning in the real world. Los Angeles, Calif., Bird Street Books, c2012.

McKay, Matthew, and Peter Rogers. The anger control workbook : [simple, innovative techniques for managing anger and developing healthier ways of relating. Oakland, CA, New Harbinger Publications, c2000.

McKay, Matthew, and Matthew, Davis, and Fanning, Matthew P. Thoughts and Feelings: Taking Control of Your Moods and Your Life. Oakland, CA, New Harbinger Publication, Inc., 2005.

McKay, Matthew, Martha Davis, and Patrick Fanning. Thoughts & feelings : taking control of your moods & your life. 3rd ed. Oakland, CA, New Harbinger Publications, c2007.

McMahon, Darrin M. Happiness: A History, 2006. New York, Atlantic Monthly Press, 2006.

Metaxas, Eric. Seven men : and the secret of their greatness. Nashville, TN, Thomas Nelson, c2013.

Meyer, Joyce, Power thoughts: 12 strategies to win the battle of the mind. 1st ed. New York, FaithWords, 2010.

___. Living beyond your feelings : controlling emotions so they don't control you. 1st ed. New York, FaithWords, 2011.

Michaels, Jillian. Unlimited: how to build an exceptional life. 1st ed. New York, Crown Archetype, c2011.

Michalko, Michael. Creative thinkering : putting your imagination to work. Novato, Calif., New World Library, c2011.

Midedamer, Talane. Coach Yourself to Sucess: 101 Tips from a Personal Coach for Reaching Your Goals at Work and in Life. New Yor, M Graw-Hill, 2000.

Moehn, Heather. Coping With Social Anxiety, Rosen Pub. Group, 2001.

Nhat Hanh, Thich. Happiness. Berkeley, CA, Parallax Press, 2009.

Norem, Julie K.The positive power of negative thinking : using defensive pessimism to manage anxiety and perform at your peak.Cambridge, MA, Basic Books, c2001.

Opitz, Michael F. Listen Hear! 25 Effective Listening Comprehension Strategies, Heinemann, 2004.

Orsillo, Susan M., and Lizabeth Roemer. The mindful way through anxiety : break free from chronic worry and reclaim your life. 1st ed. New York, NY, Guilford Press, c2011.

Osteen, Joel. You can you will : 8 undeniable qualities of a winner. First edition. New York, Faith Words, 2014.

O'Toole, Mary Ellen., and Alisa Bowman. Dangerous instincts : how gut feelings betray us. New York, Hudson Street Press, c2011.

Otto, Michael W. , and Jasper A.J. Smits. Exercise for mood and anxiety : proven strategies for overcoming depression and enhancing well-being. New York, NY, Oxford University Press, 2011.

Peale, Norman Vincent, 1898-1993. Dynamic imaging : the powerful way to change your life. Old Tappan, N.J., Revell, c1982.

___. Power of the plus factor. Old Tappan, N.J., Revell, c1987.

___. The power of positive thinking. 1st Fireside ed. New York : Simon & Schuster, 2003.

Pearsall, Paul. Toxic Success: how to stop striving and start thriving: getting what you want without losing what you need, Inner Ocean, 2002.

Peck, M. Scott (Morgan Scott). The road less traveled : a new psychology of love, traditional values, and spiritual growth. New York, NY, Simon and Schuster, 1978.

Pincott, J. editor. Success: advice on achieving your goals from remarkably successful people, Random House Reference, 2005.

Pink, Daniel H. A whole new mind : moving from the information age to the conceptual age. New York, Riverhead Books, 2005.

Pink, Daniel H. To sell is human : the surprising truth about moving others. New York, Riverhead Hardcover, c2012.

Pressfield, Steven., foreword by Robert McKee. The war of art : winning the inner creative battle.1st ed. New York City, NY, Rugged Land, c2002.

Purdon, Christine, and Clark, David A. Overcoming Obsessive Thoughts: How to Gain Control of Your OCD. Oakland, CA, New Harbinger Publication, Inc., 2005.

Rando, Caterina. Learn to power think: a practical guide to positive and effective decision making. Chronicle Books, 2002.

Rath, Tom, and Barry Conchie. Strengths based leadership : great leaders, teams, and why people follow / Tom Rath. New York : Gallup Press, c2008.

Rath, Tom, and Donald O. Clifton. How full is your bucket? : positive strategies for work and life. New York, Gallup Press, c2004.

Ricard, Matthieu. Happiness: A Guide to Developing Life's Most Important Skill. New York, Little, Brown and Company, 2008.

Richardson, Cheryl. The art of extreme self-care : transform your life one month at a time. 8th ed. Carlsbad, Calif., Hay House, 2014, c2009.

Rivers, Caryl, and Rosalind C. Barnett. The truth about girls and boys : challenging toxic stereotypes about our children. New York, Columbia University Press, c2011.

Robbins, Anthony. Awaken the giant within : how to take immediate control of your mental, emotional, physical & financial destiny! 1st Free Press trade pbk. ed. New York, Free Press, 2003.

Robertson, Arthur, K. Listen For Success: A Guide To Effective Listening, Irwin Professional Pub., 1993.

Rubin, Gretchen. The Happiness Project: Or, Why I Spent a Year Trying to Sing in the Morning, clean My Closets, Fight Right, Read Aristotle, and Generally Have More Fun. New York HarperCollins Publishers, 2009.

Rubin, Theodore Isaac. Overcoming indecisiveness : the eight stages of effective decision making, Edition: 1st ed. New York, Harper & Row, c1985.

Schuller, Robert H. (Robert Harold). Success is never ending, failure is never final. Nashville, TN, New York, NY, T. Nelson Publishers, Bantam Books, 1990, 1988.

___. Power thoughts: achieve your true potential through power thinking. HarperCollins, 1993.

Seligman, Martin E.P. Authentic Happiness: Using the New Positive Psychology to Realize Your Potential For Lasting Fulfillment. New York, The First Press, 2002.

Sethi, Ramit. I will teach you to be rich. New York, Workman Pub., c2009.

Shenk, Joshua Wolf. Powers of two : finding the essence of innovation in creative pairs.Boston, Houghton Mifflin Harcourt, 2014.

Shipside, Steve. Effective Communications: get your message across and learn how to listen, Dorling Kindersley, 2007.

Siegel, Daniel J. Mindsight : the new science of personal transformation. 1st ed. New York, Bantam Books, c2010.

Simmons, Russell, with Chris Morrow. Success through stillness : meditation made simple. New York, Gotham Books, [2014].

Sincero, Jen. You are a bad ass : how to stop doubting your greatness and start living an awesome life. Philadelphia, Running Press, c2013.

Smith, Douglas A. Happiness: the art of living with peace, confidence and joy. Columbus, Ohio, White Pine Mountain , 2014.

___. Enemies of the heart : breaking free from the four emotions that control you. Colorado Springs, Multnomah Books, c 2011.

Stanley, Andy. How to be rich : it's not what you have, it's what you do with what you have. Grand Rapids: Zondervan, 2013.

Stanley, Charles F. Emotions : confront the lies, conquer with truth. First Howard Books hardcover edition. Nashville, TN, Howard Books, 2013.

Steele, Claude. Whistling Vivaldi : and other clues to how stereotypes affect us. 1st ed. New York, W.W. Norton & Company, c2010.

Stossel, Scott. My age of anxiety : fear, hope, dread, and the search for peace of mind. First edition. New York, Alfred A. Knopf, 2013.

Stovall, Jim. The millionaire map : the ultimate guide to creating, enjoying, and sharing wealth. Shippensburg, PA, Sound Wisdom, 2013.

Strausser, Jeffrey, and illustrated by Denise Gilgannon.. Painless writing. 2nd ed. Hauppauge, N.Y., Barron's Educational Series, c2009.

Styron, William. Darkness visible : a memoir of madness. 1st edition. New York, Random House, c1990.

Sullinger, Satch, with John Dauphin. Winning with purpose : raising our game and lifting our teammates, on and off the court. Olathe, KS, Ascend Books, c2013.

Tan, Chade-Meng.Search inside yourself : the unexpected path to achieving success, happiness (and world power). New York, HarperOne, c2012.

Tafrate, Raymond Chip. and Howard Kassinove. Anger management for everyone : seven proven ways to control anger and live a happier life. Atascadero, Calif., Impact, c2009.

Taylor, Sandra Anne. Quantum Success: the astounding science of wealth and happiness, Hay House Inc, 2006.

TerKeurst, Lysa. Unglued : making wise choices in the midst of raw emotions. Grand Rapids, Zondervan, c2012.

Tharp, Twyla, with with Mark Reiter. The creative habit : learn it and use it for life : a practical guide. New York, Simon & Schuster, c2003

Thomas, Marlo, Ed. It ain't over--till it's over [large print] : reinventing your life--and realizing your dreams--anytime, at any age. Large print edition. Waterville, Maine, Thorndike Press, 2014.

Tobitani, Yumiko., [translated from the Japanese by Echan Deravy]. Quantum speed-reading : awakening your child's mind. Charlottesville, VA, Hampton Roads Pub., c2006.

Tompkins, Michael A. Anxiety and avoidance : a universal treatment for anxiety, panic, and fear.Oakland, CA, New Harbinger Publications, Inc., 2013.

Tough, Paul. How children succeed : grit, curiosity, and the hidden power of character. Boston, Houghton Mifflin, Harcourt, 2012.

Tracy, Brian. Leadership. New York, American Management Association, 2014.

Tracy, Brian. Maximum achievement : strategies and skills that will unlock your hidden powers to succeed. 1st Fireside ed. New York, Simon & Schuster, 1995.

Tracy, Brian. No excuses!: the power of self-discipline for success in your life. New York, Vanguard Press, c2010.

Trimm, Cindy. Push: persevere until success happens. Shippensburg, PA, Destiny Image Publishers, [2014].

___. Reclaim your soul: your journey to personal empowerment. Shippensburg, PA, Destiny Image, 2014.

V, Jayaram. Think Success: Essays on Self-help. 2nd. Edition. New Albany, OH, Pure Life Vision LLC., 2014.

Van Slyke, Erik, J. Listening to Conflict: finding constructive solutions to workplace disputes, AMACOM,, 1999.

Ventrella, Scott W. The power of positive thinking in business: ten traits for maximum results. Free Press, 2001.

Victoroff, Jeffrey Ivan. Saving your brain : the revolutionary plan to boost brain power, improve memory, and protect yourself against aging and Alzheimer's. New York, Bantam Books, c2002.

Watt, Margo C. & Stewart, Sherry H. Overcoming the Fear of Fear, New Harbinger Publications, 2008.

Wind, Yoram (Jerry), Crook, Colin, with Gunther, Robert. The power of impossible thinking: transform the business of your life and the life of your business. Wharton School Pub, 2005.

Wright, Simone. First intelligence : using the science & spirit of intuition. Novato, California, New World Library, 2014.

Pure Life Vision Books

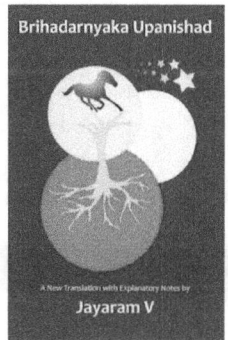  

To order please visit

http://www.purelifevision.com

Pure Life Vision Books

In 44 well written articles the author, a spiritual teacher, introduces you to a treasure trove of transformational wisdom for a life of abundance, peace and happiness. This book will stretch your mind and inspire vision. You will gain insight into the possibilities and opportunities that are available to you to achieve success, peace, and happiness in the journey of your life.

ISBN/SKU: 193576022X

ISBN Complete: 978-1-935760-22-1

Book Type: B&W 6 x 9 in or 229 x 152 mm Perfect Bound on Creme w/Matte Lam

Page Count: 406

Edition Number: 2

Edition Description: Revised

To order please visit

http://www.purelifevision.com

281

www.ingramcontent.com/pod-product-compliance
Lightning Source LLC
Chambersburg PA
CBHW080036100526
44584CB00023BA/3250